IRISH
HUNGER

PERSONAL REFLECTIONS ON
THE LEGACY OF THE FAMINE

IRISH HUNGER

PERSONAL REFLECTIONS ON THE LEGACY OF THE FAMINE

COMPILED AND EDITED BY
TOM HAYDEN

WITH A NEW INTRODUCTION

Roberts Rinehart Publishers
Boulder, Colorado

Published in the United States and Canada by Roberts Rinehart Publishers,
6309 Monarch Park Place, Niwot, Colorado 80503
Tel 303.652.2685   Fax 303.652.2689
www.robertsrinehart.com

Distributed to the trade by Publishers Group West

ISBN 1-57098-233-3

Library of Congress Catalog Card Number 98-86244

For kind permission to reproduce illustrations and text, the
Publishers gratefully acknowledge the following: 3M – Minnesota
Mining and Manufacturing Company, St. Paul, Minnesota, USA;
The National Library of Ireland. The Blackstaff Press for Paul
Durcan's *What Shall I Wear, Darling,* to The Great Hunger?; Eavan
Boland; Faber & Faber, UK/Farrar, Straus, Giroux, USA for
Seamus Heaney's *Digging*; The Gallery Press for Seamus Deane's
Return from *Selected Poems 1988*; the *Irish Times* for the October
1994 article by John Waters; Brendan Kennelly.

Every effort has been made to trace copyright holders. The editor
and publishers apologise for any errors or omissions in this regard
and would be happy to incorporate any corrections in a future
reprint of this volume.

The Editor and Publishers wish to thank all the contributors for
their time and enthusiastic response in preparing this book: Eavan
Boland, Jimmy Breslin, Gabriel Byrne, James Carroll, Tim Pat
Coogan, Seamus Deane, Luke Dodd, James S. Donnelly Jr., Paul
Durcan, Luke Gibbons, Terry Golway, Seamus Heaney, Brendan
Kennelly, Seán Kenny, Brian Lacey, Helen Litton, David Lloyd, Nell
McCafferty, Nuala Ní Dhomhnaill, Peter Quinn, Carolyn Ramsay,
John Waters, and Ray Yeates.

10 9 8 7 6 5 4 3 2

Typesetting: Red Barn Publishing, Skeagh, Skibbereen, Co. Cork, Ireland
Printed in the United States of America

CONTENTS

Dedication 7
Acknowledgments 10
Introduction 11
Chronology 17

Chapter One: Confronting the Ghosts 25
John Waters: Confronting the Ghosts Of Our Past 27
David Lloyd: The Memory of Hunger 32

Chapter Two: Remembering the Famine 49
Luke Dodd: All Our Silences Begin To Make Sense
(Interview with Tom Hayden) 50
Helen Litton: The Famine in Schools 56

Chapter Three: A Culture Lost 67
Nuala Ní Dhomhnaill: A Ghostly Alhambra 68
Brian Lacey: The People Lost and Forgot 79

Chapter Four: Identifying the Malady 93
Eavan Boland: "Inscriptions" 93
Jimmy Breslin: Leaves of Pain 95
John Waters: Troubled People 100

Chapter Five: Where the Famine Led 113
Gabriel Byrne: Famine Walk 115
James S. Donnelly Jr.:
The Great Famine and Its Interpreters 117

Chapter Six: Forgotten Lore 135

Seamus Heaney: "Digging" 135
Carolyn Ramsay: The Need to Feed 137
Peter Quinn: In Search of the Banished Children 143

Chapter Seven: Continued Troubles 159

Nell McCafferty: Whatever You Say, Say Nothing 160
Tim Pat Coogan: The Lessons of the Famine for Today 165

Chapter Eight: Transgenerational Shame 179

Seán Kenny: A Nightmare Revisited 181
Ray Yeates: My Famine 191

Chapter Nine: Making History 203

Seamus Deane: "Return" 203
James Carroll: The Shawl of Grief 205
Eavan Boland: Famine Roads 212

Chapter Ten: A Spreading Evil 225

Paul Durcan:
"What Shall I Wear, Darling, to The Great Hunger*?"* 225
Terry Golway: Famine Roots 227
Peter Quinn: Closets Full of Bones 234

Chapter Eleven: Our Dark Fathers 243

Brendan Kennelly: My Dark Fathers 245

Chapter Twelve: Recognising the Victims 249

Eavan Boland: "The Emigrant Irish" 249
Luke Gibbons: Doing Justice to the Past 250
Tom Hayden: The Famine of Feeling 263

Biographical Notes 287
Sources and Bibliography 289

DEDICATION

Iwant to dedicate this book about the Irish Famine to the memory of an Indian. He happened to be my father-in-law, Jack Williams, who descended from the Sioux Nation but spent all his life passing as a white man. His light eyes and rich Canadian accent obscured the significance of his red complexion and classic Native features.

"There were no prizes for being an Indian," Jack said of his years in logging camps in British Columbia. So he blended in, joined the union, drank his earnings, became a Fabian socialist, pored over the *New Yorker,* and complained about the ruling class. He never mentioned his Indian heritage, the humiliations, defeats and uprooting from the Black Hills that led his ancestors to Western Canada.

My wife Barbara and I took Jack on a search for his roots in the Black Hills in 1994. We spent a day with a granddaughter of Black Elk, the Sioux holy man, on the Pine Ridge reservation where modern Indian activists had battled the US government in 1973. We spent silent time at Wounded Knee, where US troops had slaughtered nearly three hundred Sioux in the freezing winter of 1890. There is no monument where the massacre took place, only a creek-bed, overgrown with bushes and inhabited by rattlesnakes. When Jack stood alone in the creek-bed, I felt his aura rearranging, as if spirits were inhabiting an emptiness in him.

One day, we drove up a long entranceway to a park commemorating Crazy Horse, the great Sioux warrior. At the kiosk, a young park attendant leaned into our car. He did a double-take when he saw Jack in the back seat. "Oh, are you a Native American sir?" he asked Jack. "Well," Jack mused, "Well, yes I am."

Respectfully, the young man responded, "Please be our guest, the admission is free for your whole family." As we drove in, Jack dryly grinned and said, "That's the first time it ever paid to be an Indian."

There are a lot of Irish today whose grandparents and great grandparents would identify with Jack. The Irish were in many ways the Indians of Europe, before the Famine deaths and forced migrations of the 1850s. They were feared by the occupiers as savage and wild. The historian Kevin Whelan describes their lives in terms similar to Indian villages in America:

> In this intimate face-to-face world . . . a rich oral culture was encouraged . . . Singing, dancing and storytelling emerged as the prized art forms. All this life was intricately interwoven . . . The vivacity and gaiety of the society, as well as its hospitality, was constantly commented on by pre-Famine visitors.

All this was destroyed, lost and nearly forgotten with the Famine. One third of the Irish people died or were forced to emigrate in just a decade. Such a massive trauma took its psychic toll in rage, shame and deep feelings of inferiority.

Poverty and prejudice in America made assimilation arduous. Alcoholism and schizophrenia ravaged Irish communities everywhere. *For a very long time there were no prizes for being Irish.*

The Irish today remember that an Indian tribe in America sent them $170 in Famine relief funds in the 1840s. Those same Indians were forced on their own "trail of tears" in the American South. One hundred and fifty years later, in 1994, a Choctaw delegation came to Ireland on the first national walk in remembrance of the Famine.

Jack Williams is dead now. What if he had lived on better terms with the Indian within him? What potential was lost? What price do we pay when those who pull the curtains of history allow us to know our roots only dimly or with shame?

In this sense Jack's story is similar to the Irish story, one of identity forever blurred by the winds of silence and sands of amnesia. It is also a universal human story, of being rooted in uprootedness.

Let me offer another example of this universality that bears a striking resemblance to Jack's story and the Irish experience. In *Black Dog of Fate,* an autobiography of an Armenian-American growing up in America's suburbs, Peter Balakian writes that he never heard the phrase "starving Armenians" or knew of the two million Armenians killed or famished in 1915 until he reached his college years. In the thickness of his family's silence, he associated "Armenia" only with the powerful presence of his old-country grandmother. But Balakian remembers a boyhood vacation with his father in the Black Hills where they met a Sioux medicine man. Peter, then a teenager, over-heard his father and the chief talking about "how old, great nations could be pushed off their own land, 'their homeland' . . . The chief nodded emphatically, yes, yes, 'homeland,' and my father said it back, 'your own homeland.'" Yet afterwards, no words were passed between the stoic father and curious son about this encounter with an Indian. "When it came to Armenia, there was a pattern of rup-tured gestures between us: my father would offer a fragment of knowledge, then retreat into silence." Change Armenia to Ireland and the story is identical.

Themes of personal identity being threatened first with destruction and later by assimilation appear throughout our liter-ature, from the diaries of Holocaust survivor Primo Levi, to the novels of Philip Roth, Barbara Kingsolver, Carlos Fuentes, Maxine Hong Kingston and David Mura, or the essays of Eduardo Galeano, Henry Louis Gates, Ana Castillo, Ann Baring and Alice Walker. The themes that reverberate in each story are those of near destruction and survival, shame and guilt, the long fuse of unre-solved anger, the recovery of pride and identity. The suffering and redemption of the despised and uprooted is the common story link-ing humanity.

The popular Irish musical *Riverdance,* for example, reenacts the native imagination of the original Irish people, followed by the trauma of Famine death and emigration, and goes on to celebrate the energizing of the Irish as they flowed and mingled with other cultures of the world, all resolving and dissolving in a wider cul-tural "river" that returns to replenish its island source.

This book is dedicated not only to the Irish, then, but to all those who have had to live with their deepest stories denied, in the hope that they and the world may respect who they truly are.

Tom Hayden
Los Angeles, California

NOTES

I am indebted to the work of historian Kevin Whelan for the description of pre-Famine Ireland which appears in his "Pre- and Post-Famine Landscape", from *The Great Irish Famine.*

ACKNOWLEDGEMENTS

To Jack Van Zandt at Roberts Rinehart and Seamus Cashman at Wolfhound Press for their personal commitment to this project. To Patricia Harty and Garrett O'Connor for the inspiration and advice they gave. To Mary Burbidge for her passionate dedication. To all the authors herein who wrote from their hearts. And to all the Famine authors who came before, and whose works informed and deepened my understanding. And finally, to the memory of the late Chuck Meissner, US Undersecretary of Commerce, who devoted himself to peace and economic development in Ireland. He was looking forward to reading this book.

INTRODUCTION
An Irish Hunger for Meaning
BY TOM HAYDEN

This book attempts to recall, commemorate and learn lessons from the Great Irish Famine of the 1840s, during which one million Irish people died of starvation and fever and another two million were forced to emigrate to new worlds.

The books stems from another Irish hunger that still gnaws, a hunger for the meaning of the Great Hunger in our lives today. This is the first collection of essays by Irish and Irish-American writers about the Famine legacy on Ireland and the Irish who came to America.

Previously there have been poems, novels, academic histories—though not many until recently—but few personal reflections such as these by writers from the two Irish communities separated by the Famine one hundred and fifty years ago.

This silence speaks. It suggests that the Famine was an unspeakable experience, and its memory a shattered one, even for a nation that imagines itself one of the most expressive in the world.

In the Irish language, the Famine is *an Gorta Mór*, the Great Hunger. The Great Famine is also widely used. But the term "potato famine" is the most common label for many Americans, tending to reduce the Famine to a freakish accident caused by an unknown fungus that happened to a backward people. In this common narrative, nature is the villain rather than British colonialism. In truth, the intensifying conversion of Irish lands from tilling to cattle grazing in the decades before the Famine caused the rise of a huge Irish-speaking peasant class which the British colonialists and Irish landlords considered "superfluous". In addition, deep-seated British religious and racial prejudice towards the Irish caused the Famine to be interpreted as an act of Providence more than a crisis requiring urgent British action. And so the Irish died in shameful pain in roadside ditches, or fever hospitals, or took the "coffin ships" to America jammed in spaces three feet by five for ballast.

After the 1850s, a powerful Famine consciousness fuelled
Irish nationalist anger for several decades, a searing wound which
underlay a nationalist fervour on both sides of the Atlantic that led
to the 1916 Easter Rising and the twenty-six county Irish Republic.

But by the twentieth century, the Famine memory dimmed
in both Ireland and Irish America under the pressures of modernity and assimilation.

Historians have struggled to analyse the silence that so often
surrounds the Famine. John Killen writes that "the trauma of the
Famine struck a deep blow to the psyche of the Irish people then
and in ensuing generations"; Terry Eagleton has concluded that
"the cataclysm stunned many of its victims into traumatised muteness", including Irish writers; Ronald Takaki describes the repression of memory as a "psychological barrier" that allowed the Irish
to protect their children from "hidden injuries and bitter memories" that they did not want passed on. Dublin journalist John
Waters asserts that this generation "should have access to this traumatised consciousness".

Tim Pat Coogan, in a Dublin discussion of this book,
pointed out that during the Northern Ireland "Troubles", an official climate that discouraged discussion of the Famine, accompanied by several "revisionist" histories that downplayed its scale,
served an "intellectual counter-insurgency" function by separating
the Provisional IRA from any historic rationale. During the thirty
years of Troubles, anyone who harped on the Famine became a
suspected terrorist sympathiser, using the Famine as a stick to beat
the British. Luke Gibbons, James Donnelly and Nell McCafferty
explore the same themes in their contributions to this book.

One myth that has been punctured recently is that
Protestant-dominated Ulster was spared the 1840s Famine, a doctrine that bolstered Unionist claims to religious and economic
superiority over the allegedly backward Catholic peasants who
starved in the rest of Ireland. But new archival research by Christine
Kinealy and Gerard Mac Atasney exposes this supremacist version
of history. Unfortunately, the records show that thousands died of
Famine in Ulster and the vast majority of those who perished in the
Lurgan Poor House (covering most of counties Antrim, Armagh
and Down) were Protestants. In the name of reclaiming history,
Irish nationalists in Portadown are seeking to raise a Famine mon-

ument in the constituency of the loyalist Reverend Ian Paisley.

But there is a deeper reason for the long silence. It is that silence is a common reaction to such profound traumas, and shame and self-blame are characteristic among survivors. Continued British dominance over Ireland after the Famine restricted the freedom of many Irish to express anger and caused an inhibition which has not fully lifted to this day. Assimilation did the rest. The pressures on the Irish and Irish-Americans to forget the past, to get on, prevailed over Famine ghosts reaching from the bog.

The purpose of this book is not to duplicate excellent works of history or fiction that already exist, but to give this "traumatised consciousness" a new Irish voice. The essays attempt to speak across the "bowl of tears" (as James Joyce called the Atlantic). It rejoices in the Irish triumph over disaster. But it rejects the amnesia about the past which so often accompanies assimilation or modernisation.

This book was first published in 1997, during the 150th commemoration of "Black '47", a time when Irish cultural pride is on the upswing and the Irish on both sides of the Atlantic are exploring the lessons of an Gorta Mór with renewed interest. Kinealy, the respected author of *This Great Calamity*, notes that "more has been written about the Famine in the last few years than was written in the previous century and a half". Other signs of the thaw are:

- The Republic of Ireland declared an official 150th-year commemoration period, and opened the first official Famine Museum, in Strokestown, County Roscommon, which is now partnering with the Famine memorial committee in Grosse Isle, the quarantine island in the St. Lawrence River where the "coffin ships" arrived.
- Former Irish President Mary Robinson, a sponsor of the Strokestown Museum, spoke eloquently of the Famine during her presidency, not only in Ireland but on state visits to famine-stricken areas such as Ethiopia.
- The globally acclaimed musical *Riverdance* is a powerful Irish evocation of the Famine dislocation and reunion with the Irish Diaspora and uprooted cultures everywhere.
- Sinéad O'Connor has caused a stir with her Famine lyrics and public statements condemning the British and comparing

Ireland to a victim of domestic abuse.

- Public schools in New York and New Jersey are incorporating the Famine into their educational curriculum, and in 1997 I was able to author similar legislation in California.
- A Famine Committee in Boston marched on the Historical Commission in 1997 and succeeded in gaining approval for a Famine Memorial on historic Cambridge Common.
- More generally, the recent explosion of Irish culture, seen not only in *Riverdance* but in a resurgence of Irish films, Celtic music, language and spirituality, may be seen as a thaw or recovery from many decades of self-doubt, feelings of inferiority, and cultural repression following the Famine.

As Killen sums up, "It is possible that only now, in the last years of the century and of the millennium, have the people of Ireland the self-confidence to seek to understand fully the causes, progress, and consequences of the Famine decade."

But some still ask: Why not let the past, with all its horrors, be at rest and be forgotten? The authors of these essays give a variety of answers.

First, there is a moral and spiritual need to express reverence for the unknown millions who suffered and died. They have been erased from history, or subjected to demeaning stereotypes. But "they were a great people", an old woman told the poet Eavan Boland as a young girl. Even today, many lie in unmarked graves all across Ireland. Thousands died at sea, or at the fever hospitals at Grosse Isle. As their survivors, we should remember and honour them properly in our rituals today.

A particularly touching story of Famine remembrance today concerns the 852 Famine dead who have been dead for one hundred and fifty years in unmarked graves on an island in Boston Harbor. In 1990, construction crews working on a sewage treatment plant turned up the bodies, desecrating the forgotten gravesite. Citizens of Boston hope to erect a memorial listing each name of the invisible dead.

Second, the deliberate avoidance of past traumas is unhealthy for individuals or cultures. The repressed past does not simply let go of us on command. The "hidden scar" (the phrase again is Boland's) is transmitted, invisibly and unconsciously, across generations. We have become, she says, "the present of the past", inferring the difference, but unable to feel or know it. In his essay, James Carroll also chooses the image of a scar, a gnarled one "encrusted around a still unhealed wound, a nightmare around a horror as yet unnamed". We have not healed from these repressed horrors; it is as if unmarked Famine graves are in each of us.

Third, proper remembrance of the Famine can contribute to building peace rather than reopening old wounds or rationalising violence. British Prime Minister Tony Blair realized this in 1997 when he personally acknowledged British responsibility for the catastrophic policies of one hundred and fifty years before. It was the first such admission by a British head of state, and it helped to revive the fragile peace process in Northern Ireland.

The road to healing passes through anger and violence, as we all too painfully know, but can never be complete without acknowledgment, apology and forgiveness. Blair's 1997 recognition of British government responsibility for the Famine unlocked the psychic and cultural levels of the peace process which then lay in ruins. On these levels, far below the abstractions of diplomacy, the healing of a historic wound needed to begin. As this is written in 1998, John Waters, who just a few years ago was the most passionate Irish critic of British denial of Famine responsibility, has become a foremost Irish endorser of Tony Blair's efforts at reconciliation.

Fourth, recovering the Irish Famine experience is vitally important to understanding the pervasive crisis of starvation that continues in the world today. The Irish-speaking peasant farmers of the 1840s were stereotyped in exactly the ways that the starving masses of Ethiopia or Bangladesh are labelled: as ignorant, backward, lazy, squalid breeders of too many children, a hopeless lot upon whom foreign aid is wasted. The cynical nineteenth-century doctrines of Malthus and Trevelyan—that famines are inevitable and result from cultural backwardness—are echoed today by many in the US Congress and World Bank. I daresay that many successful Irish-Americans are distanced from world starvation today precisely because they are severed from their own past.

But what if a clear reconstruction of the Great Hunger reveals that it was a preventable disaster? Would that not be a sign of hope, or at least a rejection of the hopelessness in the face of global poverty that paralyses so much sophisticated thinking today?

Much is at stake, therefore, in remembering the Famine. If we are willing to undertake a painful journey, to open what Peter Quinn calls our "closets full of bones", we may find new strengths with which to face the spiritual, cultural and political challenges of our future, as Irish men and women and citizens of the world.

NOTES

The John Killen references are in his excellent *The Famine Decade, Contemporary Accounts, 1841–51*. Terry Eagleton is quoted from an *Irish Reporter* 1995 interview and his fine *Heathcliff and the Great Hunger*. Ronald Takaki's essay on the Irish is from his *A Different Mirror: A History of Multi-Cultural America*. For the Famine in Ulster, see Gerard Mac Atasney's *This Dreadful Visitation: The Famine in Lurgan/Portadown* (Belfast, 1997). See also Christine Kinealy, *This Great Calamity: The Irish Famine 1845–52*. The story of the Boston Irish uncovering their Famine dead is from James Carroll, in the *Boston Globe,* 30 July, 1996. Prime Minister Blair's official apology was made 2 June 1997, and John Waters' tribute to Blair appeared exactly one year later in the *Irish Times*. The other quotations are from essays by authors contained in this book.

CHRONOLOGY

1069 AD Conquest of Ireland by the Anglo-Normans.

1500–1600 Pastoral feudalism. Ireland's population: 1 million.

1598 "Until Ireland can be famished, it cannot be subdued," Sir Edmund Spenser to Queen Elizabeth.

1601 Elizabethan Tudor conquest. Irish lands seized, "planted" with Scots Presbyterians.

1640 "The curse of Cromwell." Irish rebellion crushed with sword and famine, killing one-third of native people.

1690 William of Orange defeats James II at Oldbridge on the River Boyne.

1600s 50,000 Irish indentured servants sent to American colonies. 10,000 convicts sent to prison colonies.

1695–1709 Introduction of Penal Laws: Irish banned from voting, holding office, owning property, practising Catholicism.

1700 Irish population 2.5 million.

1720–41 Three famines reported.

1793 England authorises Catholic seminary for Ireland, at Maynooth. Priests required to take oath to British monarchy.

1798 Rebellion of United Irishmen repressed. Death of Wolfe Tone.

1798 Rev. Thomas Malthus publishes *Essay on the Principle of Population*, explaining famine as a "positive check" on population.

1700s 300,000 emigrants, three-quarters Protestant or Presbyterian, to Canada and US.

1800 Act of Union. Irish parliament dissolved, Irish promised minority seats at Westminster.

Famine. Irish population 5.2 million.

1803 Robert Emmet hanged, beheaded for 1798 Rebellion.

1816–42 4 partial or complete potato crop failures.

1826 Malthus, 6th Edition: ". . .we should facilitate. . .the operations of nature in producing this mortality. . .and if we dread the frequent visitation of the horrid form of famine, we should. . .encourage. . .forms of destruction (for example) make the streets narrower, crowd more people into houses, and count on the return of the plague."

1829 Catholic emancipation. Catholic landowners receive right to vote. But fee for voting raised from 40 shillings to 40 pounds, disenfranchising majority of Catholics.

1831–41 79 deaths from starvation for all Ireland (Derry paper).

1833 Martial law policies created.

1838 Poor Law establishes workhouses instead of welfare. "By the famine's end over a million people had spent some time enduring enormous mortality rates and all the horrors of Bedlam in Ireland's prison-like charity institutions."[1]

1841 Irish Census shows population 8,175,124 (not including sub-tenants).

1843 Repeal movement defeated at Clontarf. Daniel O'Connell calls off "monster meeting" under British military threat. Nineteenth century Catholic popular reform movement divides and collapses.

1844 Vatican reprimands Irish clergy on behalf of British. Priests instructed to "separate themselves from all secular concerns, and by work and example to inculcate subjection to the temporal power in civil matters and to dissipate popular excitements." Famine Prime Minister Lord John Russell writes, "We have tried to govern Ireland by conciliation and have failed. . .no other means are open except to. . .govern Ireland through Rome."

1845–51 The Great Hunger

1845 Britain's Devon Commission reports on "sufferings greater we believe than the people of any other country have to sustain." Estimates of seven million pounds paid in annual rent to absentee landlords.

Phytophthora infestans fungus destroys 30–40 percent of potato crop. Prime Minister Robert Peel imports £100,000 worth of "Indian Corn" (maize) from America in November to be sold to the poor at cost price through local committees dominated by Protestants of middle or upper class.

Corn is insufficient to feed population through 1846. During three months of Famine, Ireland exports 250,000 quarters of grain, 700,000 hundred weights of barley, 1 million quarters of oats and oatmeal to England. Food riots break out.

28 October: Daniel O'Connell calls for urgent reforms, including: banning all distilling and breweries in Ireland; ban on export of grain, vegetables, livestock, butter, eggs, fish from Ireland to England, purchasing of emergency provisions with revenue from existing taxes on Ireland; 10 percent tax on Irish landlords, 50 percent on absentee landlords for famine relief; public works projects like national railroad. Proposals rejected by Lord Heytesbury, the Lord Lieutenant of Ireland.

20 November: First Relief Commission meeting. 75,000, more than ever, Irish, emigrate, two-thirds to US.[2]

1846 Potato crop fails totally. In January, the Duke of Cambridge claims the famine is exaggerated and that "Irishmen could live on anything. . .there was plenty of grass in the fields even though the potato crop should fail".[3]

5 March: Parliament creates Public Works programme. Average wage 6 shillings per week (one-quarter the amount needed to support average family). Over 400,000 employed building "roads to nowhere"; 150,000 applicants rejected.

26 June: Repeal of Corn Laws (which imposed protectionist duties on crops brought into England).

648 relief committees at local levels. Required to raise local matching funds and fill workhouses.

30 June: Peel resigns under pressure, replaced by Whig Lord John Russell as Prime Minister

Whigs decide to cut back famine relief committees, and relief and public works. New policy is "Irish property must pay for Irish poverty". Shifts relief costs to Irish landlords and businessmen whose lands were being improved by the road, drainage systems, etc. Food prices to guarantee private profit to sellers, with public works wages to be less than average local wages. Grain still exported to England and Scotland for distilleries. Numbers on public works drop from 100,000 to 40,000 during August.

June–December: Riots and demonstrations by "Ribbonmen" continue.

Reports of people entering poorhouses when they knew they were dying, to ensure a decent burial.

"Young Ireland" nationalists secede from Repeal Association, form new Irish Confederation.

1846–55 500,000 evicted.[4] 106,000 emigrate, 64 percent to US. "The exodus now assumed the character of a precipitate flight."[5]

Black 1847 Potato crop at 10 percent of 1844.

January–March: 25 percent of those admitted to Fermoy workhouse in Cork die.

February: Daniel O'Connell makes last speech in House of Commons, predicting that quarter of Irish will perish without relief.

February: the Soup Kitchens Act approved. Provides "stirabout" of Indian corn, rice and water. Dysentery and scurvy occur. Many Catholics required to convert to Protestantism for soup. 15 percent of those laid off from public works not reached by soup kitchens.

Typhus epidemic begins, striking tens of thousands.

March: Sir Charles Trevelyan, head of the Treasury, orders 20 percent cut in public works. 200,000 laid off. 3 million in need of food and relief.

March: $120,000 raised in America for famine relief. Choctaw Indians of Oklahoma, victims of expulsion themselves, send $170 to Ireland.

Quakers form Relief Committee in Ireland, England and America.

St. Vincent de Paul Society formed.

8 June: "Gregory Clause" prohibits any relief to anyone having one-quarter acre of land. Purpose to make peasants give up small holdings to landlords in exchange for relief.

June: Government offers to assist emigration costs for families willing to give up their small holdings. Evictions increase. Landlords call for emigration to remove "surplus population".

22 June: New poor law targeted for Ireland. Schedules repayment with interest of loans advanced for public works. Penalty for begging in public or leaving home district is one month's hard labour.

Bishop Maginn of Derry asserts that 50,000 of his congregants are "in actual starvation"; condemns Poor Law for handing "the victims of oppression. . .over to the keeping of their oppressors, making the very persons the guardians of the poor who made them poor."

August: Free food from soup kitchens curtailed.

5 September: Senior official reports "the face of the country is covered with ripe corn while the people dread starvation. The grain will go out of the country, sold to pay rent." Trevelyan replies: "It is my opinion that too much has been done for the people." Russell asserts, "The state of Ireland for the next few months must be one of great suffering."

16 landlords killed, all in retaliation for evictions. In December, England passes Crime and Outrage (Ireland) Act. Sends additional 15,000 troops.

214,000 emigrate, almost 40 percent dying on "coffin ships". 117,000 to US, 98,000 to Canada, from where 40,000 go on to US. In May alone, 40 ships waited to embark at Grosse Isle, a quarantine island in the St. Lawrence River. In memory of 1847, Gross Isle today bears a monument to 5,294 people who "found in America but a grave".

1848 Potato blight total. It remains below the 1844 level for six more years.

Trevelyan decides to end Treasury funds to Ireland, shift cost to Irish elites. "The greatest evil we have to face", he writes, "is not the physical evil of the famine, but the moral evil of the selfish, perverse and turbulent character of the people."

The Poor Law commissioner worries that England will be accused of "slowly murdering the peasantry". Lord Clarendon writes that "I don't think there is another Legislature in Europe that would disregard such sufferings as now exist in the West of Ireland, or coldly persist in a policy of extermination."

July: Young Irelanders fail in attempted rising in Tipperary.

From 1848 to 1851, annual emigration increased from 177,000 to a peak of 245,000, falling thereafter to 134,000 in 1854 and finally to 63,000 in 1855.[6]

1849 March: new emigration assistance programme: three pence per mile for emigrants above seven, three half-pence for those under three; one pound value of clothing; ten shillings per individual for bedding and utensils.

Many placed on "coffin ships" which were designed for only one voyage, to carry timber from the US to England. Instead, owners began filling ships with emigrants as paid ballast. Ships carried 200–300 in holds designed for cargo. 30,000 died at sea, or of fever at Grosse Isle quarantine island, or shortly after arriving in Canada or US.

For the first time, *London Times* calls for "exceptional relief" as relief system bankrupts and collapses.

May: Trevelyan pushes through "rate-in-aid", which makes more solvent districts pay for poorer ones.

June: 768,902 people are on Outdoor Relief.

Cholera epidemic begins. 36,000 ultimately die.

2 June: Trevelyan writes to Quakers to ask what plans they have "for the relief of the serious distress which still prevails in some of the western districts of Ireland"; promises contribution from Russell of one hundred pounds. Quakers leave Ireland in protest.

July: the Encumbered Estates Act is passed, allowing landlords to sell their properties without paying off debts. The goal is new investors, but the result is accelerated evictions.

August: Queen Victoria visits Ireland. She writes, "you see more ratted and wretched people here than I ever saw anywhere else." She leaves "with real regret."

1850 119,628 children in workhouses at cost to state of 1 shilling per week.

June: Inspector-General reports that Famine has led to increased crime.

1851 Census shows population of 6,552,385, decline of 1.6 million since 1841. Footnote estimates that 1841 population should have increased to 9,018,799 by 1846, making a 2.5 million gap between 1846–51.

NOTES

1 Kerby Miller, *Emigrants and Exiles, Ireland and the Irish Exodus to North America*, (New York and Oxford, 1985) p.284.

2 Ibid., p.291.

3 Robert Kee, *Ireland: A History*, (London: Abacus, 1980, 1995) p.247.

4 Miller, Op cit., p.287.

5 Ibid., p.292.

6 Ibid.

Further data in this chronology is taken from several excellent sources, particularly: Christine Kinealy, *This Great Calamity*, (Dublin: Gill & Macmillan, 1994, USA: Roberts Rinehart, 1995); Helen Litton, *The Irish Famine, an Illustrated History*, (Dublin: Wolfhound Press, 1994).

Impoverished children (Illustrated London News, *20 February 1847;
courtesy of the National Library of Ireland.*)

CHAPTER ONE
Confronting the Ghosts

Go where you might, every object reminded you of the fearful desolation that was progressing around you. The features of the people were gaunt, their eyes wild and hollow, and their gait feeble and tottering. Pass through the fields, and you were met by little groups bearing home on their shoulders, and that with difficulty, a coffin, or perhaps two of them. The roads were literally black with funerals; and as you passed along from parish to parish, the death-bells were pealing forth, in slow but dismal tones, the gloomy triumph which pestilence was achieving over the face of our devoted country. . . .Under the terrible pressure of the complex destitution which prevailed, everything like shame was forgotten, and it was well known that whole families, who had hitherto been respectable and independent, were precipitated, almost at once, into all the common cant of importunity and clamour during this frightful struggle between life and death. Of the truth of this, the scenes which took place at the public soup shops, and other appointed places of relief, afforded melancholy proof. Here were wild crowds, ragged, sickly, and wasted away to skin and bone, struggling for the dole of charity like so many hungry vultures about the remnants of some carcase which they were tearing amid noises, and screams, *and strife, into very shreds; for as we have said, all sense of becoming restraint or shame was now abandoned, and the timid girl, or modest mother of a family, or decent farmer, goaded by the same wild and tyrannical solicitation and outcry as if they had been trained since their very infancy to all the forms of impudent cant and imposture. . .*

The dreadful typhus was not abroad in all its deadly power, accompanied, on this occasion, as it always is among the Irish, by a panic, which invested it with tenfold terrors. The moment fever was ascertained, or even supposed, to visit a family, that moment the infected persons were avoided by their neighbours and friends as if they carried death, as they often did, about them so that its presence occasioned all the usual interchanges of civility and good-neighbourhood to be discontinued. . .

— *Extract from* The Black Prophet, *a novel by William Carleton published in 1847*

Confronting the Ghosts Of Our Past

BY JOHN WATERS

— Irish Times, *October 1994*

Surveys, I'm told, indicate that Irish people do not want to hear about the Famine. It doesn't surprise me in the least. But it is also precisely why the subject must be talked about until we remember the things we never knew.

Any psychiatrist worth the salt on his spuds will tell you about the concept of "inhibited experience", the repression of a painful episode in the past of the human person, the denial, often over many years, sometimes over entire lifetimes, of something too traumatic to face. In the past I have put it to psychiatrists that what is true of individual people might also be true of peoples, of societies, of nations. The answer I have received has invariably been yes.

Far from being a stigma, this is actually a tremendously liberating idea. Anyone who has ever gone through the kind of personal therapy which allows the individual to bring such experience to the surface and deal with it will tell you so. Why then, as a nation, are we so reluctant to confront the ghost of our own past?

It's a complicated question. For a country like Ireland, there is a multiple problem. Not only are we reluctant to face the trauma of our own history—we are unwilling even to face the possibility that such an inhibited experience may exist in our own collective consciousness. This is because, as a consequence of the peculiarities of our history, we are both hare and hound.

Now in the late twentieth century, we like to see ourselves as an advanced Western society. Even our problems are perceived as symptoms of our modern condition. In some perverted part of the national psyche we see increases in crime, drug addiction, family breakdown and other social problems almost as reassuring evidence that we are well on the way to being as advanced as other Western societies.

All modern societies have such problems, we tell ourselves. And yet, at even the most superficial level of observation, it is clear that these problems as they exist in Ireland have an utterly different complexion to the societies we regard as our equals and "partners".

If we didn't already have the irrefutable evidence of our own eyes, there are plenty of studies and reports to show that something is not quite right on the range.

Alcoholism, for example, is a deeply entrenched problem in Irish society, and is intimately related to problems like violence and mental illness. Schizophrenia might quite plausibly be described as an Irish condition. Emigration continues to beset Irish society in a manner utterly untypical of Europe as a whole. Our levels of unemployment are already running at up to twice the levels of our partners, and are storing up a massive time bomb which threatens to explode into the new millennium.

Isn't it time we began to rethink such matters outside of the paradigms of imported Western ideologies? Isn't there a much more plausible explanation close to hand? Mightn't there be some relevance to the fact that, after eight hundred years of slavery, this country has travelled but a couple of generations into a strictly nominal form of freedom and independence? Mightn't there be some relevance to the fact that, one hundred and fifty years ago, little more than the length of two reasonable lifetimes, our nation suffered one of the most catastrophic experiences in the history of the world?

There is pain in Irish society that is not being admitted. It is there in the shapes of our society, in our congenital inability to realise our potential, and in the faces of our people. We carry it around with us and pass it silently to one another. We don't have to look too far to find its primary source. And yet, the surveys inform us that Irish people don't want to hear about the Famine.

Because we refuse to remember, we are doomed to repeat. The Famine, the most extreme expression of the violence inflicted on the Irish nation by the tyranny of the coloniser, is the door by which that colonial experience can be assessed. Viewed in its proper perspective, it reveals itself as the most powerful metaphor of life in modern Ireland. It is present as a hidden motif in much of our literature and music, for all that the creators of these works may deny it legitimacy. It casts a dark shadow over the way we live our lives in both private and public.

The Famine was simply the most violent episode in a history characterised by violence of every conceivable kind, the inevitable consequence of the destruction of Ireland's cultural, political and economic diversity. Revisionist[1] semantics about the source of the blight or the feasibility of aid efforts once the Famine had taken hold are utterly irrelevant to the meaning of the experience. The Irish economy, reduced to a virtual mono-cultural dependence, was a holocaust waiting to happen. For this reason, it is meaningless to discuss the Famine outside of the context of the colonial process in which it was rooted.

It's a long time ago, I think I hear you say. Really? Two lifetimes. Our great grandparents—yours and mine—were adults in the Famine period. That we might have been handed on its trauma and grief is but a matter of three cultural transactions, three generations of horrified silence.

What might its legacy be? Emigration, for one. But its effects are also to be seen in the warped nature of our society, in the cravenness of our dependencies, in our fear of self-belief, in the culture of amnesia in which we live our lives, in our willingness to imitate anything rather than think for ourselves.

Consider, for example, the drift of urban/rural ideologies in the present generation. We have constructed an ideology of progress which has turned concepts of "land" and "soil" into four-letter words, and thereby cut us off from the very means of ensuring our own survival. We have made virtuous the unsustainable notion that we are now an urban people and have all but destroyed ourselves in so doing. In pursuing the false god of industrialisation, we have turned Ireland into a polluter's paradise, selling off our birthright earth to the multinational sector for thirty pieces of silver. But even here, the evidence of our pathology seeks to emerge from the language and hit us between the eyes. The phrase "make the landscape pay", so much in favour among the current crop of modernisers, has about it an irony as bitter as a rotten King Edward potato. It is as though we were seeking to take revenge on the earth for the horror it inflicted upon our people one hundred and fifty years ago.

And yet we do not want to hear. Because of the elements of Western rationalism and behaviouralism which have infiltrated our culture, we perceive ourselves as in control of our destinies and our minds. We are blind to the manner in which, through song and story and word and deed and nod and wink and walk and glance, we have handed the trauma on from father to daughter, mother to son. The violence of our past is present in our present, enacted again and again in the fruitless conflicts which beset Southern society and the violence which has haunted the North for more than twenty-five years.

There is, of course, some occasional mention of the Famine, but only in a manner as to consider the issue to an ideological backwater. Like so many other matters of vital importance to our condition, it has been divided into a set of false opposites, on the one hand those who say that it was never as bad as we had been led to believe, and on the other, those who see the issue as a handy stick to beat the tribal drum. In between these polarised positions is the truth of our situation, a consciousness filled with grief and pain which has no way of expressing itself except through anger or escapism.

That is how we must begin to commemorate the Famine. We need a national period of remembering. . . All nations which have suffered traumas similar to our own have come, sooner or later, to the realisation that they must return to the past one last time in truth and reverence before they can make the first real steps into the future. The Cherokee artist Jimmie Durham has urged his own people, the victims of a not dissimilar history to our own: "It is necessary that, with great urgency, we all speak well and listen well. We, you and I, must remember everything. We must especially remember those things we never knew."

And so, let these years be years of remembering. Not out of thirst for retribution or recrimination, but out of a need for serenity and knowledge. That is how we should commemorate: by remembering, by reclaiming our history, not as a series of facts and details, but in a way so meaningful as to fill the gaping holes in our collective spirit. The designation and organisation of a Year of Remembering should immediately become the priority of all those who manage and channel the public discourse. That this commemoration be allowed to happen is the responsibility of politicians, artists, journalists, editors, psychiatrists, intellectuals and all others who claim to contribute to the betterment of this society.

In a few years, we will begin, in common with the rest of the world, a new year, a new decade, a new century, a new millennium. Moreover, in developmental and ecological terms, the human species is approaching not merely a moment of transition on a par with the Industrial Revolution, the Renaissance, or any of those other key moments of Western civilisation, but a moment with only two or three equivalents in the entire sixty-five million years of our existence in the universe. The future of our species will depend on the quality of our consciousness. The Irish experience of Famine provides us with a vital awareness which must guide us towards solidarity with the present victims of colonialism and oppression, for whom in so many tragic instances famine is not yet a metaphor.

It is inconceivable that we could have all those new beginnings without also having a need for a new dream. It is the greatest opportunity not merely in our lifetimes, but also in the lifetime of our land. Because of its unique experience, landscape and culture, Ireland could become in the next century the crucible of modernity, the place where the possibilities for peaceful co-existence might be dramatised and enacted. But before that dream must come the memory of the nightmare that we have never allowed ourselves to recall.

NOTES

1 Revisionism is a political theory in which major historical facts which would have been regarded as established are brought under new ideological principles. In the context of Famine scholarship, it is the "revision" of the nationalist anti-British credo to a new view that the Famine was less destructive than the nationalists claim or that it was caused in part by the Irish rather than by British colonialism.

The Memory of Hunger
BY DAVID LLOYD

S inger Sinéad O'Connor's controversial rap mix, "Famine", opens with the uncanny sound of a dog howling. The sound is uncanny for several reasons. Firstly, it is impossible to tell in this context if the howl is of hunger, grief or some condensation of the two. Also, it is difficult to make out whether the sound we hear is actually a dog's howl or a human imitation of the sound, a difficulty which in itself opens onto a place where the human and the natural converge and mimic one another. In addition, this animal lament accentuates the absence or the silence of what properly should be the sound of human mourning: it is as if the field of human society itself has been decimated to the extent that all that remains of its domestic and affective fabric, for which the memory of the dead is an indispensable thread, is this anguish of the domestic animal on the verge of reverting to its wildness. "Mouths biting the empty air", these sounds of dogs howling insist disturbingly on the question as to what issues from the empty mouth, what speech follows the horrors of famine, what mourning can work through the memory of mass destruction.

These are of course the themes that Sinéad O'Connor pursues. She insists that there is a repression of the memory of the Famine in subsequent Irish culture, and connects this with our deeply embedded habit of disavowing the personal and cultural damage that is in part the legacy of our colonial past, and she demands that we learn to grieve in order to heal. In relation to this demand, O'Connor's stated understanding of herself as a contemporary "keener" is entirely apposite and is a motif that we will return to later.

The uncanniness of the dog's howl lies not only in its immediate effects on the hearer. For if the sound is quite literally haunting, that is surely because it picks up and foregrounds a whole chain of representations of the Famine and its psychological effects that recur through virtually every account, journalistic, historical and fictional. In account after account of the Famine, the terrible

silence of the land is time and again counterpointed by the sound
of wailing or howling, as if indifferently human or animal. The
silence is at once the silence of depopulation and the silence of a
traumatised culture; the wail is the almost animal wail of despair
and passivity before a catastrophe that seems to exceed compre-
hension. Wordless, the wail is also anonymous, without any distinct human voice to utter it. As a recurrent motif in
representations of the Famine it marks simultaneously the disso-
lution of the Irish as makers of their own culture and history and
the historical emergence of a new kind of Irish identity whose elements are in many respects still present and which embodies a
peculiar weave of memory, damage and modernity.

The sense of shock at a catastrophe epochal in its implica-
tions is clear in a celebrated account of the Famine's effects written in its immediate aftermath:

> The "land of song" was no longer tuneful; or, if a
> human sound met the traveller's ear, it was only that
> of the feeble and despairing wail for the dead. This
> awful, unwonted silence, which, during the famine
> and subsequent years, almost everywhere prevailed,
> struck more fearfully upon their imaginations, as many
> Irish gentlemen informed me, and gave them a deeper
> feeling of the desolation with which the country had
> been visited, than any other circumstance which had
> forced itself upon their attention.[1]

Almost a century later, in what is probably the most complex
and interesting historical novel on the Famine, Liam O'Flaherty
picks up the powerful acoustic image of wailing in his description
of the advent of the blight, and with the same sense of its vocalis-
ing of despair and passivity:

> Towards the north, in the direction towards which
> Thomsy pointed, Mary and the old man saw people
> looking over fences, just as they themselves were
> doing. The people had begun to wail. In this wailing
> there was a note of utter despair. There was no anger
> in it, no power, not even an appeal for mercy. It was
> just like the death groan of a mortally wounded per-
> son, groaning in horror of inevitable death.

"It's the blight," Mary whispered. "Oh, God in
Heaven!"

. . . Mary turned away from the fence as he
approached. She began to walk back to the house. The
wailing was now general all over the alley.[2]

In a more recent account, that draws on contemporary tes-
timony, Thomas Gallagher produces a no less graphic account of
the anguished response to the blight:

Unlike the previous year, when large areas in both the
north and south were unaffected, the blight this time
spread to every area in so short a time that a kind of
wailing lament rose throughout the country wherever
neighbours gathered. Those with tin cans of holy
water flicked it into their faces, wet their fingers and
made the sign of the cross, prayed and genuflected as
though before an altar. Keeners at a wake could not
have sent up more varieties of anguish and despair
than did these Irish families at the sight of their entire
year's food supply being destroyed.[3]

Examples of the recurrence of the motif of wailing and its
relation to the passivity of the afflicted Irish peasantry could be
multiplied indefinitely and with a regularity that suggests that we
are dealing here not merely with dramatic effect but with an obsessive scenario that shapes the very meaning of the Famine as a cultural rather than a natural phenomenon.

Nor is that shaping of the Famine's meaning in any simple
way a product only of retrospect. The complex of wailing and passivity was clearly quite available to contemporary observers and
embedded in the most immediate representations of the catastrophe. Among the most powerful of such observers was William
Carleton, not least on account of his intimacy with the peasant culture from which he had emerged. His 1847 novel, *The Black
Prophet*, was written explicitly to alert an English reading public to
the horrors of starvation and accordingly records the Famine's
effects in painstaking detail:

In all these acts of violence [the food riots that occasionally broke out] there was very little shouting; the

fact being, that the wretched people were not able to shout, unless on rare occasions; and sooth to say, their vociferations were then but a faint and feeble echo of the noisy tumults which in general characterise the proceedings of excited and angry crowds. . .The ghastly impressions of famine, however, were not confined to those who composed the crowds. Even the children were little living skeletons, wan and yellow, with a spirit of pain and suffering legible upon their fleshless but innocent features; whilst the very dogs, as was well observed, were not able to bark, for, indeed, such of them as survived, were nothing but ribs and skin. At all events, they assisted in making up the terrible picture of general misery which the country at large presented. Both day and night, but at night especially, their hungry howlings could be heard over the country, or mingling with the wailings which the people were in the habit of pouring over those whom the terrible typhus was sweeping away with such wide and undiscriminating fatality.[4]

The destination of Carleton's novel does something to explain the emphasis of his representations of the starving people, which undercut the rage that was often expressed in popular attempts to halt the daily export of foodstuffs from the country throughout the Famine years. Carleton was trying to capture the sympathy of a British public accustomed, on account of their own longstanding stereotypes of the Irish as violent and the actual social unrest of the Tithe wars of the 1830s, to view the Irish as threatening and seditious. Thus he played down the anger and resistance among the poor and, throughout the novel, represents the Ribbonmen as a minority of misguided agitators. Unlike O'Flaherty, who provides a sympathetic narrative of resistance in *Famine*, Carleton emphasises the passivity and patience of the population.

In such a context, the "wailing" of the Irish becomes the sign of their helplessness in face of the "fatality" of the Famine. But the association of the Irish with "wailing" is not new; it at once picks up and, in the context of Famine narratives, transforms one of the most enduring motifs in pre-Famine English representations of Ireland's cultural peculiarities: "keening". Scarcely an English traveller's

account of Irish social customs fails to remark on the singularity of
this practice and in the period immediately prior to the Famine,
when Ireland had become both a principal locus of post-Romantic
tourism and a major site of political concern for the Empire, keening became a crucial object of study for an emerging ethnography
of the Irish national character. As a phenomenon through which the
strangeness of Irish customs and values is represented, keening
inspires a profoundly ambivalent mix of responses to pre-Famine
Irish culture, at once fixing that culture in its primitive incivility and
giving rise to disturbance and uncertainty. Reading carefully travellers' observations on keening not only connects the association of
the Famine and wailing to a longer history but contributes to our
understanding of the ongoing cultural transformation within which
the Famine was a critical watershed. It also helps to specify the racial
attitudes that underlay the administrative callousness of British
responses to the famine.

Mrs. S. C. Hall's description of a not uncommon scene of
annual hardship and shortage in West Cork around 1840 indicates
that the relationship between hunger and keening was already
established before the famine:

> At Bandon we beheld a melancholy scene—several
> carts returning to their homes in the country, which
> they had quitted in the morning with money to pro-
> cure food, but compelled to go back without it.
> Women and children accompanied them with loud
> cries; literally "keening", as if they were following a
> corpse to its place of rest.[5]

Generally, however, prior to the Famine, keening is recognised as a practice specifically related to mourning for the dead,
which is why it becomes the focus for remarks on the strangeness
and dangers of Irish emotion. Descriptions of the practice by
English writers hesitate between the recognition of its professional
and often formulaic nature and its use as a sign of Irish subjection
to and indulgence of violent and unpredictable emotion. That
emotion in turn becomes the sign of Irish political and cultural
instability. Another account by Mrs. Hall, this time of a funeral or
wake in Kerry, begins by acknowledging the organised and ritual
nature of the practice:

> The women of the household range themselves at
> either side [of the corpse], and the *caoineadh* (keen) at
> once commences. They rise with one accord, and,
> moving their bodies with a slow motion to and fro,
> their arms apart, they continue to keep up a heart-
> rending cry. This cry is interrupted for a while to give
> the *ban caointhe* (the leading keener) an opportunity
> of commencing. At the close of every stanza of the
> dirge, the cry is repeated, to fill up, as it were, the
> pause, and then dropped; the woman then again pro-
> ceeds with the dirge, and so on to the close.[6]

For many observers of the keen, part of the difficulty of
comprehending it lies in the apparent contradiction between its
wild extemporaneity and its formulaic aspects or, to put it otherwise, the difficulty lies in comprehending the performance of emotion. The sinister connotations of keening that such difficulties
give rise to are often condensed with the fact that the professional
keener generally was—or appeared to be—an old woman: "The
keener is almost invariably an aged woman; or if she be compara-
tively young, the habits of her life make her look old." (Hall, II.
P.90) In Thomas Crofton Croker's account of "Keens and Death
Ceremonies", the uncertainty that attaches to the figure of the
keener attains a peculiar intensity that is inseparable from a larger
unsettlement as to the political significance of Irish cultural practices. In this description of the funeral procession for a member of
an old Gaelic family, he oscillates between an understanding of her
expression as spontaneous, "dictated" by grief and therefore at one
with the natural sublimity of the scenery, and the acknowledge-
ment of the professonal status of the keener:

> The vast multitude, winding through some romantic
> defile, or trailing along the base of a wild mountain,
> while the chorus of the death-song, coming fitfully
> upon the breeze, is raised by a thousand voices. On a
> closer view, the aged nurse is seen sitting on the hearse
> beside the coffin, with her body bent over it; her
> actions dictated by the most violent grief, and her head
> completely enveloped in the deep hood of her large
> cloak, which falls in broad and heavy folds, producing
> altogether a most mysterious and awful figure. . .

The Irish funeral howl is notorious, and
although this vociferous expression of grief is on the
decline, there is still, in the less civilised parts of the
country, a strong attachment to the custom, and many
may yet be found who are keeners or mourners for the
dead by profession.[7]

The mystery of what lies beneath the voluminous cloak, the
impenetrability of this quasi-supernatural figure who seems at once
decrepit and powerful, rapidly becomes the metaphor for the
secret circulation of sedition for which both the keen and its language become the "cloak":

Keens are also a medium through which the disaffected circulate their mischievous principles, and this
they do without much attempt at concealment, the
Irish language being a sufficient cloak for the expression of seditious sentiments. . .[8]

What I would want to suggest, however, is that it is less the
concealed content of the keen that gives rise to disturbance than
the form itself as a striking instance of Irish cultural difference
from the English. It is not simply the seditious sense of Irish sentiments that is at stake, but the nature of Irish "sentiment" itself,
which is so deeply recalcitrant to anglicisation.

It is well known that Irish emotional or sentimental characteristics were subjected to a considerable labour of investigation
and interpretation in the course of the nineteenth century. This
labour was continuous in many respects with the longstanding
English assumptions about Irish violence and incivility. But it
received added impetus from England's political difficulties with
Ireland after the Union of 1800, particularly in relation to the
desire to integrate Ireland politically and economically into the
Empire, and was strengthened by the emergent science of ethnography and its inquiries into national and racial character.

The political and ethnographic impulses come together in
Matthew Arnold's *On the Study of Celtic Literature* which, appearing twenty years after the Famine, gave canonical expression to the
idea of the "sentimentality" of the Celtic nature and of the relation
between Irish culture and grieving.[9] Arnold's work, which draws
on other European Celticists like Renan and Martin, can be seen

as a critical moment in the long trajectory of a steadily transforming set of stereotypes about the Irish emotional economy for which the shift from the performance of grief in the often-seditious keen to the fatalistic wail of the famine-stricken peasantry is one crucial marker.

The force of Arnold's argument is that the alternately feminine, childlike or turbulent sentimentality of the Celt, which is so ineffectual in political and economic spheres, finds its cultural value only when supplemented and disciplined by Anglo-Saxon steadiness and when taken up into the larger and emerging unity of an English empire. The disposition of the Irish is subordinated to the longer history of a developing British civilisation that steadily assimilates different cultures to itself. This historical perspective absorbs any anxiety that might be provoked by the apparent incompatibility of Irish and English cultural forms, while within it the depiction of mourning makes the defeat of Irish culture seem the inevitable consequence of an ethnic *predisposition*.[10]

In this history, the shift from keen to wail is doubtless of significance in marking the transition from sedition or outcry to fatalism. At the same time, however, the historical framework within which Arnold fixes Irish ethnic characteristics is counterpointed by what we might describe as a spatial economy which explains the strangeness of Irish "sentimentality". For that sentimentality involves not merely grieving but also transports of joy and especially rapid transitions from one state to the other. The Irish emotional economy is envisaged as the "maniacal" obverse of the "dullness" of the Anglo-Saxon; it is akin to the characteristics that Norbert Elias would discern in the personality of pre-modern Europeans, or, more specifically, to the human emotional disposition prior to the regulation of emotion that emerges with the advent of the centralised political state and its corresponding "civility":

> The personality, if we may put it thus, is incomparably more ready and accustomed to leap with undiminishing intensity from one extreme to the other, and slight impressions, uncontrollable associations, are often enough to induce these immense fluctuations.[11]

The connection of the emotionally consistent or regulated personality with forms of civility reminds us that in the tradition of representations of Irish character, remarks on the "fluctuations" of Irish emotion join a system of political and moral judgement to ethnographic description. Accordingly, the proximity of emotional traits that colloquial whimsy designates "the tear and the smile" appears in the emergent ethnography before the Famine as a sign of impropriety. Impropriety has reference not simply to the moral codes of bourgeois civility as such, but to the proper spaces and the timing of emotional display. It is not just that the performance of emotion is itself an affront to the assumptions of an English observer for whom the authenticity of emotions such as grief is inseparable from its privacy and inwardness, but that within the economy of Irish emotional expression, the site of grieving is not necessarily separated, either temporally or spatially, from that of "merriment" or pleasure. The famous wake is the recurrent index of this phenomenon. The impropriety of Irish conduct is revealed at once in the fluctuations between emotional states and in the absence of marked distinctions between discrete spaces each of which is "proper" to a certain display of emotion or topic of conversation. Thus Hall's description of funeral ceremonies which we began to cite above continues as follows:

> During the pauses of the women's wailing, the men, seated in groups by the fire, or in the corners of the room, are indulging in jokes, exchanging repartees, and bantering each other, some about their sweethearts, and some about their wives, or talking over the affairs of the day—prices and politics, priests and parsons, the all-engrossing subjects of Irish conversation. . .
>
> It is needless to observe, that the merriment is in ill keeping with the solemnity of the death chamber, and that very disgraceful scenes are, or rather were, of frequent occurrence; the whiskey being always abundant, and the men and women nothing loath to partake of it to intoxication. (Hall, *Ireland*, p.87)

Multiple transgressions of the proper disposition of spaces are in evidence here. The boundaries between pleasure and pain, mourning and levity, are fluid; what begins as a gendered division of the chamber between "wailing women" and "bantering men" clearly dissolves as the women partake equally of the spirits that undermine propriety; and the mouth itself, the privileged site of oral culture, becomes the unstable and indifferent chamber of intoxication, laughter and lament.

We will return to this ambiguous territory of the mouth later, noting only how charged this orifice is for the ambivalent representation of Irishness: the site at once of fluent speech and secretive silence, lament and laughter, intoxication and hunger, guile and guilelessness. But the moral censure that greets the unsettling shifts of Irish emotional states derives from an historical order whereby English commentators seek to subordinate their Celtic others to their own forms of cultural and political modernity. Thomas Crofton Croker's judgement of the Irish character is not untypical:

> The rough and honest independence of the English cottager speaks the freedom he has so long enjoyed, and when really injured his appeal to the laws for redress and protection marks their impartial and just administration: the witty servility of the Irish peasantry, mingled with occasional bursts of desperation and revenge—the devoted yet visionary patriotism— the romantic sense of honour, and improvident yet unalterable attachments, are evidence of a conquest without system, an irregular government, and the remains of feudal clanship, the barbarous and arbitrary organisation of a warlike people.[12]

This appeal to the constitutional legality that guarantees the English spirit of independence *vis à vis* the "barbarism" and the local and effective attachments of its subject peoples, is the staple of British imperial thought throughout the nineteenth century. It implies the necessity for English interventions to bring subject peoples like the Irish to the point where they can become political subjects in a modern sense, capable of self-submission to the *regularity* of law and of attachment to abstract principles rather than affective ties.[13]

This political desire on the part of the English is inseparable from an economic judgement as to the moral character of the Irish which turns on their perceived incapacity for sustained labour (what Arnold will later call the Celt's lack of "architectonic" capacity). Croker's comments are again typical:

The present Irish character is a compound of strange
and apparent inconsistencies, where vices and virtues
are so unhappily blended that it is difficult to distin-
guish or separate them. Hasty in forming opinions and
projects, tardy in carrying them into effect, they are
often relinquished before they have arrived into matu-
rity, and are abandoned for others as vague and indef-
inite. . .The virtues of patience, prudence, and
industry seldom are included in the composition of an
Irishman: he projects gigantic schemes, but wants per-
severance to realise any work of magnitude: his conceptions are grand and vivid, but his execution is
feeble and indolent: he is witty and imprudent, and
will dissipate the hard earnings of to-day regardless of
to-morrow: an appeal made to his heart is seldom
unsuccessful, and he is generous with an uninquiring
and profuse liberality.[14]

This thesis states that the Irish lack precisely the virtues, political and economic, that would permit the development of Ireland
into a modern nation. Within English colonial rhetoric, Ireland's
backwardness can be understood as deriving from their fixation at
an earlier historical stage, that of feudalism, out of which English
political modernity has already emerged. Irish society is, at least historically, continuous with England, and only a time lag has to be
overcome. It is this lag that English reform is set to make up.
Politically, the Irish will be brought from their local and familial
attachments to reason by the systematic extension of English law;
the Irish incapacity for sustained labour or "the virtues of patience,
prudence, and industry" will be overcome by the discipline of political economy. As is well known, these interlocked projects inform
English policy in Ireland, from the attitude to the landlord system
to the question of political violence, throughout the nineteenth
century. These projects also inform the moral judgements of the
Irish held by English administrators during the Famine with catastrophic effects on efforts to provide relief.[15]

Thomas Boylan and Timothy Foley have documented well
English efforts throughout the nineteenth century to disseminate
political economic doctrine as part of a project at once economic
and political. Central to this project was the dissemination of

popular political economic tracts such as that written by the Archbishop of Dublin, Robert Whateley, which sought to use the supposed science of economics to justify the reigning social order. But the drive was not merely to school the Irish: it was to produce a new kind of person, "to change what was perceived as the Irish 'character', to substitute ordered, rational discourse. . .for rhetorical excess, thereby promoting affection for England and the Established Church."[16]

The characteristics of this new political economic subject can be fairly succinctly summarised. Critical was the capacity for sustained productive labour that the Irish were held so singularly to lack. This capacity turned on the emergence of the rationally self-interested individual whose choices and desires invisibly regulate both production and consumption. Such an individual is founded in the ethical virtues of autonomy and consistency: "he" is not swayed by effect or by outside influences, but "gives the law to himself" and becomes, accordingly, the reliable economic and political individual. All of these qualities are subsumed in that capacity for "deferred gratification" that is the hallmark of the modern individual whose corporal and psychic orientation is the future rather than the present. That individual is, needless to say, the antithesis of the Irishman described so often by Croker and others.

This catalogue of abstract qualities of the political economic individual at once obscures and reveals the fact that what is at stake is producing not merely a new set of psychic and ethical disposi tions, or even a new "social body", but in a quite immediate sense a new physical economy for the Irish body. The zones of this new body on which Ireland's possible development is founded are to be reordered in so deep a way as to transform a body that had been the site of simultaneous and shifting effects into a disciplined body which would be oriented towards the future.

This involves, along with the many other modes of discipline characteristic of modernity, the attempt to impose a distinctly modern hierarchy of the senses for which the eye and ear, the most distanced and objectifying of organs, become the privileged vehicles of taste and culture.[17] The moral discipline which seeks to transform the shiftlessness of the Irish who are "regardless of to-morrow" into prudence and economy requires the subordination of that most undisciplined of Irish orifices, the mouth.

The impropriety of the Irish, that was so consistently located in
the laxity of their mouths as sites of consumption and rhetoric, is
to be cured by a new morality which will target increasingly oral
culture and alcohol as the inveterate causes and symptoms of
Ireland's backwardness. That the moment of the Famine is generally regarded as that of the final and irrevocable demise of the
Irish language is one index of the assault on what had become an
oral culture that ensued. And though it is possible to account for
that demise in terms of the mass emigrations that took place
mostly from predominantly Irish speaking areas, or to the pragmatic realisation of those that remained that their survival
depended on proficiency in English, there is little doubt as to the
equal force of the post-famine traumatisation of a whole culture.

Nor is this an entirely superstitious or fanciful supposition
on the part of Irish people. The legitimisation of British administrative practice throughout the period lay in the intersection of the
pragmatic logic of political economy, for which the Famine represented a god-sent opportunity to clear the land of excess population, and the assertion of a providential design to punish the Irish
for their cultural profligacy.[18] That same sense of punishment, as
many have noted, produces one of the profoundest legacies of the
Famine in the peculiarly Jansenist forms of Irish Catholicism that
emerged at this time. In a very profound sense, the Famine was an
experience of punishing social and cultural discipline against which
no protest was possible. As James Clarence Mangan put it in the
most powerful of contemporary poems, "Siberia", "In Siberia's
wastes/None curse the Czar". And it is impossible to separate this
sense of discipline from either the advent of a new Irish subjectiv-
ity or the concomitant freezing of keening, as embodying both
mourning and protest, that ensues.

We can understand accordingly the peculiar dialectic of
silence and wailing with which this essay opened as marking the
importance of the Famine as an historical watershed. Of course, in
George Petrie's account, the silence is the consequence of depopulation, a depopulation which permits the social and economic
transformation of Ireland, the gradual consolidation of landholdings into small farms, and the emergence of a "nation-
building" class of farmers whose economic interests certainly
motivated their adherence to a new and puritanical morality.[19] But,

powerful as the incentive of economic interest clearly is in the combination of cultural amnesia concerning the Famine and in the corresponding need to deflect analysis of its historical and material causes and consequences into its representation as an "Act of God", that amnesia and that deflection strikingly failed in their task.

The Famine recurs, as the repressed must, in indirect and equally deflected cultural forms which continue insistently to mark the cultural singularities of pre- and post-independence Ireland. Anguished and haunting as the wail that counterpoints silence may be, it is not mourning. It is, rather, the representation of a vanishing population regarded as inhabiting the borderlines of nature and culture, as giving vent to an inarticulate and animal cry against a catastrophe to which their own cultural backwardness left them vulnerable and before which they are seen as passive. The silence that ensues is the sealing of the empty, howling mouth in a manner which consolidates the peculiarly melancholic forms of Irish cultural expression.[20]

The advent of modernity in Ireland is consequently marked by its difference from that western modernity that is elsewhere characterised by mourning as opposed to melancholy. This involves not so much a repression, whether of trauma or previous modes of pleasure, as a productive redisposition of Irish cultural forms, at the very level of bodily and effective practices, to the developmental history of modernity. At the same time, the very damage out of which Ireland's modernity may be seen to have emerged skewed Irish culture into forms which continue to manifest a deep cultural recalcitrance to any normative modernity. To put this another way, it is not in any simple way that post-Famine Ireland lost its culture; we need to understand rather that ours is a culture constituted around and marked by an unworked-through loss.

The trauma of the Famine, and the destructive processes of colonisation generally, must be registered fully in terms of the cultural damage they inflicted. To refuse to do so is to rationalise Irish history in ways which its singularities constantly elude. The project of development that got under way in nineteenth century Ireland has not so much failed as given rise to a culture that is constantly athwart rather than in time with modernity. We can comprehend this by grasping how the relation to damage as *loss* is counterpointed always by the persistence of damage as a mode of *memory*. Precisely because it is not a form of erasure or supercession, because it is not subject to even assimilation into the "higher" forms dictated by modern ideas of development, damage itself becomes the locus of survival, the pained trajectory of what lives on and, moreover, continues to resist incorporation. The question in relation to our memory of hunger, which is our version of a question that always insists for the decolonising process, is how such a resistance to incorporation articulated through the vertiginous ambivalences of damaged cultural forms, can count its psychic and corporeal costs? More importantly, how can such a reckoning lead us to transform the very damage which seams our survival and our difference into something more than survival, into alternative modes of living?

NOTES

1 George Petrie, *The Ancient Music of Ireland*, (1855), cited in Seamus Deane, *A Short History of Irish Literature*, (Notre Dame: UNDP, 1994), p.79.

2 Liam O'Flaherty, *Famine* [1937] (Dublin: Wolfhound, 1984), p.302; 304

3 Thomas Gallagher, *Paddy's Lament: Ireland 1846–1847. Prelude to Hatred*, (New York: Harcourt Brace Jovanovich, 1982), pp.5–6.

4 William Carleton, *The Black Prophet: A Tale of Irish Famine*, (London: Simms and McIntyre, 1847), pp.178–9.

5 Mr. and Mrs. S. C. Hall, *Ireland: Its Scenery, Character, and History*, Vol. I [1841] (Boston: Nicholls and Co., 1911), p.294n. Strictly speaking, of course, the kind of informal expressions of grief or anxiety implied here are not identical with the highly artful practice of keening as it is now understood. See Angela Bourke, "Performing not Writing", *Graph*, 11 (Winter 1991–2), for an account of the formal complexities and traditions of keening.

6 Hall, *Ireland*, Vol II, p.86.

7 T. Crofton Croker, *Researches in the South of Ireland, Illustrative of The Scenery, Architectural Remains, and the Manners and Superstitions of the Peasantry*, (London: John Murray, 1824), pp.172–3.

8 Ibid., pp.181–2. That the keen was often used as a means to articulate politcal anger is borne out by Mrs. S.C. Hall's more extensive account, in *Ireland*, II, pp.90–92. The keen's articulation of political or social criticism was, however, by no means confined to comment on British colonialism. As Angela Bourke remarks, "The texts that survive howl in protest and anger at death and at injustice in the world of the living, and the oral tradition offers many examples of women engaging in verbal battles with priests." (Bourke, "Performing", p.31).

9 For a discussion of Arnold's *Celtic Literature*, see my *Nationalism and Minor Literature*, (Berkeley and Los Angeles: University of California Press, 1987),

pp.6–13. On ethnic stereotypes of the Irish, which have force down to the present, and on the ethnographic writings that gave them scientific legitimacy in the nineteenth century, see L.P. Curtis's *Apes and Angels* and *Anglo-Saxons and Celts*.

10 For important reflections on allegories of loss as a function of ethnographic writings, see James Clifford, "On Ethnographic Allegory", in James Clifford and George E. Marcus, *Writing Culture: The Poetics and Politics of Ethnography*, (Berkeley and Los Angeles: University of California Press, 1986), pp.98–121.

11 Norbert Elias, *Power and Civility: The Civilizing Process, Vol.2*, (New York: Pantheon, 1982), p.238.

12 Croker, *Researches in the South of Ireland*, op cit., p.2.

13 I have discussed its developed form in the Unionist writings of Samuel Ferguson in *Nationalism and Minor Literature*, pp.83–5. John Stuart Mill's *On Representative Government*, ([1863] London: J. M. Dent, 1910) is one of the classic statements of the distinction between English readiness for government and the necessity for a government of "leading strings" in the case of subject peoples like those of India.

14 Croker, *Researches in the South of Ireland*, op cit., pp.12–3.

15 The common misconception that English administrative responses to the Irish Famine were simply informed by the economic doctrines prevalent throughout Europe at the time have been cogently challenged by Peter Gray's comparative studies of Belgian, French and Dutch responses to famine in their own nations at the same period. Paper delivered at the NYU International Conference on Hunger, May 1995.

16 Thomas A. Boylan and Timothy P. Foley, *Political Economy and Colonial Ireland: The Propagation and Ideological Function of Economic Discourse in the Nineteenth Century*, (London: Routledge, 1992), p.116.

17 Where I have discussed this hierarchy of the senses, from Kant's and Schiller's aesthetic theory to Freudian analysis, in relation to the imbrication of race and culture. See "Race under Representation", *Oxford Literary Review* 13 (Spring 1991), pp. 62–94 and "The Narrative of Representation: Culture, the State and the Canon" in Robert Bledsoe, et al, eds., *Rethinking Germanistik: Canon and Culture*, (New York: Peter Lang, 1991), pp.125–138.

18 See Peter Gray, "Ideology and the Famine", in Cathal Portéir, ed., *The Great Irish Famine*, (Cork: Mercier, 1995), pp.86–103, for a recent discussion of religious attitudes to the Famine.

19 On this consolidation of landholdings after the famine and its relation to Irish politics, see S. J. Connolly, "The Great Famine and Irish Politics", in Portéir, ed., *The Great Irish Famine*, p.49.

20 Kevin Whelan notes that "A certain amount of iron entered the Irish soul in the Famine holocaust." See "Pre- and Post-Famine Landscape Change", in Portéir, *The Great Irish Famine*, p.32.

Ejectment of Irish Tenantry (Illustrated London News, *16 December
1848; courtesy of the National Library of Ireland.*)

CHAPTER TWO
Remembering the Famine

Ejectment Murder—As Major Mahon, a gentleman holding large estates in Roscommon was returning home about twenty minutes past six o'clock on the evening of Monday, from a meeting of the board of guardians of the Roscommon union, he was shot dead by an assassin, about four miles from Strokestown. There were two persons engaged in the murder, according to our informant. Both fired; one piece missed fire, but the other proved fatal, lodging a heavily loaded discharge in the breast. The victim exclaimed, "Oh, God!" and spoke no more. Major Mahon was formerly in the 95th Dragoons, now Lancers, and succeeded to the inheritance of the late Lord Harland's estates about two years ago, the rental being about £10,000. The people were said to be displeased with him for two reasons. The first was his refusal to continue the conacre system, the second was his clearing away what he deemed the surplus population. He chartered two vessels to America and freighted them with his evicted tenantry.

—The Nation, *Dublin, 6 November 1847*

All Our Silences Begin To Make Sense

*Interview with Luke Dodd, The Famine Museum,
Strokestown Park, County Roscommon, Ireland, 1996*

BY TOM HAYDEN

The first Irish Famine Museum was established in 1994, upon the stable grounds of an old country estate at Strokestown Park, County Roscommon, where a landlord was assassinated during the Famine. The Museum introduces thousands of visitors to the Famine every year, using an extensive archive. The purpose of the Museum is not simply to provide an opportunity to reflect on the tragedy of the Great Hunger, but also to consider the continuing crisis of global famine, hunger, and disease.

LD: Back in 1989–90, when the idea for a museum to commemorate the Great Irish Famine of the 1850s first evolved, there was virtually no awareness of the impending one-hundred-and-fiftieth anniversary. Until the museum opened in 1994, the country had no facility to commemorate the Famine, an event which many now regard as the single most important in recent Irish history.

TH: Why do you think Mary Robinson took up the issue of the Famine?

LD: I don't think the Famine was explicitly mentioned in Mary Robinson's presidential campaign, but shortly after her election and as she began to evolve in the role, it began to become one of the themes which most preoccupied her. I approached her advisers in 1991 to see if she would consider becoming the Patron of the Famine Museum (more than three years before it opened). She agreed. The President passionately believes in the idea that we can only understand the present if we look to, and understand, the past. She has called the Famine a "defining" event in terms of its influence on the development of modern Ireland. It would be hard to disagree with this. However, she has also claimed that a latent memory of the Irish Famine has left Irish people with a predisposition to the plight of under-developed nations in the contemporary world.

Certainly, Irish relief agencies, for whatever reason, are at the forefront both in terms of intellectual debate and action throughout the
world, but I would tend to link this to our experience of colonialism rather than to a latent memory of famine.

TH: What is the public interest in the Famine like now?

LD: The Famine is, suddenly, everywhere. A lot happened in
1995, the first year of the commemoration. The Irish Government
established a committee to organise the commemoration of the
event. Probably the most useful and interesting event was the
Famine conference organised by New York University. While the
interest is wonderful, a lot of what has happened, to date, was a bit
superficial. It is good to see local communities organising events,
but all too often this takes the form of pageants where very white,
well-fed, late-twentieth-century, mud-daubed bodies are "dressed
up" as famine victims and buried in makeshift graves. This, it seems
to me, does little more than reduce the Famine to the level of a
spectacle by packaging it in an acceptable manner for a contemporary audience. When the pageant is over, we can all feel that we
have done our bit, but this would seem to have little to do with
commemorating the dignity of our famine dead.

TH: What has the response to the Famine Museum been?

LD: We have met some resistance to some sections of the
museum, because the museum is hard work. It is, fundamentally,
a traditional museum which relies heavily on text and documentary sources. There are a few illustrations from the period, much
of what is known is from bureaucratic sources, folklore is scarce. I
have had letters from people who have suggested that motorised
mannequins representing people on the point of death would liven
up the displays, or suggesting that a mound of bones of famine
victims be included.

TH: Like the Jaws exhibit at Disneyland?

LD: Exactly.

TH: What was the best response you got?

LD: The first summer we opened (1994) on a very busy day,
the receptionist called me on several occasions telling me that a
person from Australia wanted to see me. Being busy, I tried to put
the meeting off as long as possible, hoping to myself that this person, who didn't have an appointment, would eventually go away.
Anyway, another call came, and I went out to talk to her. She

immediately collapsed in tears, and over the course of the next hour or so as we walked around outside she told me about growing up in an Irish-Australian family where there had been an absolute embargo on talking about anything Irish, and particularly the Famine. She had spent about three or four hours in the museum, and said that gradually all the silences of her childhood had begun to make sense. She was absolutely devastated. I had a letter from her the other day, she is the mayor of a town called Newcastle. It was her visit that made me realise that the museum is potentially very powerful.

TH: Who comes here?

LD: We get a large mixture of people, a lot of Irish, and increasing traffic from the North because we are near the border and people there have a tradition of visiting heritage sites. There has been great interest in England where we have had a lot of publicity, and this has increased with the Peace Process, the idea that the Famine is the defining event in Anglo-Irish relations. The English are a good audience, they are prepared to spend time, and they are mostly completely ignorant of the long relationship between the two countries. We also get a lot of North Americans. I suppose our target market is Irish and Irish emigrant communities, really.

TH: What is the English response?

LD: Much of the British commentary, which has been brought about by the Peace Process, has not been very edifying. In the early part of 1995, many newspapers and TV news programmes peddled the line that by commemorating the Famine the Irish are showing signs of "coming to terms with their history". It's the same patronising language that they've always used, the idea that the problem is always Irish and had nothing to do with the British. I really love the quote from Terry Eagleton: "The Irish cannot forget their history because the English refuse to remember it." Nowadays, in Ireland, there is a definitive move away from the simplistic nationalistic or revisionist reading of the Famine. The Famine is now seen as a major international event, the greatest social disaster of nineteenth-century Europe. It also had a huge influence on the development of other cultures through emigration not only because of the sheer volume of those who left Ireland but because the Famine gave emigration a very particular complexion, the idea of emigrant as victim. Because of the intervention of the President, relief agencies such as *Trócaire*, and others, there is a growing awareness that the 1840s Irish experience is the forerunner of all modern famine.

TH: What are the typical responses to the museum?

LD: The audience which the museum must attract is very broad, serious academics, school children, visitors from many cultures, people with their own agendas. As the museum is self-guiding, most visitor responses come from optional questionnaires, or by mail. The response from teachers with students has been very encouraging, because the museum is ideally suited to the changing curriculum in our post-primary schools. North Americans are usually under time pressure as they arrive in bus tours, so we take them through the museum relatively quickly. We talk about things they know about, relating the Famine to the Peace Process and the way in which Irish-America has been, for the first time, mobilised in relation to the Northern situation.

TH: What is your sense of the response of the Irish?

LD: Many are shocked by the documents. The Famine is, in many ways a remote event, which is characterised in terms of abstract debates about political economy, trade, colonialism, etc. The documents from this estate root it in lived experience. They describe actual people from actual townlands. The museum tries to convey a sense of this huge class of under-privileged which existed in Ireland prior to the Famine, an illiterate, Irish-speaking subsistence culture which was wiped out by the early 1850s. I think Irish people are genuinely shocked to be confronted with an image of Ireland which has a lot in common with the images we now see of the contemporary developing world. In particular, local people respond well to the museum because they know the place very well. Most of the older members of the community have some folklore, they know the townlands, they are the descendants. To show a local person a townland just outside Strokestown where one man now lives as it was in 1847 when its population was in excess of two hundred and fifty people, or a map of the town showing hundreds of hovels on all the approach roads, is shocking.

TH: Sitting here, what do you think is the importance of Irish Americans seeing this?

LD: On one level, I think the museum frustrates the cosy picture-postcard image of Ireland in the nineteenth century which is, probably, more powerful in Irish-American culture than anywhere else. This museum is also a good introduction to the history of Ireland in the last three hundred years or so. A few visitors from the US have said that the Famine Museum is a good place to start a holiday in Ireland because it explains much of the historical background necessary for trying to understand Ireland at any level.

TH: What about a Famine monument?

LD: The Government committee certainly has one planned, but the idea frightens me a bit. Ireland already has enough bad sculpture and commemorative memorials. If something like the Vietnam Memorial in Washington were planned I would certainly support the project. Something like a memorial to the Famine needs a conceptual approach rather than a purely didactic one. I think it's a project which should be open to international tender and not merely confined to Irish artists or sculptors.

TH: Do you think the British should apologise for the Famine, in order to bring a closure?

LD: I really can't see this happening; it's just not conceivable given the attitude toward Ireland which still exists there. I think it would be eminently more useful, at the moment, if the British apologised for Bloody Sunday in Derry. I hope this won't be interpreted as rabidly anti-British, but they cannot cope with Ireland at any level. You know what is said about Ireland being the first and the last colony. The British have a lot invested in the North, and I'm not talking about in the financial sense. Maybe it will be done as part of the resolution of the Northern situation, assuming that it gets resolved.

Closure in a historical sense is dangerous. Imperial nations like Britain deal with their history through a closure, a distance. Their history is represented as unproblematic, part of a great logical narrative. In Ireland, we don't have that luxury, history is still being acted out here. The English establishment rail against Irish "nationalism". England is the most nationalistic country in Europe, but in England it is perceived as the norm. In Ireland, it is complicated by a political and territorial conflict.

TH: What should the legacy of the Famine leave us with?

LD: The legacy should be, it seems to me, to commemorate

the dignity of our famine dead and dispossessed, but to remember
them in a way which enriches our understanding of the plight of
under-privileged peoples everywhere. A formal understanding of
the 1840s famine in Ireland alone is an arid thing. Mary Robinson
has said that until famine is understood as an experience, nothing
will change. I was incredibly struck by President Robinson's press
conference when she first visited Somalia at the height of the
famine there. Throughout the trip she had remained calm and collected, in control. During the press conference she broke down
and said, simply, "I am shamed, shamed, shamed, to come from
the developed world and see these things."

The Famine in Schools
BY HELEN LITTON

LEARNING ABOUT THE GREAT FAMINE
While the Irish education system was still under British control,
some of the school textbooks did mention the Great Famine, generally with an emphasis on Ireland's helplessness and lack of self-
reliance. Some books, such as Robert Sullivan's *Geography
Generalised* (1850), infuriated Irish nationalists by their treatment,
as B. M. Coldrey describes. The 1850 edition stated:

> In 1847 a great potato famine occurred, caused by the
> almost entire failure of the potato crop. Since that dis-
> tressing period Ireland has improved in every respect.
> To this desirable result many causes have con-
> tributed—such as emigration to the Colonies, the
> operation of the Encumbered Estates Act, and the
> extension of Education.

This was revised in 1909 to read:

> In 1847 a great potato famine occurred, caused by the
> almost entire failure of the potato crop. In conse-
> quence of that distressing event and the tide of emi-
> gration which ensued, the population of Ireland has
> since then been greatly diminished, but many events
> of a desirable character have also occurred by means of
> which the condition of the people, socially and politi-
> cally, has been greatly ameliorated and the nation
> enabled to participate to some extent in the wealth
> and enlightenment enjoyed by other portions of the
> British Empire.

As Coldrey says, "This type of material angered Irish nationalists both by what it said and what it left unstressed. . ."[1]
Likewise, the textbook *Ireland 1494–1905, Cambridge
Historical Series* used for Senior Grade in Tuam, 1913–14, appears
to draw many consoling benefits from the effects of the Famine:

> The recently-made Poor Law, as may be supposed, was
> utterly unable to meet the strain of starving millions

crying out for relief; the efforts made by the
Government, gigantic as they were, but not well con-
ceived in some respects, proved to a certain extent
fruitless; and though the destitute population was for
the most part saved, many thousands of lives were
unhappily lost. . .

The mud hovel and the potato patch vanished
gradually from large and increasing areas; the face of
the landscape wore a better aspect; the Ireland of half-
starving multitudes was seen no more. . .The material
good effected was striking and great; the country
seemed transformed in many places as regards its husbandry and the breeds of its animals; some of the
towns, especially Belfast, grew immensely in population and wealth; above all the condition of nine-tenths
certainly of the peasantry was extraordinarily
improved. The misery and rags of the past seldom
offended the eye; the potato ceased to be the only
chief staple of food.[2]

Looking back now at the textbooks, even those published in
Ireland (many of which remained in use without alteration for at
least forty years), it is notable that little attention was paid to the
Great Famine as a subject in itself. The Great Famine is notoriously
a miserable catalogue of the suffering and death of thousands upon
thousands of nameless human beings, and is singularly lacking in
the stuff of patriotic glory and dramatic deeds. It is as though the
textbook authors were not really sure how to deal with this sort of
history, to make it suitable for young minds. Instead they fell back
on the traditional ways of recounting the past through the lives of
great men.

For these writers, Daniel O'Connell is the towering figure of
this period (although he died in 1845, before the famine reached
its worst depths). Much emphasis is placed on his achievements,
and it is stressed that his last days were made miserable by his fears
for his suffering country.

The miseries of famine, consequent on a failure of the
potato crop this same year [1845], the curse of absen-
teeism, the increase of pauperism and poor-rates, mis-

erable remedial legislation, and the ruined resources
of the country, all combining, presented most gloomy
prospects. A malignant fever, also, spread over the
land and carried off thousands of the people.
Weighed down by mental anxiety and failing health,
their devoted leader [Daniel O'Connell] yet put forth
almost superhuman exertions to save the starving
population. . .

   [1848] A dark cloud seemed to hang over the
fortunes of this impoverished island; famine, bankruptcy and emigration combining to expose her people to the commiserating gaze and philanthropic
sustenance and attention of alien, yet friendly, nations.

   These lowering and sad foreshadowings told with
grievous effect on the spirits and overworked physique
of Ireland's aged chief [Daniel O'Connell]. . .[3]

The Famine is, so to speak, a backdrop to O'Connell's
death, and important only insofar as it affected him. A lot of attention is paid also to the Young Ireland rebellion of 1848, with pages
devoted to the rhetoric of William Smith O'Brien and John
Mitchel; the Famine is merely seen as a backdrop to this event, and
one of its causes.

   Nowadays the Young Ireland rebellion, which received
such glorified treatment in A. M. Sullivan's *Story of Ireland*, but
which ultimately consisted of a skirmish in a field in Tipperary,
is treated very briskly indeed in history texts. In fact, it was altogether omitted from one of the most recent scholarly works on
the Great Famine as being irrelevant to that overwhelming
event. Descriptions of the Famine also featured in readers for
English classes, and in books used for Irish language classes such
as Fr. Peadar O Laoghaire's *Mo Scéal Féin (My Own Story)*[4].

   One reason why the Great Famine was not treated in the
detail we would now consider appropriate is that a lot of this
detail was not readily available. R. D. Edwards and T. D. Williams
edited a book of essays, *The Great Famine*,[5] for the 1945
Centenary, but it was academic in style and purpose and not
widely read. In 1962, however, Cecil Woodham-Smith's *The
Great Hunger*[6] unfolded the history of the Famine in an easily
accessible way, and galvanised the whole study of the subject.

Previously, school textbooks had spoken vaguely of "thousands of deaths", and limited the Famine to perhaps 1846 and 1847 only. They all agreed that corn was exported from Ireland while people starved, but that was about all they did agree on. Now the full sweep of the tragedy was made manifest, and the rights and wrongs began to be more fully discussed.

School textbooks were not the only source of information about the Great Famine. Teachers were specifically guided to use the textbooks merely as a starting point, and to discuss subjects in more detail with the class. Of course, this would depend on the individual teacher, and less interested ones would just stick to the book. Teachers were urged to concentrate on local history, using as many references as possible to places familiar to the pupils, and certainly in rural areas every village and townland would hold memories of the "Black Years".

My own history teacher, a Dominican nun now aged 83, was born and reared in Dungarvan, Co. Waterford. As a child, she was made aware of the Famine grave which overlooks Dungarvan harbour, and of the local "folly", a wall built along the top of a hill as part of Famine relief works. She also knew of people who had emigrated during or after those years, some of whom had subsequently returned. Memories of the Famine did vary widely from place to place, and it seems that in some areas it was pushed out of memory and forgotten. However in 1945, to commemorate the Centenary, the Folklore Commission conducted a country-wide survey to find out what was remembered about those years. The survey revealed a wealth of stories and folklore, some superstitious, but others obviously based on fact. It may not have been spoken of in public, but families had passed stories down among themselves.

THE ROLE OF HISTORY IN THE CURRICULUM
History, as a subject for education, featured only marginally in the lives of most Irish children in the nineteenth and early twentieth centuries. In fact in western Europe as a whole, until the mid-nineteenth century, history hardly featured on the school curriculum as a separate subject at all. In Britain and Ireland, under the Intermediate system, it was a sub-set of such subjects as English literature, Greek or Latin. History was almost unknown

in Irish primary schools before 1875, but in 1902 was made compulsory for all state-aided schools.

It was almost entirely British history that was taught in Irish schools, before the Irish Free State was founded. The aim of the system was to teach all pupils of the United Kingdom that they were part of the British Empire, a homogenous entity: "The people of these islands have one and the same language (all at least who are educated), one and the same Queen—the same laws; and though they differ in their religious worship, they all serve the same God, and call themselves by the name of Christ. . .All this is enough to make them brethren" (National Board Third Reading Book, 1861). However, by 1904 Irish schools were rejecting textbooks which had no direct relevance to Ireland, and the Gaelic Revival led to public pressure on the National Board to make the curriculum more reflective of Irish culture.

Even when history was taught, it was so-called "drum and trumpet" history—battles and kings, heroic figures and rebellions. "History. . .must be at first the study of great characters and great types. The child inevitably being a hero-worshipper, the stories must be personal and human, and alive with material achievement"[7]. There was no such thing as the history of the "common man" (or woman), no cultural history, social history, economic history. History was seen as a vehicle for training in citizenship, and to inculcate pride in one's nation.

By the 1970s, Irish Department of Education statistics were showing that the number of secondary pupils taking history had fallen perceptibly over a number of years; whereas 70% had studied history in 1960, this had fallen to 43.6% in 1970. Leaving Cert. history was taken by 32.8% of pupils in 1980. The Department of Education is at present (1997) embroiled in controversy over hints of altering the status of history in the curriculum, but the whole issue is obviously of minimal concern to most students, burdened by the necessity of studying sufficient languages and sciences to gain the places they need in an overcrowded third level system.

THE TEACHING OF IRISH HISTORY

During the years when Irish history was barely touched on in the majority of schools, it was being transmitted in the home and the community through ballads, newspapers, journals and popular history books which were read aloud, and through the tales of nurses and grandparents. Liam Deasy, later a leader of the anti-Treaty side during the Civil War, wrote: "If we learned little Irish history in the national school, the deficiency was in great measure supplied at home. . .Stories about Ireland's fight for freedom in previous generations were told repeatedly, at our fireside, while songs and ballads commemorating victories at home were frequently heard at our gathering."

Kathleen Daly, who married Tom Clarke, leader of the 1916 Easter Rising, also remembered such history, transmitted by her aunt: "From her store of historical knowledge she would keep us children entranced for hours; she had a wonderful way of recounting things so that we seemed to live the events all over again, and she wove history into the most beautiful stories for us. Mother would say, 'Have you no better sense, Lollie, keeping the children from their beds with your rambling?', but the effect of that rambling in later years brought us through one of the most difficult periods of our history with our heads up; we knew our history."

The first written history of the Great Famine was probably John Mitchel's bitter and passionate polemic, *The Last Conquest of Ireland (Perhaps)*, published in 1869. This volume, written by a Young Irelander who was transported after the 1848 rebellion, poured out a denunciation of British policy during the Famine years, and called for the repeal of the Union, and Irish independence. It contains many unforgettable descriptions of the sufferings of the people, and was probably widely read in nationalist homes.

Popular texts such as A. M. Sullivan's *The Story of Ireland* and P. W. Joyce's history books sold in huge numbers. The following excerpt from *The Story of Ireland* gives some idea of the graphic depictions to be found therein:

> Soon a darker shade came to deepen the gloom that was settling on the horizon of his future [Daniel O'Connell]. Famine—terrible and merciless—fell upon the land. Or, rather, one crop, out of the many grown on Irish soil—that one on which the masses of the people fed—perished; and it became plain the government would let the people perish too. In 1846 the long spell of conservative rule came to a close, and the

whigs came into office. Place was once more to be had
by facile Catholic agitators; and now the [Dublin]
Castle backstairs was literally thronged with the old
hacks of Irish agitation. . .[two pages follow on
O'Connell's decline and death].

Amidst the horrors of "Black Forty-Seven", the
reason of strong men gave way in Ireland. The people
lay dead in hundreds on the highways and in the fields.
There was food in abundance in the country*; but the
government said it should not be touched, unless in
accordance with the teachings of Adam Smith and the
"laws of political economy".

The mechanism of an absentee government
utterly broke down, even in carrying out its own tardy
and inefficient measures. The charity of the English
people towards the end generously endeavoured to
compensate for the inefficiency or the heartlessness of
the government. But it could not be done. The people perished in thousands. Ireland was one huge char-
nel pit.

It is not wonderful that amidst scenes like these
some passionate natures burst into rash resolves. . .[five
pages follow on Young Ireland rebellion].

In those days the Irish peasantry—the wreck of
that splendid population, which a few years before were
matchless in the world—were enduring all the pangs of
famine, or the humiliations of "out-door" pauper life.
Amidst this starving peasantry scores of political fugi-
tives were scattered, pursued by all the rigours of the
government, and with a price set on each head. Not a
man—not one—of the proscribed patriots who thus
sought asylum amidst the people was betrayed
. . . [three pages on evictions/emigration].

*The corn exported from Ireland that year
would, alone, it is computed, have sufficed to feed a
larger population.[8]

Sullivan's work has been described as "anglophobic and sec-
tarian in the extreme"[9], but it was the most popular family history
book for several generations.

Joyce's numerous editions of his *History of Ireland*[10] had a circulation of 154,000 by 1909, and, like Sullivan, held firmly to the idea of "history" as consisting of heroic individuals, with "the morality of a fairy tale"[11]. In the early twentieth century, as literacy increased, the widespread dissemination of tales of a heroic Irish past proved very useful to contemporary nationalist politicians, seeking rhetoric for their campaigns.

The Christian Brothers, striving to keep alive Gaelic culture and history without the help of the state, had always produced their own literary and historical "Readers", which combined extracts from Irish authors, and descriptions of historical events, with poems and songs. Their aim was explicitly nationalistic: "[pupils] must be taught that Irishmen, claiming the right to make their own laws, should never rest content until their native Parliament is restored; and that Ireland looks to them, when grown to man's estate, to act the part of true men in furthering the sacred cause of nationhood" (Introduction, *Irish History Reader*).

The Christian Brothers and other Catholic educators complained to the National Board about its British-oriented textbooks, but these complaints were more on religious grounds than for political or cultural reasons. In 1869, Brother John Grace, justifying their approach, told the Powis Commission (which was enquiring into Irish education) that if the Christian Brothers did not teach the main facts of Irish history, the children would learn more extremist views from other sources, without any qualifying moral standard.

When the new Irish Free State decided to increase the level of Irish culture taught in schools, history was seen as a useful vehicle for propaganda, building up a sense of nationhood and a pride in Ireland's past. This involved a concentration on heroic and noble past deeds and individuals. There was to be less emphasis on the Irish as pathetic victims, unable to control their own destinies, which had been the thrust of some earlier English-influenced versions. Professor Tierney, of University College Dublin, called for emphasis to be placed on the cultural development of the Irish people, and not "the dreary and saddening vicissitudes of the last five centuries".

The whole question of history teaching is problematic, and has led to some lively debates over the years. A TD (member of the Irish parliament) protested in 1959 that "it would be an excel-

lent thing if we could inculcate a sense of pride in our achievements as a nation in our young people and less of a sense of grievance about the years in which we failed to achieve freedom." In
the same debate, TD Lionel Booth urged that history should be
taught "so as to be of educational value, and not so as to build up
hatred and bitterness which can only serve to continue the unfortunate division of our country." Oliver Flanagan, TD, complained
in 1961 that "our children are being brought up with a feeling of
hatred towards our next-door neighbours." An Anglo-Irish
Conference of History Teachers did meet in 1974 to discuss "The
Teaching of History in Great Britain and Ireland at Secondary
Level with Special Reference to Prejudice and Bias", but without
any tangible results. As de Peitid says, "Scholarly integrity
demands that the unhappy story of English entanglement in
Ireland be told, and imaginative sympathy demands that young
Irish people feel the legitimate emotions of pride, anger and pity
which the telling of that story will naturally arouse"[12].

In 1954, a report on the Irish history curriculum of primary
schools was still stating that "only those historical events and those
personalities who would illustrate 'the best characteristics of our
people, their esteem for spiritual things, their love of culture, their
fidelity to ideals, their willingness to bear sacrifices, their desire for
freedom' were to be chosen"[13].

THE PRESENT SITUATION

Since 1995, and the beginning of the Great Famine commemorations, there has been an explosion of interest in the subject, man-
ifested through books, television programmes, newspaper articles
and films. There is no longer any risk that it can be ignored or
belittled in the study of Ireland's history. Schools are reflecting this
resurgent wave of popular awareness, that is notably taking place
outside the classroom, by adapting their own curricula somewhat.
Now the subject is given at least one chapter to itself, with usually
a second chapter on emigration. The school texts, reflecting modern ideas on making subjects more accessible to children, are lav-
ishly illustrated with engravings of the period and quotes from
contemporary documents.

The textbooks I mention relate to the Junior Certificate (originally the Intermediate Certificate); even yet, the Great Famine is

not on the curriculum for the Leaving Certificate. In 1996, the government's Famine Commemoration Committee established an essay competition for schools on the subject of the Great Famine, and efforts are being made to place it on the Leaving Cert. curriculum.

NOTES

1 B. M. Coldrey, *Faith and Fatherland: the Irish Christian Brothers and the Development of Irish Nationalism 1838–1921*, (Dublin: Gill & Macmillan, 1988).

2 William O'Connor Morris, *Ireland 1494–1905, Cambridge Historical Series*, (Cambridge University Press, 1909).

3 Rev. John O'Hanlon, *Catechism of Irish History to the Death of O'Connell*, (Dublin 1868).

4 Fr. Peadar O'Laoghaire, *My Own Story (Mo Scéal Féin)*, 1915, transl. Sheila O Sullivan, (Dublin: Gill & Macmillan, 1973).

5 R. D. Edwards and T. D. Williams, (eds), *The Great Famine, Studies in Irish History 1845–52*, (Browne & Nolan, 1956).

6 Cecil Woodham-Smith, *The Great Hunger, Ireland 1845–1849*, (London: Hamish Hamilton, 1962).

7 Tim O'Flaherty, *The Teaching of History in the Primary School*, (M.Ed. thesis, UCD).

8 A. M. Sullivan, *The Story of Ireland*, (Dublin: Gill, 1867).

9 A. S. Mac Shamhrain, "Ideological conflict and historical interpretation: the problem of history in Irish primary education c.1900–30" in *Irish Educational Studies*, Vol. 10 (1991).

10 P. W. Joyce, *An Illustrated History of Ireland*, (Dublin: The Educational Company, 1923).

11 Patrick Callan, "Aspects of the transmission of history in Ireland during the latter half of the 19th century" in *Irish Educational Studies*, Vol. 6 No. 2 (1986–7).

12 Sean de Peitid, "Teaching Irish History" in *The Secondary Teacher*, (Autumn 1972).

13 Sean Farren, "Curriculum Developments in Ireland North and South in the period 1945–1960" in *Irish Educational Studies*, Vol. 1 (1981).

Lazy-beds at Doogart, Achill Island, Co. Mayo (Howard, Island of Saints, 1855; courtesy of the National Library of Ireland.)

CHAPTER THREE
A Culture Lost

*T*o the Irish peasantry, who, more than other people of Europe, are accustomed to bestow care and attention on the funeral of their friends and relatives, the Cholera in its necessity for speedy interment, was increased in Terrors tenfold. The honours which they were wont to lavish on the dead— the ceremonial of the wake—the mingled merriment and sorrow—the profusion with which they spent the hoarded gains of hard-working labour—and lastly, the long train to the churchyard, evidencing the respect entertained for the departed, should all be foregone; for had not prudence forbid their assembling in numbers, and thus incurring the chances of contagion, which, whether real or not, they firmly believed in, the work of death was too widely disseminated to make such gatherings possible. Each one had someone to lament within the limits of his own family, and private sorrow left little room for public sympathy.

—*Charles James Lever, "St. Patrick's Eve", 1845*

A Ghostly Alhambra
BY NUALA NÍ DHOMHNAILL

I see the Famine in cultural terms, as the last and lethal body-blow to a distinct native way of life and world-view, epitomised by, but not purely confined to the Irish language. This is the culture that in one of its many high points produced the Book of Kells and an enormous corpus of mediaeval manuscript vernacular literature. It is a culture of which Joep Leerssen has said in an interview in *Poetry Ireland Review*:

> we must realise how alien the pre-Famine native tradition was. . .It must be remembered that it is a literary tradition that functions to a poetics that bypasses Aristotle, which had nothing to do with the growth of learning around the universities; where the relationship between the man of letters and the scholar is completely different to anywhere else in Europe. . .People do not realise the extent to which written culture in Ireland until the seventeenth century functioned according to mediaeval or early-modern Europe. . .the only simile I can think of is the Alhambra destroyed and the same rubble used to rebuild a different building according to a different architecture.

Leerson's image of the Alhambra is a striking one, and one that I return to again and again. In evoking this wonderful treasure of Moorish architecture he reminds us of the existence of other civilisations, other ways of being in the world which are different to the Anglo-American global cultural hegemony which is now upon us. It also reminds us in a very clear way of the existence in Ireland until a very late date, down to at least the Famine, of a subterranean, hidden, native world view, as amply described by Robert James Scally in his recently published *The End of Hidden Ireland*. It is our present total and almost willful amnesia about the hidden way of life that I see as the most lasting scar caused by the Great Famine.

I do not wish to appear heartless. Of course the severe suf-

fering and loss of life, the dreadful wretchedness and overwhelming despair of that time weighs terribly on my imagination, as it
does on many of the people of Ireland. If, according to behav-
ioural scientists it takes seven generations for the overt behaviour
patterns caused by deep emotional trauma to be bred out of a population, how long must it take for the covert ones to leave us?
Fixated as we have become by the overwhelming vision of the people of the Famine as victims, are we not forgetting something very
important: that they are representatives of a culture as different to
ours today as that of Brahmanic India? It does seem true that the
terrible imprint of the Famine and the trauma of colonisation is
something that we are finally coming to terms with. It is as if we
are waking up from a state of zombification, of a waking death
where we had no emotional memory of who it was that we were
or what it was that happened to us.

Although this process is vitally important, I think it will not
finally have worked its way through, that it will have been in some
deep and vital sense arrested in mid-action if we do not allow ourselves to become aware of this ghostly Alhambra within, of
another way of being still trembling at the edges of consciousness.
Surely the success of all colonial ideologies is predicated on this;
not only on the causing of material, physical and psychic trauma,
but on the prevention of that trauma from being expressed as it
need be—in anger and in forgiveness—so that it remains impacted
into the psyche of the colonised, just as its absence is impacted in
the psyche of the coloniser. Until we take proper cognisance of
this non-Aristotelian psychic architecture, this inner Alhambra, we
still remain severely colonised. Imperialism has finally triumphed
at the most important level of all, in the deeper recesses of our
minds. Until we face this deep level of collective amnesia about
who we are and where we come from, our existence will be at best
highly fragmented, at worst pathogenic.

This was all brought home to me most clearly one summer
when I brought my children to the Famine Museum in Strokestown
House in Co. Roscommon. I think this museum is a marvellous and
heartening enterprise. It is a sign of our recovery from the collective
trauma of the Famine that we can finally objectify it, and put it outside our psyche, the better to study it objectively, in the presence of
the Famine Museum.

The paucity of the artifacts in the museum speaks for itself. It shows the total lack of material possessions that was characteristic of the people who died in that catastrophe. It is indeed true that they were clothed only in rags, that they had no furniture at all in their hovels, that even the basic useful implements of their trades and crafts, such as spinning wheels, and fishing tackle, had already been sold in a desperate attempt to procure at any price some of the precious little food. The scale-model of a typical *clachan* village, with its shared field patterns on the rundale system, with "inner" fields devoted to intensive cultivation and "outer" fields kept for the pasturage of animals, is an interesting exhibit. The re-evaluation of the farming methods of the time, the so-called "lazy-beds", as actually being a highly efficient use of land for the type of marginal lands involved is also gratifying, and reinforces my sense of the great intelligence and industriousness and other sterling qualities of the people involved. Far from their typical stereotyping by metropolitan travellers as shiftless and lazy, they were very hard-working, as their back-breaking and tedious hand-cultivation of marginal land by spade evinces. These *clachan* dwellers knew what they were doing, and that this hard work was the most efficient way of ensuring a good harvest.

But nowhere in the museum do I get a sense of the rest of the way of life of these *clachan* dwellers. Nowhere is there an acknowledgment that 90% of these Famine-victims were Irish-speakers only. Nowhere is there an acknowledgment that a huge proportion (70-80%) of the people who left on the coffin-ships, were Irish-speakers only. They were the poorest section of the population and their lack of English was part and parcel of the double-bind that kept them in such abject material poverty. Nowhere do I get a sense of their mental and cultural life, and the high development amongst them of such art forms as did not rely on material props, such as singing, dancing, extempore and spontaneous poetry and storytelling, as well as their more formal, learned versions; even such things as the pounce and counter-pounce of quick banter and repartee.

From my childhood in the West Kerry Gaeltacht in the late 1950s, in what was still an Irish-speaking subsistence farming economy, I knew of their existence. I knew also that though poor in material terms the daily round of the life of the ordinary people could be remarkably rich in verbal culture and in mental agility and emotional satisfaction. And I only got a faint taste of that cultural richness, coming in at the late latter end of the phenomenon. What it must have been like in pre-Famine, and right up to Famine times, we can barely hazard a guess, but I know for sure that it was powerful and all-encompassing, and that even in the middle of considerable material distress "the craic was mighty". The following is one small example to prove my point. As part of his enormous collection of over 3,000 items of music, a near neighbour of my mother's family, the Rev. Canon James Goodman, of Ballymore, Ventry, later Professor of Irish at Trinity College Dublin, and a noted piper in his own right, took down over nine hundred tunes, not otherwise extant. According to the late Breandán Breathnach, the noted musicologist who was working on this material before he died, 494 of these otherwise unknown tunes were given to Canon Goodman by a single piper, Tomás O Cinnéide. Originally from my aunt's townland of Cahiratrant, O Cinnéide was living in Carraig during the famine times when he converted to Protestantism—took the soup, as it was called—chiefly because the local parish priest, a Fr. Casey, had taken his livelihood from him by forbidding him from playing the pipes at weddings and at dances.

When Parson Goodman was sent as a clergyman to Ardgroom, near Skibbereen, in Co. Cork, he took his fellow-piper, Tomás O Cinnéide with him, and Breathnach has a wonderful description of them working together in a large attic room. Tomás at this stage was slightly paralysed down one side of his body as a result of a stroke that he got, he thought himself, from a fairy *poc* (blow), received for playing fairy music at an inappropriate time and place, and without showing it the proper respect. Because of this, he was unable to play the pipes himself, but used to walk up and down the extensive attic room, whistling the tunes, and keeping proper time with his step, while Parson Goodman assiduously took down the music, and later played it back to his friend on the pipes. These tunes were written down in a large notebook. The name of each tune is more often than not given as the first line of the song. Whether or not the words of these songs were ever written down in a separate notebook or not, we cannot say, but as a child I used to dream of finding Goodman's mythical notebook, the one with all the words, words of over four hundred songs that

we know from no other source and that were written down from
one single piper from one small and terribly impoverished townland in a disadvantaged area on the extreme west coast of Kerry.
The Goodman Collection is still relatively unknown in traditional
music circles in Ireland, and is totally unappreciated by the culture
in general. That this should be so, and that this extraordinary
proof of the exuberance and cultural vitality of pre-Famine Ireland
should be still such a closely-guarded secret, is proof to me that we
have still a long way to go collectively before we will have recovered from the long term effects of the Famine.

None of this great cultural richness is made clear to us in the
Famine Museum. There is very little evidence of the existence of
Irish ever to be seen, and where it is, it is associated mostly with
the dread diseases that carried off the victims; *an fiabhras dubh*
(black fever or typhus) *an galar bhuí* (yellow or gastric fever).
Nowhere is there an acknowledgment of the fact that the overwhelming reality of the people who died was experienced and
expressed by them in the Irish language, the only language that
they knew or could speak. Is it any wonder, therefore, that I leave
the Museum somewhat dissatisfied, overcome once again, as I
always am when faced with memories of that time, by a sense of
overwhelming and unconscionable loss? Unconscionable, because
of what has been lost to consciousness, not just the tunes and the
songs and the poetry, but because the memory that they were all
in Irish—that they are part of a reality which was not English—has
been erased so totally from our minds. This seems to me to be part
of the Famine-trauma which is still not acknowledged by the post-
colonial Irish political reality. This collective memory-loss, this
convenient amnesia is still one of the most deeply-etched results of
the Famine.

* * * * *

My family has one famine story. It is not particularly remarkable
or memorable but it concerns us directly. It was told to my mother
by her grandmother, Léan Ní Chearna, who was from Gleann Fán,
that precipitous and lonely glen on the sea-ward side of Mount
Eagle, the most westerly mountain in Ireland. She came out of the
highest of the only two houses in the glen, houses that you can
barely glimpse from the road at the point where the water flows
over a bridge, rather than the bridge going over the water. (This

is called an "Irish bridge" in some dictionaries and I have yet to
make up my mind whether or not I think this is a racial slur.)

This story is not about the Great Famine of the 1840s but
about one of the many smaller famines that occurred in the more
disadvantaged regions of Ireland right up to the end of the nineteenth century and which are lumped together in Irish under the
general euphemistic title of *An Drochshaol* (The Bad Times). This
story is about the famine of 1879, when Léan saw her father die
of Famine fever; her mother had died a few years before, shortly
after the death of her youngest brother. Léan was seven the year
her father died and she told my mother years later that what she
remembered most from that awful time was how long it took him
to die. He was so weak in the bed that he could not pull himself
into a sitting position. The children had to let sheets down from
the rafters of the house so that he could use them to pull himself
up as he whispered to them his last feeble instructions. When he
finally died, five children were left orphaned, the oldest of them,
Nellie Rinn Bhuí (called after the townland that she later married
into) being at the time only fourteen years old.

Today when we look up at that lonely and desolate glen with
its small rocky fields running half-way up the mountain it is amazing that even grown adults could have fed a family of five from its
meagre soil and salt-blasted heaths, never mind being left to the
devices of a mere fourteen year old. But feed them Nellie did, even
to the extent of managing to collect a dowry of a hundred gold
guineas both for herself and for each of her three sisters, so that
they could marry into good farms to the east. The home farm was
left to the only boy, Seán Deartháir, so that the Kearney name
could stay on the land. This she managed, but the strain on both
her and her younger siblings must have been incalculable. Léan
remembered her sister as being uncommonly harsh to them all and
never forgave her for this harshness. So much so, that she never
once spoke to her after her own marriage, even when they met per-
chance by accident at the fair in Dingle. Léan, a soft woman in
many respects, was deeply stubborn on this issue. She finally
relented at Nellie's death, and to everyone's surprise was present at
her wake, family solidarity triumphing finally over deep hostility.

Each year as children, we all took part in a family pilgrimage
up the hill to Gleann Fán to visit Bríde Kearney, my mother's

cousin, and the last member of the family to live up in that wild and isolated spot. Bríde was always delighted to see us and welcomed us warmly. We children were regaled with tea and scones as this and other items of family history were rehearsed and retold. Like, for instance, the time there was such an almighty storm that it blew the whole roof off the house, rafters and all, so that it landed, holus-bolus, out on the dung-heap in front of the cottage. Seán Deartháir got such a fright on that occasion that ever afterwards, whenever there was even the slightest hint of a gale in the air, he got up out of the bed and took his bedclothes out to the stable and bedded down under the donkey cart, in the hope that if the roof were to do another such somersault, the cart would save him. At which we all used to laugh mightily, thinking of the strange vagaries of those people of olden times, but it was a wry enough laughter because we knew that we have all inherited a certain *eagla gaoithe* (fear of high winds), which still keeps us without a wink of sleep on blustery nights.

Nearby was another, perhaps more poignant reminder of *An Drochshaol* or Famine times, in the presence of a large out-cropping rock called Cloch Shéamais Bháin. This rock had given shelter to a man of the numerous Connors clan after he had been put out of his holding in the middle of the Famine by the notorious and ruthless female agent, Bess Rice. At the time of the eviction, all that had survived of Seán's immediate family were himself and a nine-month infant daughter Nance. At first, his brother Thomas and then various neighbours took them in, but one by one they got a letter from Bess Rice warning them that they were to give him no help, on pain of eviction themselves. There was nothing else for poor Seán and the infant to do but to camp out under the rock, with a few sacks of wool tacked against the outside, as their sole protection against the piercing elements. People still remember that, when he had to go down the cliffs to collect seaweed and mussels to use as fertiliser for the few meagre potato drills that he planted on land loaned to him by his neighbours, he had no one to look after the infant, but had to take her down the cliffs with him on the creel on his back. He survived this ordeal and lived on and eventually was given some sort of hut or other in the townland of Kilvicadownigh, beyond Bess Rice's jurisdiction.

The tiny infant Nance also survived and went to the new

National school that was soon opened near their home. She excelled in her studies and went on to become a "monitor" or untrained teaching assistant in the same school. She married a tailor, Táiliúr a' Chlasaigh, who was a noted story-teller and who was one of the chief informants of the American folklorist Jeremiah Curtin when he was collecting Hero- and Fairy-tales in the area in the late 1880s. Nance kept the teaching post until her son Tomáisín O'Shea was qualified as a National teacher under the new state, at which she relinquished the position to him. Tomáisín became a noted school-master and more County Council and Gaeltacht scholarships were won by his pupils than by any other school in the area. It is my proud boast to have known him myself, as he was still the school-master in Killvicadownigh when I went to school there, back in the fifties.

There is a dark side to this story, though. Ironically enough, Nance was not very good to her own father at the end of his days and it is said that she banished him to an outhouse which he had to share with the yearling pigs. It is tempting to see both her desire to excel at the lessons, her cannily keeping the good job for her son, and her cruelty to her father all as a direct result of the Famine. We have very long memories in this part of the world and these memories can often rankle with bitterness and rancour. Right down until well into this century, a man of the Connors used to come down to St. Catherine's graveyard on Pattern day and do a triumphant hornpipe on the grave of Bess Rice, the erstwhile persecutor of his relations. It was, and is, an eloquent gesture. In dead spite of her, there are members of the Connors clan still alive and thriving and happy in the place, while her name, bereft of progeny, has long died out.

* * * * *

There are other pointers that seem to show me that a non-Aristotelian psychic space, an inner Alhambra, shimmers within us, just beyond the reaches of consciousness. This is a world-view that the tragedy of the Famine wiped from our consciousness, and that it ill-behoves us to leave neglected, if we want to try and overcome the trauma of that time. One place it can still be found not only thriving but even winning the battle against Anglo-American blandness is in the musical tradition. As Fintan Vallely has written in *Graph*:

Somewhere in most Irish people is a subversive, con-
ditioned intuitive understanding of active suppression
of language, forced emigration, political frustration
and resistance to Anglo-Western world conformity.
One expression of this is in Gaelic football. Music and
language dredge deeper, take on and retain all this—a
variety of applied, absorbed, ascribed and adopted
associations, some real, many mythical. Socially music
(and part of its appeal) is on the smoky, a-moral never-
go-to-bed anti-work-ethos side of life.

Vallely later goes on to say, "Traditional music in Ireland
touches the historically-conditioned dispossessed, rural, rebel or
simply nonconformist strata that are never too far beneath the surface with a large number of us and define our difference from
other nationalities."

The fact that traditional music is being incorporated into
mainstream commodity pop music, a fact bemoaned by many, is
seen by Vallely in a different light, as rather the proof that it has
ridden out the storm, and won. It has shaken off the "top-down"
sanitised view of music culture foisted on it by the parish priests and
their efforts to "improve" people according to the Victorian model
(a direct result of the loss of culture and confidence caused by the
Famine.) As Vallely says, "Through doggedness and essentially subversion of this myopic political fallout, people like Breandán
Breathnach have been instrumental in turning all that around,
gradually building up a generation of like minds (among players
and consumers) who now wield the ideological power at all levels
of this society." This is very much music to my ears, as one of the
fall-outs of the Famine in my own family was the adoption two generations back of such a rigorous work-ethos that even singing and
whistling were forbidden in the house, never mind dancing, or
wasting time or money on a musical instrument. This had the net
effect in just one short period of time of changing a reasonably
musical family into a whole generation who were, and remain,
tone-deaf, who do not to this day possess a note in their heads.

One other area of real breakthrough is in the greatly
renewed interest and outburst of creativity in the Irish language,
especially in its less Aristotelian registers, such as the oral tradition in general and the special branch of area-specific place-lore

in particular that goes under the general term of *dinnseanchas*
and which has been greatly revitalised, renewed and reappraised
by writers such as Tim Robinson. This has been from time
immemorial one of the great branches of knowledge of the
Gaelic world. For countless millennia in the oral tradition and
for the fifteen hundred years of the written Irish language tradition, it has been central to the culture. Through *dinnseanchas*
we can possess the land emotionally and imaginatively without
any particular sense of, or actual need for, titular ownership. It
gives us a marvellous "objective correlative" on which we can
hang the powerful and ever-changing dimensions and personages of our *paysage interière*. It is a magnificent monument to
the collective memory of the Irish people, and a source of great
wonder and delight to me personally, because without the medi-
ation of this dimension of the human imagination, rocks and
grass and water are ultimately only rocks and grass and water. In
this deeply resonant and highly-articulated repertoire of myth,
legend, folk-knowledge and local narrative we can find an imaginative impulse at work, a shadowy but nevertheless quite palpa-
ble imaginative delineation of that rose-red inner Alhambra that
I have already mentioned.

Dinnseanchas itself encodes the collective memory of the
Famine in its pointing out of famine graves and its delineation of
certain spots as "hungry grass", where famine victims died, and
where if you walk on them, you will be overcome by a sudden and
overpowering hunger or weakness that might even be lethal.
(Hence the good country habit of always carrying some item of
food, be it only a crust of bread, in the pocket.) But at an even
deeper level, *dinnseanchas* encodes the collective trauma of the
Famine. Again and again in the stories told about the landscape
features of Corcha Dhuibhne, the Dingle Peninsula, which is the
part of Ireland that I know most intimately, a certain pattern
emerges.

Always and ever there is a barely submerged female principle or image, just beneath the surface of the collective subcon-
scious, whether like the *piast* or monster of Loch Crawley it was
because she was confined by the forces of Christianity under a
cauldron in the depths of a lake, or like the ever-giving Magic
Cow, *an Ghlas Ghaibhneach*, she was misused by being milked into

a sieve and as a result ran back into the sea whence she first came. Sometimes, like the legendary Carbuncle of Lough Geal on the Connor Pass, whose story entranced the otherwise doggedly empirical Lloyd Praeger, she rises to the surface once every seven years and lights up the dark night through the brilliance of her shining.

Just like the legendary fairy islands that emerge in like fashion off our coastline, whether Hy Brasil, or Little Arann or Cill Swithin or Dún-idir-dhá-Dhrol, all this female force is waiting for is a brave act of repossession. This is imaged in the stories in many different ways. Sometimes it is by throwing some of the clay of the real world on the mythical island that we recover it; other times it is through the planting of a lighting ember, or the stealing of a magic cape from the guardian of the place that we finally force it up on to dry land. There it emerges into consciousness, and appears to all clothed in the wonder and exuberance of an inner Alhambra.

The People Lost and Forgot
BY BRIAN LACEY

I n his study of the use of folklore as evidence for the Great Famine, Cormac O Gráda quotes from a source in the Donegal Gaeltacht of Rann na Feirste:

D'imigh an spórt agus an caitheamh aimsire. Stad an fhilíocht agus a'ceol agus a damhsa. Chaill siad agus rinne siad dearmad den iomlán agus nuair a bhisigh an saol ar dhóigheannaí eile ní tháinig na rudaí seo ariamh ar ais mar a bhí siad. Mharbh an gorta achan rud.

> (Fun and recreation disappeared. Poetry, music and dance stopped. The people lost and forgot all of that and when life improved in some respects these things didn't come back as they had been. The famine killed everything.)[1]

The trauma of the Famine produced a sort of amnesia from which they (and we) never recovered. It is the job of modern researchers to help us to try to remember.

For over twenty years, I have been professionally involved with "remembering" aspects of the Irish past. As an archaeologist, I have had to look at the very earliest phases of our prehistory when the island was first colonised and opened up for settlement by our aboriginal ancestors. More recently as a museum director, and as a historian of Derry in which I live, I have found myself dealing with all aspects of the city's turbulent past, right up to the day before yesterday.

Derry, built on its hills overlooking the River Foyle, is a city of political and historical perspectives, as well as topographical ones. Here, the past is continually in discourse with the present. In this city it is very hard to get away from remembering the past. Quite apart from its monuments and troubled politics, every year seems to bring some major historical commemoration, each of which raises serious questions for us in the present.

One of the museums of which I am in charge in Derry, the Tower Museum, has acquired the reputation of honestly facing up to some of the less pleasant aspects of our history, including our recent past. It was voted Irish "Museum of the Year" in November 1993, and, on 1 September of the following year (the first day of the eighteen-month IRA ceasefire), I was told that it had also won the British "Museum of the Year" award. To us that seemed like a nice irony and, if nothing else, interesting timing. It is the only museum to have held both of those titles, and as far as I know, the only museum to deal directly in its displays with the "Troubles" and the historical events which gave rise to them.

In the citation for the latter award, the (by no means radical) judges, headed by the Labour peer, Lord Morris, candidly said that the museum had been "planned and brought to fruition with immense faith and courage in the middle of a civil war". The British Secretary of State for Education, Gillian Shephard, who had to present the prizes and sit on the platform while the citation was read out was, to say the least, annoyed by the use of the term "civil war". However, despite our decision to deal with such controversial topics in the museum, the only real attempt to interfere with our editorial independence came from the Northern Ireland Tourist Board. They were worried that our emphasis on some of the more "interesting" aspects of our history and culture would be bad for business. We robustly disagreed. Eventually, without too much argument, we achieved our original intentions.

When we were establishing the museum, a few years ago, the designer suggested that we should have a display relating to the Great Famine. As we had no relevant contemporary objects he suggested something quite clinical, perhaps some graphics and models on the natural history of the potato with an explanation of how the blight had come to Ireland. After some thought I rejected the idea, arguing that to me that would be like having a display on the nature of gas in Auschwitz.

The Famine was certainly more than an ecological disaster. The old jibe that "God sent the blight but the British brought the Famine" is an indication, however unsophisticated, that human hunger has more to do with politics than with natural agencies. How can the awfulness of that hunger and the failures in official response be represented in an exhibition? It is not easy, as others

have discovered, to represent the Famine in the context of a
museum. Despite the best of intentions on the part of the organ-
isers, there have been many criticisms of museum exhibitions dealing with the Famine, in places like the National Famine Museum
at Strokestown, County Roscommon, and the Ulster Folk and
Transport Museum at Cultra outside Belfast.

We faced similar problems at the Tower Museum and ended
up with a simple information panel outlining the basic facts of
those years, and a small diarama depicting nineteenth century
"Poverty, Famine and Eviction" in general terms.[2] Is this a cop-
out or a compromise? I think it is a compromise, but not with the
history, or with our funders, our employers or our visitors. Instead
it is a compromise with the limitations of the museum as a mode
of communication. There is a difference between a museum and a
memorial. By its very nature, and because of the lives of most of
the people who were its victims, the Famine left few objects. In
the absence of contemporary objects (the very essence of a
museum exhibition) we are all faced with a lacuna. Maybe that has
its own symbolism.

Lists of inscribed names is often the way our societies deal
with this type of dilemma. One thinks of war memorials everywhere—in town squares, on the battlefields of the Somme, at the
Vietnam monument in Washington DC. There was such an original object connected with the Famine in Derry. The Catholic
bishop of Derry in the 1840s, Dr. Edward Maginn, was outspo-
ken in his criticism of the inactivity of the Whig government of
Lord John Russell. He had the priests of his diocese compile a list,
for the period November 1846 to April 1847, of the deaths
through starvation of their parishioners. On Mayday 1847, these
lists, wrapped in a black covering, were formally placed among the
diocesan records, labelled with a chilling inscription recording
"the Murders of the Irish Peasantry, perpetuated. . .under the
name of economy". In a museum today that would be, literally, a
stunning object. So far, unfortunately, it has not come to light.

As a child, I heard quite a lot about the Famine; how the
combination of a natural disaster with British government incom-
petency and, at best, indifference had led to the death of a million
people and forced another million to emigrate. The emphasis was
definitely nationalist with the blame entirely directed towards the

British who were governing all of Ireland during the Famine. As an adult, of course, I've learned the complexities of the event in its own time. But it is still difficult to do other than blame the British government of the day. They may not have wanted or caused the Famine but they certainly saw it, in their terms, as a fortunate "act of God" which might sort out the Irish "problem" once and for all. As in the "Troubles" of our own times, there was "an acceptable level" of death which, if it could be confined to Ireland, need not unduly disrupt the normal workings of the United Kingdom. Despite the "revisionist" attempt to play down the issues of blame, recent historiography on the Famine, if anything, strengthens the criticism of British government policy at the time.[3]

However, like many Irish people, I have also found myself having to ask who is to blame for the famines which have occurred in my own lifetime. What role has my behaviour and lifestyle played in the starvation of millions of my own contemporary fellow humans? Have I, never mind others (including governments) learned anything from remembering and commemorating the Irish Famine of one hundred and fifty years ago?

As we know well in Derry there are often problems about historical commemorations. The latter are rarely concerned only with the past. Invariably they have an agenda more related to present day issues than with the event they are ostensibly commemorating. In this city we have lots of experience of the problems surrounding the public remembering of the past. The heroic role played by the citizens' army which defended the city during the Siege of 1689 (including severe food shortage and famine) is worthy of being commemorated by all who believe in human freedom, including (if not especially) by those who think of themselves as Irish republicans. However, given the current near monopoly of this topic by the unionist section of the population, what ought to be a communal commemoration of the universal struggle for liberty has become instead a tribalistic and sectionalist celebration, in which the capacity for human division rather than unity has come to be emphasised.

The Northern Ireland "Troubles" effectively began on 10 August 1969. On that day each year the Protestant Apprentice Boys march to commemorate their understanding of (and, for them, the contemporary significance of) the "Relief of Derry" in 1689 from the Catholic forces which had besieged their ancestors. Opposition by Catholics to what were perceived as the triumphalist aspects of that march led to the Battle of the Bogside and twenty-five years of the "Troubles". Almost unbelievably, in the midst of the ceasefire, on 10 August 1995 the marchers insisted on returning to their controversial 1969 route along the seventeenth-century city walls. The result was three days of confrontation between the police and opposing nationalists, with consequent rioting, street battles, plastic bullets and a return to destruction.

In such a divided society, while it might be possible to get some agreement on the need and the value of remembering historic events, it is a lot more difficult to secure consensus on the contemporary aspects of these commemorations. Irish nationalists, for example, have struggled for years with the problem of Armistice ("poppy") Day on 11 November. While there is little difficulty in recalling the defeat of Nazism and honouring the sacrifice of those (including the large number of Irish men and women) who gave their lives in both world wars, there is, nevertheless, a suspicion that at least some of the commemorative ceremonies organised here still have more than a hint of British imperialism about them.

As a teenager growing up in Dublin, I can remember very well the powerful emotional affects of the 1966 commemorations of the fiftieth anniversary of the Easter Rising. On one level it was a celebration of the lives of those who had helped to bring an independent Irish state into existence—the swan-song of the de Valera era. However, some have argued that these 1966 events had an influence on the revival of the particular brand of physical force nationalism which was to come to the fore in the worst excesses of the "Troubles". In January of the year before these commemorations, there had been the momentous meeting of the two Irish Prime Ministers, Terence O'Neill and Seán Lemass. This had gone ahead at Stormont despite the futile snowball protests of the Reverend Ian Paisley. A new way of dealing with North–South relations seemed possible then. Sadly, this was not yet to be the way forward.

In 1991 the Irish government seemed extraordinarily reluctant to support the commemoration of the seventy-fifth anniversary of the Easter Rising—the founding event of the Republic of which it was in charge. Apart from the self-denial (as if Americans chose to ignore the Boston Tea Party) this was likely to be the last opportunity to honour officially the few remaining people who had been alive and involved in the original events. Diplomatic manoeuverings with the British government over the Northern Ireland question and the joint membership of our two countries in the European Union, never mind domestic issues, probably did raise some difficulties about such commemorations. But why should the country be embarrassed by its own past?

Official Ireland has seemed equally reluctant until very recently to remind us of the Famine. There were hardly any events in the 1940s to mark the centenary of the Famine. Widespread poverty and the existence of soup kitchens in Dublin at that time would have made comparisons with the economic advances achieved since independence a somewhat hollow experience. The fact that partition had carved out the economically most prosperous part of the country would not have sufficed as an adequate excuse.

On this one-hundred-and-fiftieth anniversary, however, the situation has been very different. Organisations from the government down, and communities throughout the country, have been vying with each other to mark the occasion. The government of the Republic has even grant-aided some Famine commemorative projects in Northern Ireland. One historian has suggested that we are in danger of suffering from what he called "Famine fatigue". However, there has not been universal approval for all the commemorative projects. A major television series *The Hanging Gale* was much criticised. Museums, as we've noted above, have the difficulty that the Famine, by definition, left very little artifacts. The subject of the Famine is very difficult. It was not an heroic costume drama like the Battle of the Boyne or a romantic epic such as the Easter Rising. It has been noted that there are very few songs about the Famine. Folklorists have pointed out how, in their sources, the Famine has been remembered (almost downplayed) on the level of a personal or family tragedy. There is little sense of the realisation of a national disaster. It is human nature, of course, to black out the worst details of the traumas which assail us but then we have an even greater struggle if the time comes when we need to remember them. It is clear that here is a great need for

much more serious research on the Famine, both at local and
national level.

Apart from its direct impact at the time, it seems certain that
the Famine has continued to have an influence on the lives of
many of us down to the present. These influences may be obvious
in terms of the emotions such as anger and frustration generated
by learning about the obscenities of the Famine through academic
or "unofficial" history. But there are some influences of which we
are not as conscious. We are the successors of the survivors of the
Famine not of its greatest victims. Although it would be hard to
identify any element of "survivors' guilt" in our behaviour,[4] commentators frequently point to the generosity of Irish people in
responding to contemporary famines in the developing world. The
anti-British feeling, among some of the descendants in America of
those forced to emigrate as a result of the Famine, is often attributed to strong race memories.

The Famine and its direct consequences had a powerful
influence on two of the most fundamental aspects of our lives as
human beings. It does not seem too strong to say that it "bug-
gered-up" our attitudes to the Irish language (and perhaps in
some respects to language in general) and to the whole area of sex.

The Irish language has been losing out to English for several
hundred years but post-Famine Ireland seems to have just given it
up. There is nothing unusual, as Joseph Lee has pointed out,[5] in a
subordinate culture acquiring the language of its dominant neighbour. This is fairly common throughout the European continent.
In such situations bilingualism is the norm, as it might have been,
and should be, in Ireland. But here, as well as acquiring English,
we surrendered Irish. Official and economic pressures made
English essential for engaging in intercourse with the expanding
world of government and commerce. More peculiarly, the Catholic
church made it essential for engaging with the world of the spirit.

In Séamus O Grianna's book *Caisleáin Óir*, dealing with the
people of the Donegal Gaeltacht of Rann na Feirste at the end of
the last century, the *Fear siopa* (Gombeen man), Pádraig
O Dálaigh, says:

> *Tá an Béarla usáideach. . .Bainimse caitheamh aimsire*
> *mór as. Thig liom mo chomhrá a dhéanamh leis an D.*
> *I. agus le sagart na paróiste.*

(English is useful. I get a lot of fun out of it. I
can converse with the D.I. (District Inspector of the
Royal Irish Constabulary) and with the parish priest.)[6]

The point being made is that all the important people in his
local society spoke English. By speaking English himself he could
be part of that establishment. It was the same for everyone; the
Irish language only condemned people to be part of the economically down-trodden.

In the same story the seven-year-old boy Séimí has to go to
confession. Two priests are there.

Agus na daoine ag caint eatarthu féin nach raibh aon
fhocal Gaeilge ag ceachtar acu, agus gur dhoiligh do
shean-daoine bochta, gan léann gan Béarla, a gabháil
ar faoisde chucu. Chuala Séimí an comhrá seo, agus sin
an uair a bhí mo dhuine bocht san fhaopach. Níorbh é
a chuid peacaí a bhí ag cur bhuartha air anois ach díob-
háil an Bhéarla.

(And the people were talking among themselves
that neither of them (the priests) had a word of Irish
and that it was difficult for the poor, old people, without education or English, to go to confession to them.
When Séimí heard this conversation, the poor fellow
found himself in a fix. It wasn't his sins that were troubling him now but devil the English [did he have].)

When we lost the Irish language it was not just our vocab-
ulary that was diminished. The Gaelic language had been the
principal means by which the people of this island had understood
and interpreted this island and their wider world for over two
thousand years. What wisdom, what knowledge of the environment, what world view was lost we will never fully know. We can
get some glimpses of it, of course, through folklore and literature.
However, having grown up as an English speaker in Ireland my
own involvement with the Irish language as an adult has left me,
in some ways at least, with a sense of loss, a sense of what might
have been. It would be wrong to overstress this. Everyone knows
how the Irish have succeeded with the English language. But
there was more we could have inherited.

The English word "heritage" has become much debased. In

the Thatcherite language of the 1980s and 1990s it seemed to mean only those aspects of the past which could be packaged and sold. Compare it with the equivalent French *Patrimoine*, a word which seems to reflect all the greatness of France which a citizen of that country inherits just by being born there. The word *Oidhreacht* in Irish in comparison (whatever about its etymology and technical meaning) seems to summon up, for me anyway, a sense of what I have not inherited. The cultural paradox is that my heritage was not inherited.

The other fundamental area which was influenced by the Famine was our attitudes to sex. Gaelic Ireland had been an open, earthy society—an agricultural society dependent on the fertility of land and animals. It closely observed and understood nature and procreation. This rural economic base provided the paradigm for much of its social and interpersonal relationships. In more ways than one, the Gaelic Irish were married to the land. In the case of their kings and chieftains this was literally so. These males were inaugurated by being united in a fertility ceremony (*feis*) with the goddesses and spirits of the territory over which they were to reign. Christianity tried to eliminate these concepts, but for over a thousand years it had little success.

Despite the prudery and voluntary censorship which has operated here for the past century or so, increasingly younger authors and researchers are pointing out the passionate themes of Gaelic poetry and song. The candid love poems addressed to his male patrons by Eochaidh O hEochusa who was the official retained poet to the Maguire family of Country Fermanagh in the late sixteenth century, are just one example of this.[7] Discussing the themes of the traditional *sean nós* (old style) songs, of which he is one of the foremost exponents himself, Lillis O Laoire says "*an rud nach raibh cead a rá sa ghnáthchaint dúradh i módh fíliochta é...Tá na hamhráin ghrá lomlán de phaisean agus de chrá croí agus caint ghlan ghéar iontu*" (what was not permitted to be spoken of in ordinary speech was expressed in terms of poetry...The lovesongs are saturated with passion and heartbreak in an intense direct language).[8]

A woman at a Fianna Fáil Ard Fheis not so long ago, very powerfully arguing against the introduction of divorce in the Republic, castigated those who said that the 1937 Irish constitution was not written in stone. It might not be she conceded but "it was written in blood—a thousand years of blood." She was no doubt ignorant of the fact that for most of that thousand years the Gaelic Irish had practised divorce widely and had made provision for it fully in their legal system. She was probably unaware also that the very word used to describe the party convention which she was attending, *feis*, is derived from an old Irish word meaning "to spend the night, to sleep with", its sexual meaning clearly obvious.

Pre-Famine Ireland did not have the sexual hang-ups which were to dominate the country for the past one hundred and fifty years and which, thankfully, are now rapidly changing. Tim Pat Coogan put it bluntly:

> Sex being one of the few outlets from their wretched-
> ness, the Catholic peasantry produced children in such
> numbers that not even the virulent fevers of the time
> could prevent a population explosion which the fail-
> ure of the potato crop in the 1840s turned into a
> nightmare.[9]

The Famine did indeed change everything. Ireland (or to be more exact the politico-economic system in Ireland) had not been able to feed her people—the population had to be reduced. I do not mean that there was a conscious decision to affect this, but at a personal and family level decisions were taken and sexual life lived according to "the priority of economic man".[10] In a society where contraception was unknown there was only one way to achieve this. Sex itself—libido—had to be reduced. Post Famine Ireland had remarkable demographic characteristics. The population fell by half in the succeeding half century and yet Irish families continued to be among the largest in Europe. However, the age at which people got married rose, and fewer and fewer people got married. Many lay people, never mind the clergy, remained celibate all of their days. The impact on individual human lives is incalculable. It is hinted at in the darker pages of our literature and in some of the official statistics. Joseph Lee has pointed out that lunacy rates quadrupled between 1850 and 1914.[11] He also suggests that these figures would have been worse if it had not been for the consoling effects of the prevailing Catholic ideology which extolled chastity and the benefits which would flow as a result in the next life.

There was of course a cyclical aspect to this clerical advice. The Famine had not hit all sections of the population equally. The numbers of agricultural labourers, cottiers and small farmers all declined over the next half century while the figures for the wealthier farmers increased. There was a class element to the Famine. The clergy came from that section of the population which had done well (at least in the long run) out of the Famine—the larger farmers and the commercial classes. In *Caisleáin Óir* Séimí's grandmother tells him *"nach bhfuil a fhios agat nach dtig sagart a dhéanamh ar iascaireacht"* (don't you know you can't make a priest out of fishing). Small farmers and fisherman could not afford the costs of educating their sons for the priesthood. That clergy, coming from a rising Catholic middle class, propagated a moral ideology which had, in the long run, not only the effect of reducing the overall population of the country but also of strengthening and increasing the influence of the class to which they belonged.

History may not be able to teach us about anything other than the scope of human nature for good and evil, but to neglect the past, or to refuse to examine particular parts of it, is to ignore the varied nature of that humanity. The Great Famine was a terrible period in our history. We may never be able to comprehend its awfulness, but we should try.

NOTES

1 Cormac O Gráda, *An Drochshaol—Béaloideas agus Amhráin*, (Baile Átha Cliath, 1994), p.3. The translation is mine, as are the others below.

2 The major contribution in Derry of the city and museum service to the Famine commemoration will be the restoration of the old workhouse and its fitting out as a library and local history museum.

3 Christine Kinealy, *This Great Calamity: The Irish Famine 1845-52*, (Dublin: Gill & Macmillan, 1994, US: Roberts Rinehart, 1995).

4 For a discussion of the concept of "survivors' guilt", and similar controversies in the debate surrounding the historiography of the Famine, see Christine Kinealy, "Beyond Revisionism—reassessing the Great Irish Famine", *History Ireland*, Vol. 3 No. 4, Winter 1995, pp.28-34.

5 Joseph Lee, *Ireland 1912-1985*, (Cambridge, 1989), pp.663-4.

6 Séamus O Grianna, "Aois Discreidimh" in *Caisleáin Óir*, (Corcaigh, 1976), p.22.

7 James Carney, *The Irish Bardic Poet*, (Dublin, 1967).

8 Lillis O Laoire, "An Ceol Dúchais i dTír Chonaill" in W. Nolan, L. Ronayne and M. Dunleavy (eds), *Donegal History and Society*, (Dublin, 1995), p.749.

9 Tim Pat Coogan, *The Troubles*, (London: Hutchinson, USA: Roberts Rinehart, 1995), p.9

10 Joseph Lee, *The Modernisation of Irish Society 1848-1918*, (Dublin, 1973), p.5.

11 Ibid., p.6.

Potato Diggers (Illustrated London News, *1849; courtesy of the
National Library of Ireland.*)

CHAPTER FOUR
Identifying the Malady

Inscriptions
BY EAVAN BOLAND

About holiday rooms there can be
a solid feel at first. Then, as you go upstairs,
the air gets
a dry rustle of excitement

the way a new dress comes out of tissue paper
up and out of it, and
the girl watching this thinks:
Where will I wear it? Who will kiss me in it?

Peter
was the name on the cot.
The cot was made of the carefully-bought
scarcities of the nineteen-forties;
oak. Tersely planed and varnished.
Cast-steel hinges.

I stood where the roof sloped into
paper roses,
in a room where a child once went to sleep,
looking at blue, painted lettering;

as he slept
someone had found for him
five pieces of the alphabet which said

the mauve petals of his eyelids as they closed out
the scalded hallway moonlight made of the ocean at
the end of his road.

Someone knew
the importance of giving him a name.

For years I have known
how important it is
not to name
the coffins, the murdered in them,
the deaths in alleyways and on doorsteps—
in case they rise out of their names
and I recognise

the child who slept peacefully
and the girl who guessed at her future in
the dress as it came out of its box
falling free in
kick pleats of silk.

And what comfort can there be
in knowing that
in a distant room
his sign is safe tonight
and reposes its modest blues in darkness?

Or that outside his window
the name-eating elements—the salt wind, the rain—
must find
headstones to feed their hunger?

Leaves of Pain

BY JIMMY BRESLIN
— The Recorder, the Journal of the
American Irish Historical Society, *1977*

At first, it seemed to be nothing. It was a curled up dark brown leaf of about the size of a good lock of hair and it was preserved in glass in a room in the Fairlow Herbarium in Cambridge, in Massachusetts. A typewritten card alongside the leaf said that it was taken from an infected potato plant in Ireland during the Famine of 1845–51. I looked at the leaf, read the card and began to walk away and, of course, did not leave. Here in this glass case was the weapon used by the earth when it turned against men and nearly ended a nation, the leaf which determined the character of its people, wherever they were, for generations at the least.

Behind the glass case, on long shelves, was an impressive line of books. There also was in the room a man who could help me decipher some of the written matter. I decided to forget about taking one of the morning shuttles to New York. I sat at a table. Usually when you are around relics of things Irish, you hear in your mind a song or have the feel of a smile. This time, the hand went for a book.

At the time of the Famine, the man in charge of the room observed, mycology, the study of fungi, was only beginning. People from a couple of places in the world went to Ireland to collect blighted plants and then took them back to their laboratories to study. But they could give Ireland no help. By the time the Famine was ending, the potato fungus was only being given a name: *phytophthora infestans*. One of the things most vile about the use of a dead language is the manner in which the message of horror becomes lost in the struggle to absorb the inhabitual syllables.

The man in the Fairlow Herbarium suggested one of the books, *The Advance of the Fungi* by E. C. Large. The author noted that in good weather the potato fungus reproduced sexually. However, when conditions were constantly wet and chilly, the fungus reproduced asexually, and at great rapidity. On two occasions during the Famine years, there was a chill rain that did not seem to end. Fungus appeared wherever the land was wet. Potato leaves became brown and started to curl up and the potato underneath became purple and mushy. With no food, over a million died and millions fled.

The book says that experiments over the years appeared to show that the blighted potato was edible. Because of the fungus causing the inside of the potato to break down, much of the starch turned to sugar, thereby giving the potato a strange sweet taste. This is something which can be said in the safety of a laboratory. But while a million were dying, people tried to eat the potatoes and found they could not. The potato originated from the Andes Mountains of Peru, where it grows in many varieties. However the English, who introduced it to Ireland in the sixteenth century, planted only one variety, the clone, and it is susceptible to the wet fingers of fungus. With no second variety of potato plant to withstand the disease, the blight became total. The Irish, ignorant of all this, planted any eyes which seemed even vaguely uninfected and prayed that the next crop would be clean, and the new plants were as infected as the ones from which they came.

As I was reading this, I began to think of the crumbling stone building on Bantry Bay, in Cork. The ruin stands right on the bay, at a point where the rocky shore builds up to great cliffs that go along flat, deep water until the water begins to rise and fall in great swells and suddenly the land ends and now it is ocean, not bay, slapping against the bottom of the cliff and sending spray high into the air, up to the top of the cliff.

The ruin sits in a tangle of rough brush and is difficult to reach. In 1845, at the height of the Famine, the place was a granary. Each day, while Irishmen died with their mouths stained green from eating grass, the British worked this granary and filled sacks that were placed on ships and sent to England. Near the end, when there were no people able to work in fields and supply the granary, the British announced that the granary would be donated to the people. It could be used as a Children's Home, which is a twisted way of saying what it actually became: a morgue for children who died of not having food. The bodies of children were stacked floor to ceiling in the granary.

And now, in this room in Cambridge, with the time passing and the man in charge finding me still more to read about fungus and Famine, the line in the English language I always think of first walked through my mind in all its stateliness and wisdom: "Too long a sacrifice can make a stone of the heart."

The sons of this Famine burned an orphanage in New York City. It was the Coloured Orphan Asylum, of course; when the maimed poor lash out anywhere, they seek not the blood of Dukes and Earls, but rather of victims such as they. The Coloured Orphan Asylum was on Fifth Avenue, between 43rd and 44th Streets. At three p.m. on Sunday, 12 July 1863, a crowd of nearly four thousand Irish broke through the front gate of the orphanage, rushed across the lawns and broke inside. The orphanage officials managed to sneak four hundred terrified black orphans out of the back door and take them to the safety of a police station. The mob of Irish meanwhile ransacked and burned the orphanage. And throughout the city, mobs of Irish, their hearts shale, their souls dead, rioted and killed blacks.

I always thought it was important to know what happens to men when their insides become stone. The violence, the illegal acts are not to be condoned. But I always want to know why it is that all people, even those of your own, lose control of the devils inside them. Perhaps something can be learned.

The riots in New York are called in history books "The Draft Riots", but at the time the newspapers referred to them as the "Irish Riots". The government in 1863 set up a military draft for New York, a lottery, but one from which any citizen could buy himself out for $300. Which excluded the Irish, who barely had money for dinner.

The first drawing was held on Saturday, 11 July. When the names were published in the Sunday morning newspapers, growls ran through the tenements where the Irish lived. Soon, people were out in the streets, carrying anything that would hurt, and with their first violence, their first beatings, their first fires, the word struck them, as similar words have sunk into any thrashing crowds, throughout history. In Odessa, the crew of the Potamkin mutinied and the people were fighting the troops on the steps rising from the harbour and them somebody screamed the word: "Jews!" It became not a fight against authority any more; it was a pogrom. And in Manhattan, in 1863, here were the Irish, the sons of famine, out in the streets against the injustice of a system that would allow the rich to buy out of a danger in which the poor

must perish. And suddenly, inevitably, as the water of a wave turns
to white, the word races through the crowd: "Niggers!"

On 32nd Street between Fifth and Sixth Avenues, a black
was hung from a tree and his house burned. An army officer who
had tried to stop the mobs was trapped on 33rd Street, between
2nd and 1st Avenues. He was beaten to death, and the mob played
with his body for hours, as a kitten does with a spool. At six p.m.,
on the second night of the rioting, a mob of six hundred Irish
attacked a house on the corner of Baxter and Leonard Streets in
which twenty black families lived.

The police arrived at this point, two platoons of them led by
three sergeants, listed in the records as Walsh, Quinn and
Kennedy. The patrolmen under them all were Irish. At this time
ninety per cent of the police force were Irish: Irish with their trait
of loyalty. And loyalty was stronger than stone. There was no question what the police would do: protect the black families and then
attack the mob, this mob of Irish. Attack them and beat them and
club them and force them to break and run and then chase them
down the street and beat them so they would have no stomach to
return for more.

During the three-day riot, the rioters killed eighteen blacks.
There could have been thousands killed without the police intervention. The police and army units killed twelve hundred rioters.
Seven thousand were injured. General Harvey Brown, in charge of
the army troops, said of New York's Irish police department:
"never in our civil or military life have I ever seen such untiring
devotion or such efficient service."

In the history of the Police Department of the City of New
York, it was the act which first caused people to call them "The
Finest." That it came as the result of having to put down savage
assaults by Irish is something which should neither be hidden or
explained away. Remember it. It happened just over one hundred
and thirty years ago, which is a short time as the history of the
earth is measured. Remember it, and do not condone it. But at
the same time know about it. Know by being told what Yeats knew
by instinct: the effect of something like this leaf in the glass in the
room in Cambridge.

I gave the man back his books, said thank you and left the
Herbarium and went to the airport in Boston for the shuttle to

New York. I had to be at a wake in Brooklyn, in the Bedford Stuyvesant neighbourhood. My friend Mabel Mabry's nephew, Allen Burnett, had been murdered. He was walking along Bedford Avenue and somebody shot him in the back because Allen would not give up his new coat. After the wake, I rode in the cab past the place were Allen was murdered. Bedford Avenue at this part, Kosciusko Street, is empty. The buildings have been burned and the sidewalks are covered with glass. In an empty lot alongside a boarded-up building, a pack of dogs rooted through garbage that had been thrown there during the day. Weeds grow in the lot. The weeds made me think of the curled up dark brown leaf I had seen earlier that day.

Troubled People

BY JOHN WATERS

34-20-107 St.
Corona 68
NY
Oct. 24 1962

My Dear Tom,

Thanks for your nice letter received and I am sorry to be so impatient but I was afraid that I might not have put the right address on or not enough postage but I am glad you got it allright, you have got a nice family the childrens pictures are lovely, your little girl Marian looks just like my Ann when she was her age I would love to see you all I hope some day to make a trip over there. I hear from Aunt Maggie quite often since Kevin died, she told me Martin has got a nice place not far out from the town, she gets around quite a bit she saw Pat in Mt Edward and was to see Rose in Uncle Michael's place but I believe she had built a new house down at the crossroads I suppose you don't get down that way very often, I had a letter from James P. he was having the station too bad he didn't get married years ago it must be pretty lonesome for him all alone, Tom it must be tough to be out of work so long but I hope you will be allright and have no bad after effects after the accident. Jimmy Dan looks very well I haven't seen any of their wifes Dan's wife and children were out to see us a few years but late years we havent kept in touch. Denny had quite a few serious operations in the past but he looks very well now, and Dan looks great.

This letter reads like an everyday dispatch of family gossip and news, but it is actually a story of Famine. It was sent thirty-odd years ago by my grand-aunt Nora to her nephew, Tom Waters, who was my father. Most of the people in the letter I knew only by name. I met my grand-aunt Maggie maybe once or twice. I presume Kevin was her husband. Martin was my uncle, my father's brother. I knew him well, as I will explain. I don't know who Pat was, or Rose. I never knew of that particular Uncle Michael. James P, or James Patrick, was also a brother of my father, the eldest of five boys. As for the rest— Jimmy Dan, Dan or Denny—I don't know who they were. I'm fairly certain that they are all now dead.

On the surface, this letter says nothing, but underneath it tells the history of my father's family. This was a family which scattered to the four winds, lost touch and could not bear to restore anything except the most superficial of contact. This was a family in which dislocation, dispersal and exile were everyday concepts, part of the reality of life.

All of the people in the letter who were known to me were strange, troubled people. My father was a man who carried a deep hurt within him. I am only beginning to know that now, six or seven years after his death. I still do not know what precisely that hurt signified.

In my first book, *Jiving at the Crossroads*, I wrote about how my father used to collect tools and store them in a room in our house. The room was full of tools, from floor to ceiling, most of them wrapped in newspaper and tied with twine. My father was not content with one or two of everything. He would have maybe a dozen hammers, all wrapped and tied. And then, one day, he would need a hammer, to hammer in a nail. But he would not unwrap any of the hammers in his room. Instead, he would go to a shop and buy another hammer, hammer in the nail and then wrap that hammer up in newspaper, tie it with twine and place it with the others. This, too, is a story of Famine.

James Patrick, my father's eldest brother, lived in the home place at Mount Edward, County Sligo. The family cottage was falling down, but he lived there on his own almost to the end. He did not go out, and saw other human beings only on rare occasions. Then, one night, his cottage mysteriously caught fire and he was taken to hospital in deep shock. He died within weeks. This, too, is a legacy of Famine.

My uncle Martin left Ireland in the 1950s to go working building the roads of England. Every week, he sent most of his wages home to my father to bank for him. After a few years, he came back and bought his nice place not far from Sligo town. But

he couldn't settle there, and a few years later he sold up and tried
to buy a place some distance away. He bought a farm from an
elderly couple, but just before the sale could be completed, their
two sons intervened to try and stop them selling. The deal ground
to a halt, and a legal wrangle began to try and restore possession to
my uncle. That was in 1970. More than a quarter-century later, my
uncle is over ten years dead. He never lived a day on his new farm.
It was occupied by one of the two sons of the old couple. Martin
died in 1985 of pneumonia following a nervous breakdown, a broken man. The elderly couple from whom he bought the property
are long dead. Their son is still in illegal occupation of the property. A couple of years back, as legal representative of my late uncle,
I was made legal owner of the property and issued with an order
for possession. I was told I had a stark choice: evict the man or leave
the issue to the mercy of the Statute of Limitations. I declined to
evict. Why? Because this is a story of Famine.

In Ireland today, nothing is as you might expect it to be. And
at the same time, nothing is what it seems. We do not talk about
our history as though it were our history; we talk about it as though
it were somebody else's business. The idea that we, in our own
homes and families, are the walking, talking, living consequences of
that history is not something we want to engage with.

Given the extreme, traumatic nature of our historical experience, you might reasonably expect Ireland to be a front of radicalism and subversion—a society which, having been abused and
cheated and raped and pillaged, would at the very least bear witness
to that experience and express solidarity with those who continue
to suffer the same fate. On the contrary, we have a frighteningly
conservative society, which is prepared to bend over backwards to
gain acceptance from Europe's erstwhile colonisers. Even where the
legacy of history festers on the surface, we refuse to make the obvious connections. In the past couple of decades, we have seen the
people of the Republic, privately and through the voices of their
public representatives and media, work ceaselessly to distance themselves from the continuing consequences of their own history, just
across the border.

This is why I say that nothing is quite what it seems. I believe
that the things we say in public are very often not what we mean,
but what we imagine we are expected to say. Underneath the ritu-

alistic condemnations of IRA violence and republican aspiration, is a different reality, a reality which is not expressed in the public conversation. It is the reality beneath the surface of Aunt Nora's letter.

This is what I have found most interesting about the emerging discussion on the Famine, in the emerging consciousness of that catastrophe since the beginning of 1995. The story of the Great Famine provides perhaps the most graphic example of the distortion of history which the modern appetite for denial has created. Not only does the event itself, as the most catastrophic event in a most catastrophic colonial history, provide a window on the Irish experience of colonialism. But in the way that story was dealt with heretofore we have a perfect encapsulation of the condition of modern Ireland in terms of its ability to know itself. The evasion of its truth tells us everything about the evasion of the wider truth of Irish history. That the successors of the victims of such an appalling atrocity as the Great Famine would themselves seek to sanitise that event is something which defies all logic, except the logic of post-colonialism. And that is a term we are not encouraged to use. It is the condition that dares not breathe its own name.

When you cut away all the fudge, the meaning of the Famine is irrefutable. Even the revisionists cannot argue with it, so they just don't talk about it. Or they talk about the peripheral aspects, like the source of the blight or the consistency of the soup provided in the relief effort, such as it was. When you talk about the Famine, you have to cut the bullshit. When I speak about it in public, I make a point of saying, unequivocally, that the Famine was an act of genocide, driven by racism and justified by ideology. At first, I have noticed, there is a slight intake of breath. People look at one another. It isn't that they don't think what I have said is the truth, but that they didn't know you were allowed to talk like that any more.

It is interesting, I tend to observe, that the emerging new wave of historians and writers who have done most to bring about the gradual change we now begin to perceive have come from the Irish diaspora, a generation or two removed from Ireland. I speak of people like Christine Kinealy, Terry Eagleton and Liz Curtis. I note how I have found that, in the expatriate communities of British cities there is often a greater awareness of Irish history, and of its meaning, than one finds at home, certainly down south. I allow that perhaps it is necessary to have that distance to have the freedom from the host of complexes which cloud our view of our own history and in that sense lock us into it. These historians and academics, starting from a sense of compassion and hunger and righteous anger, have sought for us the things we lacked to explain ourselves and the way we felt. As a result, they have come under fire from both sides in the tit-for-tat battles.

Then I say it again. An act of genocide, driven by racism, justified by ideology. This, I say, is the inescapable conclusion from reading the accounts of the Famine written by English historians. It is the truth. It is also the truth as we have felt it all our lives.

And yet it is not a truth you often hear expressed. Why? The answer is that, like abused people everywhere, we, rather than the abusers, carry the guilt and shame of our own degradation.

The truth is that modern generations of Irish people have not begun to understand that the people who died in the Famine were their own people. In order to make sure they do not have to make this leap of imagination, they have created ideologies of revisionism, pseudo-modernism and anti-nationalism, to cut themselves off from their ancestors. If these ancestors can be categorised as primitive, ignorant and uncivilised, then the most you have to do is pity them from a distance. I always say, too, that if we are truly to remember the Famine, we have to be able to imagine the suffering of at least one of those who died, one of those who left, or one of those who were left to die. We think we are remembering, but in reality we are creating new forms of forgetting. At best, what we feel toward them is an objective sympathy, diluted by time, as though they were just an interesting historical case study which might be worth investigating in order to become better informed.

Most people in the Republic, for all that they may have strong opinions, believe the unfinished business of the Six Counties to be nothing to do with them other than as a troublesome embarrassment to the Republic's efforts to become a civilised European society. This factor has seriously contaminated any possibility of a truthful engagement with history, leading to a vicious circle of denial and confusion, which has enabled the wound to fester and expand. Listening to present day political discourse in the Republic, one could get the impression that the point of history was to provide a battering ram for the various factions—nationalists, post nationalists, revisionists, post revisionist nationalists—to make their arguments, and beat one another over the head. In some ways this is necessary, but is frequently destructive and at best misses the point.

Quite often the divisions which appear to be about the past represent also the divisions of today. This is inevitable and probably quite healthy. Clearly history has to do with the present: we explore the past to understand why things are the way they are. But that can sometimes be taken as permission to shift the emphasis of history to try to bring about the kind of present we believe ought to be. This is clearly dangerous, and certainly there was, in previous tellings of Irish history, a measure of myth-making and over-simplification. The Christian Brothers version of Irish history may have been well-intentioned, but, when exposed to the explosiveness of the renewed conflict in the North, unleashed a paralysing backlash of self-hatred and denial.

Post-colonial syndrome is a very complex condition, and one of its characteristics is the creation, in the years immediately following independence, of an excessively insular version of the nation. This occurred in Ireland during the 20s, 30s, 40s and 50s. One of the characteristics of this was a historiography which emerged to feed national self-confidence. I do not believe that this was wrong, in its essence, but it was certainly simplistic, and this allowed those infected with other variations of post-colonial syndrome to claim that it was not the truth. For example, the equation of Irish nationalism with Catholicism was a myth which provided a handy straw man for revisionists to knock down. There was little understanding in the country of the process which was underway, or of the comparisons with other post-colonial nations which might have proved useful. The death of Pádraig Pearse, the only republican leader with the remotest grasp of the condition, and of the scale of the freedom project which it necessitated, was a critical loss. So we were left with the second-15, who fed us simplistic half-truths, believing that we were children. Curiously, this was precisely the way the English had treated us as well.

But equally dangerous is a rewriting of history on the basis of a belief that these dangers can be avoided by detachment. In the past generation, much of the history we have been offered of our country and our people has been infected with a different kind of bias, a bias which attempted in some way to counterbalance the version of the previous generation. There was, as the historian Dr. Brendan Bradshaw has put it, an attempt to replace myth with anti-myth. This arose partly because of the desire of a modernising elite in the Republic to dispense with the baggage of its traumatised past. This elite believed it could do this without pain or loss. And its anxiety to expunge the past was increased by the commencement of the Northern conflict at the end of the 1960s. There is no doubt that that conflict has had serious ramifications in the South. These may be the least of all the ramifications, but they do exist, and they have an increasing relevance now in the post-ceasefire period. I think we in the Republic ran away from the problem of the North, and in particular from its historical causes. And because we wished to deny the effects of history "up there", we also developed a need to deny its effects on ourselves "down here". This led to almost total denial. We had imagined ourselves as a fully fledged, totally self-realised, independent "modern" society, so this could have nothing to do with us. We confined ourselves to ritual condemnations of violence, as though it had nothing to do with us. This denial was not a neutral factor in the conflict, but contributed to its development. So yes, we should talk about violence and our opposition and repugnance towards it, but we should also talk about our failure to understand why, for some people in the North, it was something they had to contemplate. Perhaps our denial reduced the options and increased the sense of hopelessness.

As if the denial of nationalist Ireland was not entrenched enough, the guilt spawned by Provisional IRA violence threw up a generation of Irish commentators and historians who thought they could see themselves more clearly if they tried to see themselves as others did. Or course, because that is the nature of the post-colonial condition, they ended up seeing themselves with English eyes. They called this "detachment". Detachment; Objectivity; Balance; Empiricism—these are words I believe we should be suspicious of, because they can conceal a more subtle form of bias or agenda, which does not reveal itself so readily.

But I have also noticed that once people have been given permission to speak this truth, they quickly begin to connect it to other truths which lay buried inside. Many of these truths relate

to the conflict in the North. Most people in Ireland do not believe
what they read in their newspapers or listen to on radio and television. They have quite different beliefs to those which are
expressed for them by their supposed representatives in the public
arena. These beliefs do not exist at the conscious level. Like the
undercurrent of Aunt Nora's letter, they emerge as a subtext of
normalised denial. I'm not talking about what revisionists call
nationalist "sentiment", but about the buried feelings which the
discussion on the Famine is allowing to emerge.

We have arrived at the possibility of a movement of synthe-
sis between the two extreme interpretations of recent Irish history.
One of the traps of the post-colonial mindset is the urge to give
voice to the coloniser's version of history. This condition runs rife
through the media, political arena and universities of the Republic,
and consequently through the entire public conversation. The
post-colonial condition creates a lot of diversion to prevent the
colonised people from understanding the reality of their condition.
A particular slant emerges, without self awareness, from the more
destructive feelings which result from a traumatised history—feelings of guilt and shame and self-hatred—and this requires a constant intelligent self interrogation to prevent distortion. In the
recent past, Irish historiography has not always had that self-inter-
rogation. As a result, we experienced a period of historiographical
tit-for-tat warfare. It was as if there was no truth except the truth
of the victors.

Thinking isn't enough. We think as we have been taught to
think. If we are to get to the truth, we have to trust the way we
feel. This is not the same as "sentiment". Sentiment is a half-way
house between thought and feeling, and so is not reliable by the
standards of either.

The telling of our story, whether in journalism, literature or
the writing of history, should best be approached with the heart
and soul as well as the mind and hand. Because although the substance of history is fact, its truth depends on feeling. If we believe
at all that we are more than physical beings, that we have a spiritual dimension, we must be conscious that there is a truth in the
way we have come to feel about the experience of history, and also
in how we feel as a result of that experience. We are the products
of history, socially, politically, morally, spiritually, psychologically.

So a historiography that denies the validity of those feelings is not wholly trustworthy. In a sense the point of history is always about feelings. What do we feel about who we are? Why do we feel like that?

Last year I interviewed Patrick Graham, a superb painter from Mullingar. I was attracted to him because his work seems to come out of some place in the historical commonage of pain, which seems to seek a cleansing of the humbug and the lies. I asked him if this seeking emerged from a personal sense of loss or from something else. He said that, yes, some of it was about his own past, his childhood. But most of it was much deeper and mysterious than that. It went beyond his own life. It was accessible to him, but only in silence, in communion with the landscape. "Walking in certain areas in Ireland, there is an ache that is not part of consciousness. I cannot walk in some graveyards in this country, or in some parts of the country, without feeling this kind of liquid sense of being absolutely lost. And then of anger. And this aching for a people I don't personally know, but whom I feel in my bones somehow. And that's what I paint." And he added, "What I'm talking about is being born with a sense of abuse. But a sense of being abused historically."

What he was saying is that there is such a thing as societal feelings, societal pain, societal hurt, and that these feelings have an integrity of their own. He was also saying that we are stuck with our history, that we cannot escape it no matter how hard we try, and that sooner or later we must face the truth of it. And this, I believe, is a function of history which we have come to disrespect, especially in the Republic of Ireland. Quite often, in our desire to be eminently reasonable, to show our willingness to forget as well as forgive, we have disrespected our own deeper feelings or the feelings of our parents or forefathers, or our fellow countrymen. I think we have for a long time disrespected the feelings of the nationalist population of the six counties. That is what shame and misplaced guilt can do.

The problem with a history like ours is that it is a self-locking device. It locks its own people out of any understanding of what it has done to them. Often, being the victim of an especially traumatic history means that through displacement, poverty, or shame, you have misplaced amounts of knowledge about your

own past. And this can lead to feelings which lack historical sub-
stantiation. When this happens in a rational society, the feelings
become suspect.

History is, of course, knowledge and fact, as well as feeling.
But I think the impulse to search for fact always comes from feeling, and that is essentially a good thing. I think we should trust
feelings more. We should interrogate them, yes, but we should not
dismiss or jettison them lightly. Do these feelings correspond with
what we know? If not, why not? If not, perhaps we are simply missing some knowledge that would help to explain them?

This, for me, is the great relevance which the Famine has. Of
course, it is important to honour those who suffered and died by
remembering them. And it is important, too, to acknowledge the
hard truths of their suffering. But the main reasons we have to
commemorate those events is to do with today. The Famine left
an endless array of legacies which live with us to the present
moment: the haemorrhaging of our young, the corruption of our
spirituality, the destruction of our independence of spirit, the final
assault on our sense of self. But it would be an even greater tragedy
if that calamitous event, which carries such a shocking emblematic
truth about our history, were to be used to lock us out forever
from the truth of our history.

That is why attempts to talk about the Famine have led to
such controversy. I was, I admit, surprised by the ferocity of the
attacks I attracted once I began to talk openly about the Famine.
One self-styled intellectual said I was trying to re-fight the war the
IRA had lost. Another told me on a live radio debate that I should
stop whinging about the Famine—"It wasn't all bad," he said. "It
did, after all, lead to the modernisation of Ireland."

Now I have begun to understand that I had touched on a
very sore nerve—the most irrefutable episode in the history of
English colonialism in Ireland. I believe that the viciousness of
some of these attacks is indicative of a sense of panic which may
mean that this is the last stage of the post-colonial process.

There is a truth, and it belongs to all of us, not to the win-
ners or to the losers—to all of us. The cease-fires gave us a great
opportunity to look anew at the historical roots of our common
difficulties. They gave us a chance to stop and look at what was
actually going on, and to undo the misunderstandings which have

prevented us from being of use to one another. We in the
Republic have not met the demands of the situation very well. We
have been timid. We have allowed ourselves to be bullied. We
stood idly by.

*****

The letter from my grand-aunt Nora changed tone about three-
quarters of the way through. It began to relate what came across
as an afterthought but was in fact the true purpose of the letter. It
was the facts of the final days of Michael Waters, another of my
father's brothers who had gone to the United States as a young
man. We had known almost nothing about this "Uncle Michael",
except that he was a melodeon player who had been in some war
with the American army. I have a strong memory of being taken
out from school one morning as a young boy, together with my
elder sister, and taken by our father to a High Mass in the local
church. I had been at a lot of High Masses, as an altar boy and
singer, but this one was different. There was no coffin and no con-
gregation. Myself, my sister and our father sat in the front row.
There was nobody else in the church except a couple of old ladies
sheltering from the rain.

The truth of Uncle Michael's death will never be known,
but it was believed that he was beaten up in the street for the few
cents he earned from playing his melodeon. He was taken to hospital, remained in a coma for some weeks, and then he died. None
of us knows where he is buried.

The last paragraph of Aunt Nora's letter tells not just the
story of his life and death, what it meant and what it should not
be allowed to mean, but also the story of Ireland's history in the
past millennium, and in particular since the Famine. It is the
pathology of the personal as the pathology of the public. Our own
shame about our degradation prevents us from speaking the truth.
In the mind of modern Ireland, the Famine was a hit-and-run:

> *Tom it was only through some of the men in the hospital*
> *we found out what happened to Michael, he was able to*
> *tell nothing what happened his head was all banged up*
> *and the Dr told me there was blood clot. he was found in*
> *the snow, could have been a hit and run driver. it was*
> *away down town where there isn't much traffic and he*
> *could have been there for hours before he was found, so*

there was nothing we could do. the government took very good care of him in their hospital the priest was with him every week. Michael was a good boy and all the family loved to see him come Lord have mercy on him.

Love to all from Aunt Nora

*Woman in Clonakilty begging for money to bury her dead child,
Co. Cork (Cork artist James O'Mahony, Illustrated London News,
13 February 1847; courtesy of the National Library of Ireland.)*

CHAPTER FIVE
Where the Famine Led

*H*ow did the effects of the famine generally show themselves?

The most fatal effects of starvation in the appearance of the poor people was a swelling about the face and a peculiar turn of the eye; the eye was made sharp and closed, and made long; the extremities of the feet became swollen, and the upper part of the feet less swollen, they were deformed; they were not well able to walk, and they became languid and careless about what became of them.

— *Evidence given by Rev. Meehan to the Poor Law Inquiry, 1849*

To those who have never watched the progress of protracted hunger, it might be proper to say, that persons will live for months, and pass through different stages, and life will struggle on to maintain her lawful hold, if occasional scanty supplies are given, till the walking skeleton becomes in a sense of inanity—he sees you not, he heeds you not, neither does he beg. The first stage is somewhat clamorous—will not easily be put off; the next is patient, passive stupidity; and the last is idiocy. In the second stage, they will stand at a window for hours, without asking charity, giving a vacant stare, and not until peremptorily driven away will they move.

*In the last state, the head bends forward, and they
walk with long strides, and pass you unheedingly.*

— *Asenath Nicholson in Kingstown (now Dun Laoghaire), Co. Dublin (1846)*

Famine Walk

BY GABRIEL BYRNE

Each year in Co. Mayo, there is a famine walk in commemoration of those who died during the Famine. Famine victims from all over the world come to the beautiful West of Ireland to take part. They trace the path of the doomed and weary, starving people who struggled along the same way through the Pass of Doolough, hopelessly seeking refuge from their devastating plight of eviction years ago. The Choctaw Tribe in Oklahoma, who had been forced from their lands in 1831, donated money to the local population.

We cannot see the end of the long road. It winds between the hills, shadowed now and then by dark clouds which threaten rain.

But no rain falls this summer day.

Only the wind grows cold as evening comes.

And we march on. Hundreds of us.

Ten miles through this valley so sadly beautiful and watchful as ever it has been, witness to the turning of countless days into countless centuries.

We are a cheerful group. Irish, American, African, Bosnian. From all places. There is the laughter of children. The music of pipes. The echo of stout shoes on the hard road. Random stops. Impromptu speeches. Remembering the famine dead, who died on this road and others like it one hundred and fifty years ago. And I remembering the stories my own mother told me, that she got from her mother told by hers in turn of those bitter years. Images that haunted my childhood. Haunt me yet. Images of genocide, starvation, death. The hollow-eyed skeletons.

Stains of green around their mouths from eating grass to stay alive.

Babies sucking on milk-less breasts.

Helpless fathers watching wives and children slowly die day by day.

And all the while, ships bursting with grain, oats, livestock leave the harbours.

Bound for England under armed guard.

It was a story I could not truly comprehend asking why with a child's clearsighted logic. Only later I came to understand the sad history of our people. Their suffering. Their ultimate triumph and survival. I am of that people and of that past. Today, by remembering, I honour them.

My friend Chief Gary Whitedeer, of the Choctaw Nation speaking before we set off reminds us that the dead are always with us. Today, they will be walking alongside us, he says.

I remember once my father pointing to an empty road asked me what I saw. Nothing, I replied. Look closer he urged, and you will see not just the trees and the hedgerows, but the ghosts of all the people who have ever walked this road. Every street, every road is crowded with them. The past is always with us, the earth absorbs our blood and our tears.

Later, the bar is packed. Music plays. Fiddle and bodhrán. The singing of *sean nós*. A man from El Salvador tells the story of his people. Their struggle for freedom. We listen. We know. We understand. Our suffering unites us. A great hurt has been done to our collective soul he says. The scars have not healed. Yet seeking revenge of retribution will not bring peace into our hearts. Do not condemn in hatred he pleads but forgive in love. The room falls silent for some moments and then the music begins again. Floating out over the street of the town to the sleeping valley beyond.

The Great Famine and Its Interpreters, Old and New

BY JAMES S. DONNELLY, JR.

For many years now revisionist historians have delighted in debunking nationalist interpretations of the Irish past. They have been especially busy in correcting what they view as those simplistic and emotional accounts in which Ireland and the Catholic Irish are portrayed as victims of English imperialism or Protestant sectarianism, or both together. In general, revisionism has had a triumphal march, slaying one dragon of nationalist historiography after another. Eventually, however, there came to be such a discrepancy between what the revisionists professed and what many Irish people still believed that in certain quarters the revisionist enterprise became the subject of ridicule. In December 1984 a notorious and uproariously funny lampoon of revisionism, as practiced by certain Trinity College historians, appeared in the satirical weekly magazine "In Dublin". In what purported to be a flattering review of a supposedly new book entitled *The Famine Revisited* by one Roger Proctor, the reviewer, whose name is given as Professor Hugh T. Lyons, tells us with a straight face that Proctor has turned the accepted interpretation of the Great Famine on its head:

> Proctor produces an array of evidence to show that most of those who died in the Famine years were neither small farmers nor cottiers, but were in fact landlords, their families and their agents.
>
> The details recounted are harrowing. Richard Mortimer, a landlord in East Kerry, kept a diary for the years 1846 to 1847. He records how, after giving away all his family goods to his tenants (whom he assumed to be starving), he watched powerlessly while his aged father, his wife, and seven children died, one by one, of hunger in the dark winter of 1847. What makes the Mortimer case particularly shocking is that

it now emerges from a study of the London money
market accounts that two of the Mortimer tenants,
Tadhg O'Sullivan and Páidín Ferriter, actually invested
considerable sums of money in London in those very
years.[1]

More recently, the entire revisionist enterprise received a
much more serious challenge from Dr. Brendan Bradshaw in that
citadel of revisionism, the journal *Irish Historical Studies*. His article, "Nationalism and Historical Scholarship in Modern Ireland",
published in November 1989, took the whole revisionist school
to task for its pursuit of a kind of scientific, objective, value-free
examination of the Irish past. In this approach, Bradshaw charged,
the revisionists had employed a variety of interpretive strategies in
order to filter out the trauma in the really catastrophic episodes of
Irish history, such as the English conquest of the sixteenth century, the great rebellion of the 1640s, and the Great Famine itself.[2]
In fact, the Famine provided Bradshaw with the best evidence for
his case, revealing what he considered "perhaps more tellingly than
any other episode of Irish history the inability of practitioners of
value-free history to cope with the catastrophic dimensions of the
Irish past". In the fifty years since the emergence of their school
of history in the mid-1930s, they had managed to produce "only
one academic study of the Famine", and when the revisionist Mary
E. Daly published a brief account in 1986, she too, according to
Bradshaw, sought to distance herself and her readers "from the
stark reality". Seconding criticisms of Daly's book made by
Cormac O Gráda, Bradshaw asserts that she did this "by assuming
an austerely clinical tone, and by resorting to sociological
euphemism and cliometic excursi, thus cerebralising and thereby
de-sensitising the trauma."[3]

Bradshaw's views have aroused heated controversy, even *ad
hominem* attacks, and the debate is likely to continue for quite a
long time.[4] Without subscribing fully to his arguments, I believe
that he is essentially correct in asserting that numerous revisionist
historians have not honestly and squarely confronted what he calls
"the catastrophic dimensions of the Irish past". I wish to examine
this question with reference to the Great Famine, focusing especially on the issue of the extent to which the British government
was responsible for mass death and mass emigration because of the

policies which it did or did not pursue. We may begin with the
only two major book-length studies of the Famine to appear so far
in this century, which differed markedly in character, interpretation, and audience.

For revisionists, the publication in 1962 of *The Great
Hunger: Ireland, 1845–1849*, by Cecil Woodham-Smith was not
an altogether welcome event.[5] These academic historians no
doubt envied the book's commercial success; *The Great Hunger*
was immediately a best-seller on two continents, and its premier
status as the most widely read Irish history book of all time has
only grown with the years. But far more troubling to the revisionists was the "ungoverned passion" to which numerous reviewers of the book succumbed. Vigorously protesting against this
"torrent of muddled thinking", the late F. S. L. Lyons called
attention in *Irish Historical Studies* to a striking aspect of the popular response:

> Ugly words were used in many reviews—"race-mur-
> der" and "genocide", for example—to describe the
> British government's attitude to the Irish peasantry at
> the time of the Famine, and Sir Charles Trevelyan's
> handling of the situation was compared by some
> excited writers to Hitler's "final solution" for the
> Jewish problem. This response to Mrs. Woodham-
> Smith's work was not confined to Irish reviewers, nor
> even to imaginative authors like Mr. Frank O'Connor,
> but cropped up repeatedly in English periodicals also,
> occasionally in articles by reputable historians.[6]

Among such reputable scholars, Lyons must have had in
mind A. J. P. Taylor, the distinguished, if controversial, historian
of modern Germany, whose review of *The Great Hunger* appeared
in the *New Statesman* and was later reprinted under the title
"Genocide" in his *Essays in English History*. At times Taylor
sounded just like the famous revolutionary nationalist John
Mitchel. In the late 1840s, declared Taylor with a sweeping reference to the notorious German extermination camp, "all Ireland
was a Belsen". He minced no words: "The English governing class
ran true to form. They had killed two million Irish people." And
that the death toll was not higher, Taylor savagely remarked, "was

not for want of trying". As evidence, he offered the recollection of Benjamin Jowett, the Master of Balliol: "I have always felt a certain horror of political economists since I heard one of them say that the Famine in Ireland would not kill more than a million people, and that would scarcely be enough to do much good."[7]

Woodham-Smith herself was reasonably restrained in her conclusions, and Lyons absolved her of responsibility for what he saw as the emotionalism and the wholly inappropriate comparisons of the reviewers.[8] But at the same time he accused her of other serious faults: vilifying Charles Trevelyan, the key administrator of famine relief, and exaggerating his importance, failing to place the economic doctrine of *laissez faire* firmly in its contemporary context and glibly using it as an explanatory device without acknowledging the looseness of this body of ideas, and in general committing the cardinal sin of the populariser—choosing narrative and description over analysis. Admittedly, her merits as a populariser were great. "No one else," conceded Lyons, "has conveyed so hauntingly the horrors of starvation and disease, of eviction, of the emigrant ships, of arrival in Canada or the United States, of the terrible slums on both sides of the Atlantic to which the survivors so often found themselves condemned." And if all that students wanted to know was "what happened in the starving time and how it happened", then *The Great Hunger* would supply the answers. But they would simply have to turn elsewhere if they wanted "to know the reasons why"—a rather unkind ironic wordplay with the title of Woodham-Smith's famous book about the British role in the Crimean War.[9] Apparently, Lyon's stinging criticisms of Woodham-Smith were widely shared by other members of the Dublin historical establishment. In University College, Dublin, in 1963, history students encountered as the essay topic of a final exam the dismissive proposition, "*The Great Hunger* is a great novel".[10]

In saying that students of the Famine who wanted to know the reason why would have to turn elsewhere, Lyons had in mind the academically acclaimed but much less famous book entitled *The Great Famine: Studies in Irish History, 1845-52.* Edited by R. Dudley Edwards and T. Desmond Williams, two of the founding leaders of modern Irish historiography, this book was published in Dublin in 1956 (and in New York in 1957) after rather extraordi-

nary editorial delays. Thanks to the detective work of Cormac
O Gráda and the openhandedness of Ruth Dudley Edwards, the
internal history of this collective and poorly managed historical
enterprise has now been laid bare.[11]

Surprisingly, given the academic and revisionist halo that
eventually came to surround it, this project had its origin in a suggestion made in the early 1940s by Eamon de Valera, then the
Taoiseach, to James Delargy (Séamus O Duillearga), the Director
of the Irish Folklore Commission. Offering modest government
financial assistance, de Valera proposed the production of a commemorative volume in time for the centenary of the Great Famine
in 1945 or 1946.[12] If de Valera expected such a volume to have a
nationalist and populist bias, he was to be sadly disappointed. We
are not at all surprised to learn that de Valera, who liked to tax the
British with seven or eight centuries of oppression, greatly pre
ferred Woodham-Smith's book, with its attack on British politicians and administrators, to the scholarly work edited by Edwards
and Williams.[13]

The editors of and contributors to *The Great Famine*, whatever their other faults, could not be accused of emotionalism or of
politicising their tragic subject. They appear to have been quite
anxious to avoid reigniting old controversies or giving any coun-
tenance to the traditional nationalist-populist view of the Famine.
The overall tone was set in the Foreword, where Kevin B. Nowlan
soothingly observed:

> In folklore and political writings the failure of the
> British government to act in a generous manner is
> quite understandably seen in a sinister light, but the
> private papers and the labours of genuinely good men
> tell an additional story. There was no conspiracy to
> destroy the Irish nation. The scale of the actual outlay
> to meet the Famine and the expansion in the public-
> relief system are in themselves impressive evidence that
> the state was by no means always indifferent to Irish
> needs. But the way in which Irish social problems so
> frequently overshadowed all else in the correspondence
> of statesmen testified in a still more striking manner to
> the extent to which the British government was preoc-
> cupied with the Famine and distress in Ireland.[14]

The worst sins attributed by Nowlan to the British government were its "excessive tenderness" for the rights of private property, its "different (and limited) view of its positive responsibilities
to the community", and its inevitable habit of acting "in conformity with the conventions of (the larger) society".[15] High politicians and administrators were not to be blamed; they were in fact
innocent of any "great and deliberately imposed evil". Instead,
insisted Nowlan, "the really great evil lay in the totality of that
social order which made such a famine possible and which could
tolerate, to the extent it did, the sufferings and hardship caused by
the failure of the potato crop."[16] In other words, no one was really
to blame because everyone was.

That their collective volume essentially failed to answer the
basic question of British responsibility was recognised by at least
one of the editors at that time. Very soon after the book was published at the end of 1956, Dudley Edwards confided to his diary,
"If it is [called] studies in the history of the Famine, it is because
they [the contributors?] are not sure all questions are answered.
There are still the fundamental matters whether its occurrence was
not due to the failure of the sophisticated to be alert."[17] By "the
sophisticated" I assume that at a minimum he means the political
elite in Britain. Indeed, Edwards was aware much earlier, in 1952,
that a merely mechanical yoking together of a series of specialist
contributions on such subjects as politics, relief, agriculture, emigration, and folklore would "fail to convey the unity of what was
clearly a cataclysm in the Butterfield sense". The need to comprehend and to portray the disaster as a whole was, she felt,
inescapable. If this were done, it would "also answer the question
of responsibility, so unhesitatingly laid at England's door by John
Mitchel."[18] But in the end, when the book was published, no
comprehensive narrative was provided, and partly as a result, the
powerful Mitchel's most fully developed indictment—*The Last
Conquest of Ireland (Perhaps)*—does not even appear in the bibliography. Given the bias already discussed, this omission was
entirely appropriate.

Let us now consider Mitchel's *Last Conquest* at some length.
Clearly, one reason why Mitchel repels modern revisionist historians is that his language is so vehement in tone and so extreme in
the substance of its accusations. Occasionally, these accusations

were personalised, as against Trevelyan. The awful sight of fam-
ishing children—"their limbs fleshless, their bodies half-naked,
their faces bloated yet wrinkled"—children seen as he travelled
from Dublin across the midlands to Galway in the winter of 1847,
prompted the vitriolic remark: "I saw Trevelyan's claw in the vitals
of those children; his red tape would draw them to death; in his
government laboratory he had prepared for them the typhus poison."[19] But usually Mitchel cast blame much more widely over
British politicians and officials, employing bitterly ironic language
that swept aside all restraint. "To make an addition to the national
debt," he declared, "in order to preserve the lives of a million or
two of Celts, would have seemed in England a singular application
of money. To *kill* so many [Celts] would have been well worth a
war that would cost forty millions."[20] The aim of British relief
measures ("contrivances for slaughter",[21] he called them) was
really nothing else but mass death: "Steadily but surely, the 'government' people were working out their calculations; and the
product anticipated by 'political circles' was likely to come out
about September (1847) in round numbers—two millions of Irish
corpses."[22] But the fullest statement by Mitchel that British policies amounted to genocide came near the very end of his book,
where he asserted that:

> [a] million and a half of men, women, and children
> were carefully, prudently, and peacefully slain by the
> English government. They died of hunger in the midst
> of abundance which their own hands created; and it is
> quite immaterial to distinguish those who perished in
> the agonies of famine itself from those who died of
> typhus fever, which in Ireland is always caused by
> famine. . .The Almighty indeed sent the potato blight,
> but the English created the Famine.[23]

What exactly was it that convinced Mitchel, and by what evidence did he seek to convince others, that British politics were
genocidal in both intent and result? First, there was the government's "strict adherence to the principles of 'political economy'"
in spite of, or indeed because of, its consequences: the export of
huge quantities of grain and livestock to Britain in the midst of
famine; the refusal to sell relief supplies at less than market prices;

and the wasteful expenditure of large sums on "unproductive" public works.[24] Mitchel was especially incensed by the government's refusal to close the ports to the outward shipment of grain and livestock, and he skilfully exploited the issue. "The great point," he declared, "was to put the English Channel between the people and the food which Providence had sent them, at the earliest possible moment." Not only did life-sustaining Irish corn flow freely over to England, but sometimes it came back again to Ireland with full English commercial profits and other charges added to the price. This encouragement of exports made a mockery, insisted Mitchel, of imports of cheap food under government auspices in 1846, or later from philanthropic bodies in America. A "government ship sailing into any harbour with Indian corn was," he claimed, "sure to meet half a dozen sailing out with Irish wheat and cattle."[25] And the exports encouraged by Britain had the effect of nullifying American aid. If Ireland "should again starve (as she is most likely to do), and should still be under British dominion," he sternly advised, "let America never, never send her a bushel of corn or a dollar of money. Neither bushel nor dollar will ever reach her."[26]

Mitchel badly misinterpreted what was really happening in the critical area of food supply. In fact, Irish grain exports decreased substantially during the Famine years, and imports, after a fatal delay, eventually soared.[27] Even so, modern historians cannot reject the Mitchel perspective entirely. The stoppage of exports after the disastrous harvest of 1846, and before the arrival of large supplies of foreign grain early in 1847, might well have greatly slowed the onset of mass starvation and disease by providing a bridge between extreme food scarcity and relative abundance.[28] Even apart from the precise facts of the matter, the open movement of food out of the country, no matter how diminished in scale, was certain to inflame the feelings of the hungry and starving at the time, and just as certain to be long remembered and portrayed as a graphic illustration of alleged British malevolence.

The force of Mitchel's case against the British government, however, was (and remains) much stronger when he turned to consider the cost and character of those relief measures that he branded as "contrivances for slaughter". Repeatedly, he condemned the utter inadequacy of the British government's financial contribution and the gross unfairness in a supposedly "United Kingdom" of throwing almost the entire fiscal burden (after mid-1847) on Ireland alone. "Instead of ten millions in three years (1845–48), if twenty millions," insisted Mitchel, "had been advanced in the first year and expended on useful labour. . ., the whole famine slaughter might have been averted, and the whole advance would have been easily repaid to the Treasury."[29]

Especially irritating to Mitchel was such parsimony toward Ireland in contrast to the earlier readiness of the British government and parliament to spend £20 million in 1833 in compensating slave-owners and in "turning wild the West India negroes".[30] The offensive language stemmed in part from Mitchel's pro-slavery views and in part from his bitter disgust that the British should apparently have shown greater regard for the plight of West Indian Blacks than for the famine-stricken Irish. Mitchel also portrayed in the darkest colours the economic results of the application (in the Poor Law Amendment Act of 1847) of the Whig maxim that Irish property must support Irish poverty: "the ratepayers were impoverished, and in most of the 'unions' could not pay the rates already due and were thus rapidly sinking into the condition of paupers. . ., throwing themselves on the earnings of others;. . . the poorhouses were filled to overflowing, and the exterminated people were either lying down to die or crowding into emigrant ships."[31] And when the Irish poor-law system teetered on the brink of collapse in 1849, prompting the Whig government to bring forward a special scheme to aid bankrupt western unions (the Rate-in-Aid Act), the burden of furnishing relief was still confined exclusively to Ireland. "Assuming that Ireland and England are two integral parts of an 'United Kingdom' (as we are assured they are)," Mitchel declared almost gleefully, "it seems hard to understand why a district in Leinster should be rated to relieve a pauper territory in Mayo, and a district in Yorkshire not."[32]

Mitchel detected the genocidal intent of the British government not only in its refusal to accept the essential degree of fiscal responsibility but also in the relief machinery itself and in the way it was allegedly designed to work. He drew an infuriating picture of a murderous bureaucracy, murderous partly because it was tragically bloated, impossibly cumbersome, and dreadfully inefficient.

In his judgement the administration of the Board of Works was manifestly in this condition during the horrendous winter of 1846–47 and the following spring. But what really made the bureaucratic structures of "relief" murderous, in Mitchel's view, were the goals they were intended to serve. Whatever relief was made available to the hungry and the starving, whether in the form of employment or of soup or of a place in the workhouses, was ultimately designed to break the grip of the Irish farmer and cottier on his house and land, as a prelude to death at home or emigration and exile abroad. Mitchel was perfectly convinced that the consequences of British policy were not unintended but deliberately pursued, and he said so forcefully and repeatedly.

Although the British government did not directly promote mass emigration, Mitchel poured scorn on the idea that the huge exodus was voluntary in any meaningful sense. If landlords cleared estates by means of the quarter-acre clause and chased "the human surplus from pillar to post", so that relief under the poor law "becomes the national way of living, you may be sure there will be a deep and pervading anxiety to get away. . .". At that point, asserted Mitchel, the hypocritical and sanctimonious "exterminators" would "say to the public, 'Help us. . .to indulge the wish of our poor brethren; you perceive they want to be off. God forbid we should ship them away, save with their cordial concurrence!'"[33]

At first glance, Mitchel's accusations may seem far-fetched, wildly erroneous. And some of them surely were, such as the claim that before moneys voted by parliament at the behest of Peel's government early in 1846 became available to relieve distress, "many thousands had died of hunger";[34] or the claim, made in a diatribe against food exports in the midst of famine, that "many a shipload (of Irish grain) was carried four times across the Irish Sea" to satisfy the injunctions of *laissez faire*.[35] But other charges contained a core of truth, or an important aspect of the truth, even if they were not wholly accurate. In this category were the murderous effects of allowing the harvest of 1846 to be exported, the refusal to make the cost of fighting the Famine a United Kingdom charge, and the decree that from mid-1847 onwards Irish ratepayers (landlords and tenants) must bear all the expense of relieving the destitute.

The harsh words which Mitchel had for Trevelyan do not seem—to me, at any rate—to have been undeserved, even if the

professional historian would choose different language.[36] After all,
in the closing paragraph of his book *The Irish Crisis* (1848),
Trevelyan could be so insensitive as to describe the Famine as "a
direct stroke of an all-wise and all-merciful Providence", one
which laid bare "the deep and inveterate root of social evil"; the
Famine, he declared, was "the sharp but effectual remedy by which
the cure is likely to be effected. . .God grant that the generation
to which this opportunity has been offered may rightly perform
its part. . ."[37] As one historian has observed almost charitably,
"such a view was itself unconducive to substantial government
intervention to relieve peasant suffering."[38] Nor is there much
truth in the suggestion sometimes made by revisionist historians
that the importance of Trevelyan, the assistant secretary of the
Treasury, has been greatly exaggerated. Never was Treasury influence and control in more ascendancy.[39]

Even John Mitchel's insistence on the perpetration of genocide becomes more understandable when certain crucial facts and
their interrelationship are kept in mind. Among the lessons that
"the most frightful calamities" of 1846–47 had driven home,
according to the incorrigibly blinkered Trevelyan, was that "the
proper business of a government is to enable private individuals of
every rank and profession in life to carry on their several occupations with freedom and safety, and not itself to undertake the business of the landowner, merchant, money-lender, or any other
function of social life".[40] Admittedly, the massive public works and
the ubiquitous government-sponsored soup kitchens had violated
the doctrinaire *laissez faire* views thus espoused by Trevelyan, but
that is precisely the point: they were gross violations which very
recent experience, as interpreted by Trevelyan (and Whig ministers) in late 1847, had shown should never be repeated. And of
course they weren't, even though the greater part of famine mortality was yet to come.[41]

As if to make amends for its misguided profligacy through
the summer of 1847, Russell's Whig government then moved to
fix almost the entire fiscal burden on the Irish poor-law system.
The 130 poor-law unions into which Ireland was divided were
each self-contained raisers and spenders of their own tax revenue;
the poorest unions in the country were to go it alone, their ratepayers sinking under the accumulating weight of the levies needed

to support a growing mass of pauperism. It mattered not in the eyes of the British government whether this weak fiscal structure was really capable of keeping mass death at bay. What mattered was the supposedly universal and timeless validity of a then cherished economic doctrine. "There is," declared Trevelyan in late 1847, "only one way in which the relief of the destitute ever has been or ever will be conducted consistently with the general welfare, and that is by making it a local charge."[42] It was on this principle that British policy rested from mid-1847 onwards, with the result that, as Trevelyan himself said (and said proudly), "The struggle now is to keep the poor off the rates".[43]

What we would consider serious defects of this tragically excessive reliance on the Irish poor-law system were not necessarily regarded as such by Trevelyan or Whig ministers. Certain key features of the Irish poor law, especially the notorious quarter-acre clause and the less well-known £4-rating provision, led directly to mass evictions, to the infamous clearances. British officials and Irish landlords mentally insulated themselves against the inhumanity and often murderous consequences of mass evictions by taking the view that clearances were now inevitable, and that they were essential to Irish economic progress.[44] The potato failure had simply deprived conacre tenants and cottiers of any future in their current status. "The position occupied by these classes," Trevelyan insisted in *The Irish Crisis*, "is no longer tenable, and it is necessary for them to become substantial farmers or to live by the wages of their labour."[45]

Although a towering mass of human misery lay behind the twin processes of clearance and consolidation, Trevelyan (and many others) could minimise the human tragedy and concentrate on the economic miracle in the making. Among the signs that "we are advancing by sure steps toward the desired end", remarked Trevelyan laconically in *The Irish Crisis*, was the prominent fact that "the small holdings, which have become deserted owing to death or emigration or the mere inability of the holders to obtain a subsistence from them in the absence of the potato, have, to a considerable extent, been consolidated with the adjoining farms; and the middlemen, whose occupation depends on the existence of a numerous small tenantry, have begun to disappear."[46] Is it not remarkable that in this passage describing the huge disruption of clearance and consolidation, the whole question of agency is pleasantly evaded? Tenants are not dispossessed by anyone; rather, small holdings "become deserted", and the reasons assigned for that do not include eviction. But whatever the reasons, the transformation is warmly applauded.

There is thus no cause to think that Trevelyan would have disagreed with the Kerry landlord who affirmed privately in October 1852 that "the destruction of the potato is a blessing to Ireland".[47] This was the common view among the landed elite. Lord Lansdowne's agent W. S. Trench put the same point somewhat differently in September of the same year: "Nothing but the successive failures of the potato. . .could have produced the emigration which will, I trust, give us room to become civilised."[48] But the connecting line that ran from the blight to mass evictions and mass emigration embraced the poor-law system imposed by Britain. As the economist Nassau Senior was told in 1852 by his brother, himself an Irish poor-law commissioner, "The great instrument which is clearing Ireland is the poor law. It supplies both the motive and the means. . .It was passed for the purpose of relieving England and Scotland at the expense of Ireland; it will probably relieve Ireland at the expense of England and Scotland."[49]

British ministers could also regard with perfect equanimity yet another major consequence of the operation of the poor law during the Famine. This was the severe strain which it placed on the solvency of many Irish landlords. The Irish landed elite was generally viewed hypercritically in British political circles. Indeed, in British mythology of the Famine the feckless, improvident, and irresponsible Irish landlord was second in sinister importance only to the idling and duplicitous Irish pauper labourer. British officials traced many of the worst evils of the Irish economic and social system to what they considered the landlords' criminal neglect.[50] For this reason the poor rates which landlords in impoverished parts of the south and west found so crushing in the late 1840s served in Trevelyan's eyes the highest social and moral purposes. "The principle of the poor law," he declared, "is that rate after rate should be levied for the preservation of life, until the landowners and farmers enable the people either to support themselves by honest industry or to dispose of their property to those who can and will perform this indispensable duty."[51]

Thus it was a distinct gain when many Irish landlords were driven into bankruptcy by the burden of poor rates and other Famine-related losses. Their insolvency was part of that wider opportunity provided by "an all-wise and all-merciful Providence" which must now be seized. By making it much easier for the clamouring creditors of bankrupt or heavily indebted Irish landlords to move against them, British ministers aimed to confer on a backward Irish agricultural system the elixir or magical healing of British capital and enterprise. This was the acknowledged strategy behind the famous Encumbered Estates Act of 1849 and its abortive predecessor.[52] How much importance the Whig government attached to this legislation was signalled by Trevelyan in *The Irish Crisis*: "The fact is that the main hope of extrication from the slough of despond in which the small-holders in the centre and west of Ireland are at present sunk is from the enterprise and capital and improved husbandry of the class of owners commonly known by the name of landlords."[53] Clearly, the landlords whom Trevelyan and the Whigs had in mind were not the current Irish landed elite, whose members he accused of relinquishing "their position in rural society".[54]

What, in conclusion, should we make of all this? First, it is now much easier, I hope, to see why John Mitchel could plausibly accuse the British government of genocide against the people of Ireland in the late 1840s, and why his indictment should have had such resonance at the popular level. In my view the cost in human life of both what the government did and what it omitted to do was enormous. As to the bold charge of genocide, Mitchel was wrong. A. J. P. Taylor was right when he said of those who presided over British relief policy (Lord John Russell, Sir Charles Wood, and Trevelyan) that "they were highly conscientious men, and their consciences never reproached them".[55] But an analytical survey of the means, ends, and results of British policy does not, in my judgement, leave much scope for the persistent inclination of revisionist historians to adopt what we might call a forgive-and-forget attitude.

Why they would want to do this, or why they might have done this even unconsciously, is itself an interesting and somewhat perplexing question. Part of the explanation is no doubt that they have been disinclined to judge the British response to the Great

Famine harshly when the recent governmental record of fighting famine around the world has left so much to be desired, even after striking advances in technology and communications.[56]

Another part of the explanation may well be the probably correct perception that even limited endorsement of the Mitchel indictment would give political aid and comfort to revolutionary Irish nationalists in our own time, whose version of this catastrophic episode in Irish history is a simplified rendition of Mitchel's. Still another reason may be related to the obvious fact that Mitchel wrote *The Last Conquest* with a determined propagandist purpose, and it was his view, or at least the view of which he was the greatest exponent, that became and long remained by far the dominant popular interpretation among Irish Catholics at home and abroad.[57] Historians, of course, are not in the business of echoing past propaganda or of endorsing the popular myths used to forge new nations. Revisionist historians have seen it as their special duty to explore such myths. But they must also seek a fuller understanding of the degree to which Mitchel's enormously effective propaganda corresponded to reality or illuminates it, and they cannot allow the political concerns of our own day, however well intentioned, to deflect them from this essential task.

NOTES

1 *In Dublin*, 13 Dec. 1984, p.36.

2 Brendan Bradshaw, "Nationalism and Historical Scholarship in Modern Ireland", *Irish Historical Studies*, xxvi, no. 104 (Nov. 1989), pp.329–51.

3 Ibid., pp.340–1.

4 See especially the essays by Hugh Kearney and Gearóid O Tuathaigh in Ciaran Brady (ed.), *Interpreting Irish History: The Debate on Historical Revisionism, 1938–1994*, (Dublin, 1994), pp.246–52, 306–26. See also Kevin Whelan, "Come All Your Staunch Revisionists—Towards a Post-Revisionist Agenda for Irish History", *Irish Reporter*, ii (Second Quarter, 1991), pp.23–5, L.P. Curtis, Jr., "The Greening of Irish History", *Eire-Ireland*, xxix, no. 2 (Summer 1994), pp.7–28.

5 Cormac O Gráda has called attention to the negative reception given by Irish academic historians to Woodham-Smith's book. See his pamphlet *The Great Irish Famine*, (Basingstoke, Hampshire, 1989), pp.10–11.

6 Lyons's review appeared in *Irish Historical Studies*, xiv, no. 53 (Mar. 1964), pp.7–9.

7 A. J. P. Taylor, *Essays in English History*, (Harmondsworth, Middlesex, 1976), pp.73, 75, 78.

8 Lyons's review, p.77.

9 Ibid., pp.78–9.

10 O Gráda, *Great Irish Famine*, p.11.

11 Cormac O Gráda, '"Making History" in Ireland in the 1940s and 1950s: The Saga of *The Great Famine*', *Irish Review*, no. 12 (Spring/Summer 1992, pp.87–107).

12 Ibid., pp.87–8.

13 Ibid., pp.96–7.

14 Kevin B. Nowlan, "Foreword", in R. D. Edwards and T. D. Williams (eds.), *The Great Famine: Studies in Irish History, 1845–52* (New York, 1957), p.xi.

15 Ibid., pp.xiii–xiv.

16 Ibid., pp.xiv–xv.

17 Quoted in O Gráda, '"Making History"', p.95.

18 Quoted ibid., p.100.

19 References in this essay to Mitchel's *The Last Conquest of Ireland (Perhaps)* will be to the so-called "author's edition" published in Glasgow by Cameron, Ferguson, & Co. See Mitchel, *Last Conquest*, p.148.

20 Ibid., p.94.

21 Ibid., p.102.

22 Ibid., p.126.

23 Ibid., p.219.

24 Ibid., p.107.

25 Ibid., p.112.

26 Ibid., p.134.

27 P. M. Austin Bourke, "The Irish grain trade, 1839–48", *Irish Historical Studies*, xx, no. 78 (Sept. 1976), pp.164–8.

28 Even Bourke concedes this point (ibid., p.165).

29 Mitchel, *Last Conquest*, p.152.

30 Ibid.

31 Ibid., p.211.

32 Ibid., p.212.

33 Ibid., p.140.

34 Ibid., p.105.

35 Ibid., p.121.

36 For an unconvincing exculpation of Trevelyan's conduct, based on the wrong-headed notion that he was simply the servant of his changing political masters, see P. M. Austin Bourke, "The Visitation of God"? *The Potato and the Great Irish Famine*, (Dublin, 1993), pp.170–7.

37 Charles E. Trevelyan, *The Irish Crisis*, (London, 1848), p.201.

38 David Arnold, *Famine: Social Crisis and Historical Change*, (Oxford and New York, 1988), p.111.

39 It could be argued that Trevelyan's importance and influence were inflated by the divisions over famine policy that existed among members of the Whig government led by Lord John Russell. See Peter Gray, "British Politics and the Irish Land Question, 1843–1850" (Ph.D. Dissertation, Cambridge University, 1992).

40 Trevelyan, *Irish Crisis*, p.190.

41 James S. Donnelly, Jr., "The Administration of Relief, 1847–51", in W. E. Vaughan (ed.), *A New History of Ireland*, v: *Ireland under the Union*, pt. I, 1801–70 (Oxford, 1989), pp.316–31.

42 Trevelyan, *Irish Crisis*, p.185.

43 Ibid.

44 The two great Irish landlords who sat in Russell's cabinet held and advocated such a view. See Gray, "British Politics", p.205.

45 Trevelyan, *Irish Crisis*, p.164.

46 Ibid., pp.195–6.

47 James S. Donnelly, Jr (ed.), "The Journals of Sir John Benn-Walsh Relating to the Management of His Irish Estates, 1823–64", *Journal of the Cork Historical and Archaeological Society*, lxxx, no. 230 (July–Dec. 1974), p.119.

48 Nassau W. Senior, *Journals, Conversations, and Essays Relating to Ireland*, (2 vols., 2nd ed., London, 1868), ii, 3.

49 Ibid., pp.40–1.

50 See, e.g., Trevelyan, *Irish Crisis*, pp.25–30.

51 Ibid., p.163.

52 R. D. Collison Black, *Economic Thought and the Irish Question, 1817–1870*, (Cambridge, 1960), pp. 35–40; James S. Donnelly, Jr. "Landlords and Tenants", in Vaughan, *New History*, v, pt. I, pp.344–9.

53 Trevelyan, *Irish Crisis*, p.172n.

54 Ibid.

55 Taylor, *Essays*, p.75.

56 Arnold, *Famine*, pp.119–42.

57 Among the numerous works in which John Mitchel's views were echoed, special mention should be made of T. P. O'Connor's *The Home Rule Movement, with a Sketch of Irish Parties from 1843. . .*(New York, 1891), pp.40–125; and Michael Davitt's *The Fall of Feudalism in Ireland, or the Story of the Land League Revolution*, (London and New York, 1904), pp.47–65.

Deserted famine village of Moveen near Kilrush, Co. Clare
(Illustrated London News, *22 December 1849; courtesy of the*
National Library of Ireland.)

CHAPTER SIX
Forgotten Lore

Digging
BY SEAMUS HEANEY

*Between my finger and my thumb
The squat pen rests; snug as a gun.*

*Under my window, a clean rasping sound
When the spade sinks into the gravelly ground:
My father, digging. I look down*

*Till his straining rump among the flowerbeds
Bends low, comes up twenty years away
Stooping in rhythm through potato drills
Where he was digging.*

*The coarse boot nestled on the lug, the shaft
Against the inside knee was levered firmly.
He rooted out tall tops, buried the bright edge deep
To scatter new potatoes that we picked
Loving their cool hardness in our hands.*

*By God, the old man could handle a spade.
Just like his old man.*

*My grandfather cut more turf in a day
Than any other man on Toner's bog.*

Once I carried him milk in a bottle
Corked sloppily in paper. He straightened up
To drink it, then fell to right away
Nicking and slicing neatly, heaving sods
Over his shoulder, going down and down
For the good turf. Digging.

The cold smell of potato mould, the squelch and slap
Of soggy peat, the curt cuts of an edge
Through living roots awaken in my head.
But I've no spade to follow men like them.

Between my finger and my thumb
The squat pen rests.
I'll dig with it.

The Need to Feed

BY CAROLYN RAMSAY

My grandmother grew senile when she was in her late seventies and cataracts clouded her eyes. She would sit on our living room couch, her hands busily working a rosary and tissue, her brow creased with worry about images on a television screen she could barely see.

"There's a man at the window," she'd call blindly in a thin voice. "Will someone make him a sandwich? He's hungry."

My grandfather and I would catch eyes and he would slap the air with annoyance, as if to say, "Don't listen to her." When no one responded, she'd lean forward to heave herself from the sofa. "Let me get him something to eat."

My grandfather would grip his arm around her shoulder and pull her back to the sofa, scolding: "God bless us and save us, Mother. There's no one at the window. Just sit down."

This happened over and over, several times a day, confusing and alarming my nine-year-old self. The image of a head at the window frightened me. I couldn't understand my grandmother's impulse to feed someone lurking in the alley. What if he were a robber or murderer? If you fed him, wouldn't he just keep coming back? I finally asked my mother what my grandmother meant and she explained that during the Great Depression, hungry men walked the alleys of West Philadelphia begging for hand-outs.

"My mother always gave them a sandwich or some leftovers," she said. "We were poor but she always found them something to eat."

It might also have had to do with the fact that her parents emigrated from a country where over a million of the people had starved to death, but that was never mentioned.

The memory of my grandmother, in the confused last days of her life, pushing herself blindly off the couch for the sole purpose of feeding an imagined hungry man left a profound impression on me. Either because of her powerful modelling or on the twisted threads of heredity, I acquired my grandmother's urge to feed people. When the soup kitchen where I once worked asked me to write a recruitment letter, I wrote about my grandmother. I've donated holiday turkeys, money and clothing to another soup kitchen and fed hundreds of people in my home each year. I've fiddled with a short story about a gourmet soup kitchen and fantasised about planting fruit trees in poor neighbourhoods to create a ready supply of fresh, nutritious food.

These are not the typical pre-occupations of professional women with families in Los Angeles. I don't know another working mother who worries about feeding people the way I do. My friends either don't cook at all or have full-time maids to prepare family meals. It has taken me years, on the other hand, to learn to focus on just feeding my family—not the entire world.

On late nights when I've pounded chicken and chopped vegetables alone in my kitchen while my family sleeps, I've wondered what precisely my problem is. I've always associated it with my Grandmom Duffey, but she also carried a heavy pocketbook filled to the brim with pennies and I don't hoard money. Part of me passes off the feeding urge as a slightly embarrassing compulsion, although its emotional depth and power indicates otherwise. After dropping food at a soup kitchen for the first time a decade ago, I had to steer my car to the side of the street because I was sobbing so hard that I couldn't see. There's such unremitting sadness at the root of this drive to feed people that I've come to assume that it links me somehow to the dark events of Ireland in the mid-1800s.

I can't know this. No famine stories made their way from my migrating great-grandparents to me, or even to my parents. "The Irish aren't real talkers," my mother once said. When I consider how my grandmother's need to feed an imagined ghost has followed me for thirty years though, it seems likely that her famine-surviving parents' attitudes toward food made a deep impression on her. How could they not?

When I think of my grandmother before the cataracts and senility, I picture her always standing in her tiny kitchen, shredding cabbage with her soft wrinkled hands, asking over and over if everyone had had enough to eat, or reluctantly slicing bruises, the bad spots, from a banana for me. "When I was a girl, we called them the good spots," she'd say, gently admonishing my wastefulness.

Although my grandmother was born in Philadelphia, her parents were both from Ireland. Their migration stories are beautiful and mythic, blessed with the Irish gift for romance and optimism. Even before telling the first one, my mother said she doubted its veracity. "I'm sure the reason I'm American is because of the Famine," she said.

The story goes that my grandfather's mother was from an upper middle-class Dublin family and fell in love with a fisherman named James Duffey. Her parents didn't approve, so they sent her to a proper Catholic boarding school in Philadelphia to make her forget him. James missed her so much that he sailed his fishing boat all the way across the Atlantic to marry her.

My grandmother's mother told stories of a happy childhood in Kells, County Meath, where she mischievously picked apples from trees around the famous monastery there and threw them at the praying monks. She too emigrated for a man she loved, she told my aunt, and never saw her family again. Neither Irish woman ever even mentioned the Great Famine or its devastating aftermath to their grandchildren. There was nothing about difficult journeys on creaking ships that are part of most American migration stories. It was almost as though leaving one's family and country were necessary sacrifices for love.

The stories must be interpreted in the context in which they were told, of course. While baby-sitting their grandchildren, these Famine-era women answered the inevitable questions about their lives. It would be natural to romanticise, wouldn't it? Children are so serious and impressionable; a grandmother knows that.

What little I know of my mother's family's Famine experience is a treasure trove compared to what I know about my father's family. My sister spent years studying our ancestry at the Library of Congress in Washington, DC but could never find the Ramsays' point of immigration. Ramsay is a Scottish and English name but my father joked and sang with a mimicked Irish brogue. We always considered ourselves Irish, exclusively, and Catholic. We identified with the Irish persona of tough, inner steeliness cloaked in charm. The Kennedys personified the American version of the archetype; I was named for Caroline.

The facts and stories I know of my family don't explain my grandmother's emotional need to feed people or mine. Since I was a teenager cooking spaghetti dinners for my brothers, I've fed hundreds of people in my home and in the soup kitchen. I've grown hundreds of vegetables and handed them out to friends and neighbours. The summer I was pregnant with my son, I grew enough vegetables for a family of ten and stocked the pantry until cans of soup, tuna and fruit spilled out when you opened the cupboard door. I did this even thought the quick mart a block away was open all night.

We have two refrigerators in our home and both are always packed—plates of lemon chicken rest precariously on jugs of milk and boxes of cake. Friends come to my house and head straight for the refrigerator, even when they have no intention of eating. They want to see what treats are inside. At the moment, there are brownies baked from scratch; fresh peaches, cherries, grapes and plums; homemade cranberry, ginger and peanut sauces in jelly jars with peeling labels; six loaves of bread, five cartons of ice cream and forty bottles of soda. There's far too much food for this household of three spaghetti-thin people: my husband, seven-year-old son and myself.

My friends, I worry, think I'm either showing off or suffering such low self-esteem that I feel chained to the kitchen. "Stop it with the cooking, will you? You're making me look bad," a friend said the other day. I was embarrassed. I couldn't articulate my compulsion about feeding people and worried maybe I was showing off. It seemed ridiculous to tell her food is sacred to me.

When I fantasise about what I'd do if I were rich or powerful, as every American does, I don't think about buying a fancy car or a mountain retreat. I honestly wonder how many orange, pomegranate and persimmon trees I could plant along the streets of this sunny, fertile city. That way, hungry people could eat without the shame of begging. One day, I was obsessing about the trees and who would care for them and whether I could set up a system whereby the poor could harvest the fruit and sell it on street corners in Beverly Hills. I was apparently talking at such a pitch, my husband finally said gently, "Don't worry, honey. You'll do it. You'll make it happen."

When I read articles about American businesses abandoning inner city neighbourhoods, I predict that old factories and industrial plants will be razed or destroyed and replaced by squatters' farms. I have not read of another person predicting such a fanciful outcome.

This deep empathy for the hungry comes from a woman whose life can be characterised only as abundant. There is something about hunger in particular that calls to me in a way that ordinary empathy for orphaned children, handicapped old people or endangered animals does not.

When I saw Jim Sheridan's movie *The Field*, I believed I found the causal link between my grandmother, our mutual obsession and me. The character Bull McCabe makes a speech about the Famine scattering his people "to the four corners of the Earth." I stopped breathing when I heard that. I felt a nervous, pit-of-the-stomach resonance of truth suddenly revealed. I was sure my ancestors had fled Ireland because of the Great Famine, that they had found prosperity and, because of guilt or sadness, needed to feed the hungry. I carried this belief even though I knew nothing of their stories.

Now that I've heard the stories, I'm frustrated. If they were so happy and prosperous there, why did they leave Ireland? Is it possible a sensitive child could pick up vestiges of survivor guilt unspoken by generations not inclined to gab about a devastating event? My great-grandparents, who were born in the 1860s, were obviously affected by the Great Famine but chose not to recall their memories for their grandchildren. To formidable old women in a bustling city and new country, it may have seemed like a distant piece of hard history they had been lucky to escape.

It's also possible that the Famine endures in the Irish collective unconscious, the way the Holocaust in Germany resides within Jews who have never experienced anti-Semitism. It's a wound on the Irish psyche that still aches, is still not healed. We each may interpret it differently, based on our experience. Because of my grandmother, I want to feed the hungry.

When I mentioned to friends of Irish ancestry that I was writing this essay, each told a story. One said her affluent mother always prepared too little food for her family—six chicken legs for a family of seven, for example—so that each dinner began with a scramble for food. Another friend's Irish-American grandmother limits herself to tea and so little food that she must occasionally be treated for malnutrition. She does this despite a full bank account.

That friend dreams of creating a meal-cooking co-operative for nursing mothers who are too tired to prepare the nutritious nightly dinners that their bodies crave.

Many of us have obsessions about food that, due to the long silence about the Famine, we've struggled to comprehend. Americans believe so strongly that they create their own destiny, apart from their families and culture, that the Great Famine probably seems remote and insignificant to many. That the stories are being told now is a gift to us. It was a story of the Famine that helped me to make sense of my urge to feed people and give it a proper place in my personal mythology. For that I'm grateful. In the sudden spate of media regarding the Famine, the image that hit me hardest was not of starving children or crumbling poor houses, but of grassy hillsides divided by grey stones in the tiniest of plots, plots that once supported entire families for a year.

That image moved me, although not as powerfully as the memory of my grandmother pushing herself blindly off the couch to feed an imagined hungry man. I can't know my family history, can't fully understand why that memory haunts me so. In the insistent need to cook, carry plates to a full table and find food for the hungry, I sense a truth though. I believe it's the same impulse that haunted my grandmother at the end of her life, so each night, I let it pull me to the stove.

In Search of the Banished Children:
A Famine Journey

BY PETER QUINN

"That's what makes it so hard—for all of us. We can't forget."
— Long Day's Journey Into Night

Memory is unique to each one of us, and it is familial, tribal, communal, the seepage into our minds of other memories, an intravenous inheritance, the past in our bloodstream, elixir, narcotic, stimulant, poison, antidote.

I was raised in a family that asked few questions about the past. We lived in a world whose boundaries seemed solid and settled. We knew who we were, took it for granted as naturally and unthinkingly as gender or eye colour. We were conscious of being Irish to the degree that almost everyone in the Bronx of the 1950s was conscious of an identity rooted outside New York and America. But our Irishness was largely synonymous with Catholicism and the Democratic Party. It didn't involve much, if any, awareness of Irish history or literature. I never heard my parents mention Yeats or Synge or Joyce. As far as I knew, "Brian Boru" was a bar on Kingsbridge Avenue.

The event that first brought my family to America, the Great Famine of the 1840s, was barely part of my family's conscious memory. My father's maternal grandfather, Michael Manning, left Ireland in 1847. He lived into the first decade of the twentieth century and died in a tenement (so the building is described on his death certificate) on the Lower East Side of New York City. Born in 1904, my father remembered Michael as an old blind man, kindly and attentive.

Michael was born in the 1820s and left Ireland in one of the worst years of a sorrowful decade in which over two million people, a quarter of the population, took their leave. "The scale of that flight," as David Fitzpatrick has written, "was unprecedented in the history of international migration." Beyond this, I know little of Michael Manning's life. I suppose he was a tenant farmer, part of the mass of Irish peasants who worked holdings of less than five acres and lived in "fourth-class" accommodations—one-room cabins built of turf or loose stone. Two-fifths of the pre-Famine population existed under such conditions.

There was never any family lore about what Michael Manning did or the specific place where he lived. Just as there were no heirlooms handed down to us from Ireland, not a trunk or dish or stick of furniture, there were no stories or reminiscences rooted in some particular corner of the countryside. It is mostly a blank.

Michael's wife, my great grandmother, was Margaret Purcell. Perhaps Michael met Margaret on the journey over or perhaps they were already married and left together. I'm unsure. Soon after they arrived in America, Michael and Margaret came to the village of Fordham, then a part of Westchester County, in which, I was told, relatives of Margaret had already settled. Michael worked a farm they owned, or more likely leased, across the road from the College of St. John, which Archbishop Hughes had recently entrusted to the Jesuits, and supposedly earned extra money by cobbling the boots of the reverend fathers. My grandmother, Margaret Manning, was born on that farm, in what is now the central Bronx, in 1868.

Eventually, Michael ended up back in Manhattan, drawn perhaps by the prospect of a job. By the time she was in her teens, his daughter, my grandmother, was working as a seamstress. Michael eventually came to live with her and her husband. He seems to have spent his life as a man of no property and little luck.

My father, who was more interested in the past than my mother, or at least more willing to talk about it (she militantly disliked and discouraged such activity), sometimes seemed to weave his stories from the twin spools of truth and fancy.

Michael Manning, for instance, had a brother Richard who sailed to Galveston, Texas, in the same year that Michael left for New York. (According to my father, Richard had only the vaguest notion of his destination and how far away he would be from New York.) Although there is no surviving picture of Michael, there is a faded daguerreotype of Richard taken in New Orleans in the 1870s. In a spidery, hesitant scrawl, it is inscribed on the back, "To my dear brother Michael." Richard died in a cholera epidemic in 1876.

My father, however, was fond of recounting a tale in which Michael and Richard were almost reunited during the Civil War. Michael, the story went, worked as a hand on the boats that ferried Confederate prisoners from Virginia to imprisonment on Blackwell's Island, in the East River, and Richard, who had joined the famous "Louisiana Tigers", was one of those prisoners. Neither brother was aware of how close they had come to meeting one another until the war ended and they resumed their correspondence.

It is possible that there is truth in this story. Working on a prison boat may well have been one of the many jobs Michael Manning held throughout his life. Richard perhaps served in the Confederate army. Yet the neat recapitulation of the Civil War's fratricidal tragedy is so transparent that I regard it as a romantic embellishment on the otherwise unadorned lives of these two men.

At one point, in pursuit of an Irish passport, I did some research into the life of my mother's mother, Catherine Murphy (née Riordan), who listed her place and time of birth as Blarney, County Cork, in November 1868. I could find no person of that name born in Blarney within two years—plus or minus—of that date. A friend of mine, a priest in Ireland, undertook an exhaustive search for me and turned up the 1858 marriage certificate of Catherine's parents, Patrick Riordan and Mary Looney (both listed "labourer" as their occupations; Mary, at age 18, is described as a "spinster"). He also found the baptismal records of four infants from this marriage who apparently died soon after their birth. The trail grew cold after this. I still don't know where and when Catherine was born.

The immigrant past I inherited was more generic than specific, a shared sense of the "No Irish Need Apply" prejudices that our forebears had faced and overcome. I knew Catherine Riordan worked as a maid, and detested the job, but I have no idea where she was employed or by whom. There were no individual lives that were offered to us as examples, Horatio Alger-style, of how to get ahead, no family lore minted into a coinage that was to be treasured and reinvested, a moral patrimony passed from one generation to the next, emblazoned with the hortatory motto, "Go thou and do likewise."

The only real record of their lives that I have is from their self-described "betters," the social critics and reformers whose well-intentioned interest in the "other half" was almost always tinged with condescension, if not outright contempt, an attitude which in the case of the Irish drew on old and enduring stereotypes that were common to Anglo-Saxon culture on both sides of the Atlantic.

Writing about the New York slums in 1890, Jacob Riis remarked on the inability of segments of the population to pull themselves up and move on to something better. He found the Irish in particular, who had arrived *en masse* in the 1840s, susceptible to this inertia: "The result is a sediment, the product of more than a generation in the city's slums, that as distinguished from the larger body of this class, justly ranks at the foot of tenement dwellers, the so-called 'low Irish.'" (Today we call these second- and third-generation slum dwellers "the underclass" and blame their condition on government programmes.)

In the view of Riis—a view that had been shared by Charles Loring Brace and other early philanthropists—the Roman Catholicism of the Irish and their romantic Celtic temperaments hobbled their progress and made them lag behind admirably ambitious immigrants like the Germans and Scandinavians.

"Down in the streets," Riis wrote, "the saloon, always bright and gay, gathering to itself all the cheer of the block, beckons the boys. In many such blocks the census-taker found two thousand men, women, and children, and over, who called them home.

"This picture is faithful enough to stand for its class wherever along both rivers the Irish brogue is heard. As already said, the Celt falls most readily victim to tenement influences since shanty-town and its original free-soilers have become things of the past. If he be thrifty and shrewd his progress henceforward is along the plane of the tenement, of which he assumes to manage without improving things."

The prevailing angle from which we get our view of how the great mass of poor and working people lived (and most often they were the other three-quarters or nine-tenths, not half) has usually been from above, with all the inevitable distortions and omissions this implies. As given to us, these lives seem flat, grey, undifferentiated, an existence without density or subtlety, without the emotional complexity that marks every human community, wherever it is found.

For their part, the poor have traditionally not only lacked the education and time to record their lives, they have also lacked the interest. The stories the poor carried with them were rarely about their own particular travails and tragedies. These events weren't remarkable or exceptional but the everyday context of life itself. For people steeped in rural existence, or only recently in transition from it, the storytelling they were familiar with was communal rather than individual. It offered mythic explanations of evil, death, failed crops, cures, curses, the feared or welcomed interventions of heroes, fairies, angels, saints, or God Himself.

Once arrived in the cities of America, these stories quickly shrivelled in meaning and significance. The old may have continued to tell them, and the young pretended to listen, but the landscape and mindscape that nourished them were lost forever. Besides, there were new fables to take their place, new tales and incantations, the mass-manufactured entertainments of vaudeville and Tin Pan Alley, dime novels, newspapers, sheet music, variety shows.

Even if the opportunity presented itself for the Famine Irish to make a full accounting of their story, it is questionable how many would have done so. In their day, the assertion of victimhood—of subjection, mass poverty, starvation, flight—was not a way to gain attention or claim a voice in the country's political conversation.

American triumphalism was at full tide. Irish self-assertion usually tried to mirror the arguments made in favour of Anglo-Saxon exceptionalism. The emphasis was on Irish virtue, on the purity of their religion, the antiquity of their origins and the bravery of their soldiery. Like England, Ireland had long been a nation of stouthearted peasants and high-minded noblemen. Ireland, however, had been undone by treachery and by superiority of numbers. So the story went. Even John Mitchel's famous howl of protest was short on individual examples of what the Famine did, on the class aspects of the suffering and want among the poor, and long on English perfidy.

Of all the many New York Irish families I know who can trace their American origins back to the Famine migration, not one possesses a single artifact or memory from that time. Yet over a million Irish crossed South Street into America in that single decade. Given the sheer volume of this passage as well as its nature—described by the historian Robert James Scally as bearing "more resemblance to the slave trade or the boxcars of the holocaust than to the routine crossings of a later age"—and the immense disaster in Ireland that caused the most horrific spectacles of civilian suffering in nineteenth-century Europe and drove most of them to leave, the silence around these events seems at first hard to explain.

Here again, I think, this silence in part describes the plight of the poor throughout history. Out of all the millions who have endured deprivation and brutalising poverty, out of all the families pulverised by punishing degrees of want, how many memoirs are there? How many detailed renderings of the conditions of the destitute—of broken hopes, lives, communities—do we have from the hands of those who suffered these events? Hasn't it been the experience of every group to let the dead bury the dead, to get on with the business of survival and hide or romanticise a record of degradation that might be embarrassing as well as painful?

It is not hard to imagine why many of the Famine immigrants chose not to instil in their progeny a vivid recollection of what was left behind in Ireland or encountered in America. "My mother was left, a stranger in a strange land, with four small children," James Tyrone tells his son in Eugene O'Neill's master play, *Long Day's Journey into Night*. "There was no damned romance in our poverty."

The Famine migrants suffered not only physical want and deprivation, a lack of food, the debilitating rigours of living on the road, of a journey across the Irish Sea or the Atlantic often under brutal and dangerous conditions, but deeper scars as well. The effects of their own powerlessness, of humiliating dependency on landlords and government officials, were imprinted on their minds and souls, on their communal character. "The Famine," as one Wicklow farmer put it, "left the survivors so sad in themselves," and "made many a one hard too."

Dead children are not such stuff as dreams are made of. Or mass graves. Or tuberculosis, cholera and typhoid. Or illiteracy and rude physical labour. Or alcoholism. The memory of the streets of

New York during the Draft Riots of 1863—the worst urban insur-
rection in American history, of the pent-up rage of the Famine
Irish, of firing from rooftops at Federal troops, of looting, arson
and lynchings, was never likely to be cherished and passed down.

The saga of the Famine Irish is studded with reminders of
the bitterness these people carried with them. It is there in the
story of the Irish deserters from the American army who went over
to the Mexicans and formed their own brigade, the San Patricios.
Preferring to fight with the Catholic Mexicans against the
Protestant Americans, the San Patricios were the only group of
deserters in American history to band together in the service of a
foreign enemy. Those who were caught were hanged *en masse* by
the Americans.

The Famine echoes in the court-martial of Michael
Corcoran, the commander of the 69th New York Militia.
Corcoran served in the treasury police in Ireland during the
Famine and resigned in protest against the policies of Her
Majesty's Government. After arriving in New York, he became a
founding member of the Fenian Brotherhood, the secret revolu-
tionary society built upon the Famine's legacy.

In October 1860, the Prince of Wales (the future Edward
VII) made the first visit of a member of the Royal Family to the
United States. His arrival in New York created a high degree of
excitement, except among the Irish where His Royal Highness was
known as the "Famine Prince". As part of the official welcome,
Governor Edwin Morgan ordered the militia to march in the
Prince's honour, but Corcoran refused, and the regiment stood by
him. In perhaps the only instance of such an ethnic mutiny in
American history, Corcoran accepted a court-martial rather than
obey. The onset of the Civil War in April of 1861 saved him from
punishment.

The Famine immigration changed the American ethnic
equation. The rural Catholic culture of the Irish, the beliefs and
mores of peasants accustomed to living in tight-knit, pre-capital-
ist communities with little experience of the yeoman individualism
of English or American farmers and few of the entrepreneurial
skills of other immigrants, introduced a new element of confusion
and conflict. White America would never have the same degree of
homogeneity that it did before the Famine.

Beginning in the 1840s, New York and other cities entered a period of rioting and public violence that wouldn't be repeated again until the 1960s. In addition to the week-long horror of the Draft Riots, the city witnessed what is still the bloodiest single incident in American urban history, the Orangeman's Day Riot of 1871, when the militia opened fire on a crowd protesting at a Protestant parade through a Catholic area, shooting a hundred people and killing over forty.

As a result of the swelling numbers of Papist foreigners being washed up on the East Coast, many of them destitute and unskilled, few with any experience of villages and towns in the European or American sense, some with little or no facility in English, the largest third-party movement in American history took wing. "America for the Americans" was its cry. Though subsequently overshadowed by the slavery question, the anti-Catholic, anti-Irish, anti-foreign impetus this movement embodied remained strong and could be easily stirred. In the aftermath of the Famine, controls were put on immigration that hadn't existed before.

The great wave of immigration set off by the Famine swept over America and changed the face of the country. In terms of sheer brawn and sweat, the Irish would provide much of the cheap labour that built America's infrastructure of canals and railways. The work was brutal and unremitting. Tensions between American bosses and Irish labourers often ran high. In the coal fields of Pennsylvania, the Molly Maguires became synonymous with labour radicalism and terrorism, and the mass hanging of twenty of them in the 1870s, most from Donegal, was intended as both punishment and warning.

The summary description that Peter Way gives of Irish canal workers in the pre-Famine period might as easily be applied to a large number of the Irish who arrived in its wake:

> They were paid poor wages, toiled under severe conditions, and regularly found themselves without work. As a result, they and their families were drawn into a marginal existence along public work lines, lucky to live at a subsistence level and wholly exposed to the vagaries of the market. . .[T]hey served the essential function of feeding industry's fluctuating need for labour. They were the miners and sappers of capitalism, sent in to

undermine the old order and to lay the foundations of
the new, dispensed with when the war was won. Few
made it up through the ranks, or even out of the
trenches, regardless of which industrial army con-
scripted them.

As the century wore on, the panicked, desperate nature of
the Famine years receded. The three million people who formed
the broad base of Ireland's social pyramid—those cottiers and
labourers who lived at a subsistence level—had either died or left.
The new immigrants from Ireland were more likely to have some
experience of farming besides potato cultivation. A growing number would head west to try their hand at homesteading.

In the cities, the Irish created their own neighbourhoods
and a tightly-woven network of parishes, unions and social and
political organisations. In a single generation the Irish went from
the most rural people in Western Europe to the most urbanised in
North America. As Kevin Whelan has pointed out, "the cities of
the Irish were in America, not in Ireland." Here, they began the
process of recovering from the shattering experience of the
Famine, of unbending from the defensive crouch it had forced
them into, of building a new identity in America that preserved
their deep sense of being Irish as it prepared them to compete in
a country in which the hostility they faced was interwoven with
possibilities for advancement that had never existed before.

With the advent of other immigrant groups, especially the
Slavs, the Eastern European Jews and Italians, the Irish became
less foreign or threatening. They evolved from pariahs to role
models. The peasant horde of the Famine eventually transmogri-
fied into Pat and Mike, Bridget and Kate, the sentimental, sometimes pugnacious, mostly good-hearted ethnics. Hollywood
would enshrine this brand of Irishness in the national psyche in
the form of those tough-talking, street-wise Irishmen (the depiction of identifiably Irish women was usually restricted to mothers
and nuns) immortalised by James Cagney, and wise, kindly priests
such as Fathers Pat O'Brien, Bing Crosby and Spencer Tracey who
never failed to discern the angel beneath the dirty face.

The political, religious and labour organisations formed by
the Famine immigrants became the basic infrastructure of Irish-
American life for the next one hundred and twenty years. A century

after my great-grandfather Michael Manning landed in New York, I attended Catholic grammar school, high school and college in the Bronx, in institutions all founded in the 1840s by the Famine generation. I did my graduate studies across the street from the fields Michael Manning had worked and was taught by men whose predecessors' boots he had repaired and shined. My education was paid for by my father's political career, in the Bronx organisation run by Ed Flynn, and my father in his turn had been pushed ahead by his father, a union organiser. Though rarely remembered or discussed, the inheritance of the Famine surrounded us.

The cohesiveness of the Irish was often remarked upon. Their own culture put an emphasis on communalism and sociability, and the entrenched antipathy of many Americans to all things Irish and Catholic helped to turn those traits into necessities. But the Famine also set in motion what one historian has called "a vagabond proletariat" that went wherever there were jobs which required little more than muscle and a shovel. Sometimes these migrants stayed together. Not infrequently, I think, they wandered off, or their children did, their descendants rapidly losing any conscious sense of an Irish past or identity.

I was reminded of these Irish vagabonds by Don Graham's 1989 biography of Audie Murphy, *No Name on the Bullet*. The most decorated American soldier in the Second World War, Murphy grew up in North-Central Texas. On his mother's side, Audie descended from old Southern stock. His father, Emmett Murphy—or Pat, as his friends called him—had a decidedly different pedigree. Pat's father, George Washington Murphy (oh, how the Irish loved that name! The way it rang with the notion of the British Empire turned upside down!), came to Texas from Louisiana in 1872.

The original Murphys, George Washington's parents, arrived in New Orleans as part of the Famine migration. Perhaps, like my own great granduncle Richard Manning, they had landed in Galveston and then travelled to New Orleans to rejoin a substantial Irish community. In any event, about the same time Richard died from cholera, George Washington Murphy travelled to Texas in search of an American future that turned out to have a lot in common with the Irish past. As Graham tells us, the Murphys were decidedly unsuccessful, and Audie's father was a tenant farmer remembered by many for what seemed his feckless inertia:

> Emmett Murphy wasn't a very good provider. He might have worked hard in his life—there were neighbours who said he was a good worker (but many more who said he wasn't)—but what he did never seemed to amount to much in the long run. Or the short run, for that matter. He liked to go to town and play dominoes, and he didn't mind gambling a little bit if he had any walk-around money, which most of the time he didn't. After the war, Audie wrote that his father "was not lazy, but he had a genius for not considering the future."

It is possible to find in Emmett Murphy's life Irish continuities that don't exist. Maybe Emmett was just another poor white tenant farmer scraping out a hard-scrabble existence. But it requires no historical sleight of hand to discover in the description of Emmett—in the man's love for music and for company, in his poverty, drinking and resignation to life's failures and futilities, in the disapprobation of his more earnest, determined neighbours—the tendrils of the Irish past, of the Famine and of its pain.

The Irish Famine of the 1840s and the Jewish Holocaust of the 1940s are very different events and should not be confused or equated. Neither a passing pogrom nor a sudden outburst of ethnic violence nor a wartime atrocity nor, as in the case of the Famine, the turning of a natural catastrophe to the brutal purposes of social engineering, the Holocaust was a death sentence levelled against every Jewish man, woman and child under German rule. No exceptions. None. The full force and organisational power of the modern industrialised state was dedicated to bringing about the total eradication of the Jews. As terrible and as traumatic as the Famine was, as formative of all that followed in Irish and Irish-American history, it was not this.

In the underlying justification of official policies and in the attitudes of those who survived, however, there are similarities. By the time the potato blight struck, the fixed and time-honoured image of the Irish in mind of the British public was of a people whose main role in the United Kingdom was as problem,

scourge, infection, perpetual nuisance, source of national weakness
and unrest.

The Times was expressing a widely shared view when in
1847, at the height of the Famine, it editorialised that "by the
inscrutable but invariable laws of nature, the Celt is less energetic,
less independent, less industrious than the Saxon. This is the
archaic condition of his race. . ." Within a century, buttressed by
the medical and scientific logic of eugenics and racial biology, the
National Socialists had codified nature's "invariable laws" into the
state's and, in applying them against the Jews, taken the underlying logic to its psychotic conclusion.

Among the survivors of both events what is at once strikingly similar is their silence. Each group had watched its world be
shattered in such a way that demolished the comforting illusion of
Providence having set a limit to human suffering. The survivors of
the Holocaust resisted looking back. It would take the rigorous
proddings of a new generation of historians and documentary
filmmakers to piece together the record of astounding cruelty and
unparalleled depravity which had been inflicted on the Jews of
Europe, a process driven in part by the attempt of Nazi apologists
to deny the Holocaust had ever happened.

Such a challenge was never made against the Famine. There
were no arguments about the scope or impact of the disaster that
had befallen Ireland. Nationalists and government officials,
Protestant missionaries and Catholic bishops, relief workers and
journalists, all agreed on the epochal nature of what had taken
place. Though the responsibility for the magnitude of the suffering and dislocation might be argued, the dimensions of the event
provoked little debate.

The American temperance crusader and relief worker
Asenath Nicholson, who undertook her own eccentric and com-
passionate mission to famine-stricken Ireland, left behind a record
of what she had witnessed in which she wrote this:

> The work of death now commenced; the volcano, over
> which I felt Ireland was walking, had burst, though its
> appearance was wholly different from anything I had
> conceived; a famine was always in Ireland, in a certain
> degree; and so common were the beggars, and so many
> were always but just struggling for life, that not until

thousands were reduced to the like condition. . .did
those, who had never begged, make their wants
known. They picked over and picked out their blackened potatoes, and even ate the decayed ones, till many
were made sick, before the real state of the country was
made known; and when it fell, it fell like an avalanche,
sweeping at once the entire land. . .[T]he wave rolled
on; the slain were multiplied; the dead by the way-side,
and the more revolting sights of families found in the
darkest corner of a cabin, in one putrid mass, where, in
many cases, the cabin was tumbled upon them to give
them a decent burial, was somewhat convincing, even
to those who had doubted much from the beginning.

Somewhere in the mass of statistics compiled on the
Famine—bowls of soup distributed, evictions, deaths from fever,
departures, etc.—are my ancestors. Over the years, as I poked at
the fringes of those lives, as I tried to piece together some coherent record of the long day's journey of my family from Famine
Ireland to the Bronx of my childhood, I came to realise that in their
particularity, in their individuality, these people were beyond my
knowing. They had been swallowed by the anti-romance of history,
immigrant ships, cholera sheds, tenement houses. They had dissolved into genetic influence, pigment of skin, size of feet, shape of
nose, into unconscious inheritance, presumptions, fears, ambitions,
into thin air: the exhalation of the past that shapes the present, like
the glassblower's breath in the bubble of hot, melted sand.

Even amnesia, the absence of remembrance, cannot erase
the imprint of the past. Recalled or unrecalled, memory is embedded in the way we love, hope, believe. Tamed, sublimated, suppressed, it will not disappear. It pulls on us like the moon's
elemental urgings on the sea. Full, gibbous, eclipsed, obscured by
clouds or enthroned as regent of the sun, memory has its sway, a
distant, immediate, irresistible direction: neap and spring tides.

Memory is more than a recollection of discrete events, battles, inaugurations, assassinations. It is more than history proper.
Memory is a reel of endless, haunted gossip, a montage of snip-
pets, remnants, patches, whispers, wisps, the way our parents held
us, the acceptance or reluctance in their arms, shadows on the
nursery wall, smell of cut grass, chalk dust, mother's breath.

Eventually, in my search for my family's past I turned away from history. I tried to reach beyond the quantifiable, factual material of the historian to explore the territory that belongs to imagination alone: the ordinary moments of ordinary, unrecorded lives.

I set out to write a novel. At an early stage in the process, I visited Ireland and travelled to my sister-in-law's relatives outside Skibbereen, in County Cork. I stayed with her uncle, Willie O'Regan. Willie brought me to meet a relative of his, Bernard O'Regan, then in his nineties, who as a boy had known some of the people who had lived through the Famine, which had devastated the area around Skibbereen.

Sometime after the turn of the century, when he was a small boy, Bernard remembered watching an old man of strange gait struggling up the boreen to the O'Regan house.

Bernard had heard his parents talk of the man and of the reason for his twisted legs and awkward stride. As a child during the famine time, the man had collapsed from hunger and been taken for dead. Rather than see him consigned to a mass grave, the boy's mother consented to his legs being broken so he could be fitted into the only coffin that was available. When his legs were snapped the pain forced out a deep moan that saved him from being buried alive.

That old man is in my head. He walks the lanes of Ireland and the streets of New York. He is at home in both places. He has the face of Richard Manning in the photograph. He is glad to be alive. Though his stick-like legs are bent and there is a queer swivel to his hips, he has no pain, and when he dances, it is impossible to tell his legs were ever broken at all.

Bridget O'Donnell and her children, Famine beggars
(Illustrated London News, *22 December 1849; courtesy of the*
National Library of Ireland.)

CHAPTER SEVEN
Continued Troubles

The time has not yet arrived at which any man can with confidence say that he fully appreciates the nature and the bearings of that great event which will long be inseparably associated with the year just departed. Yet we think that we may render some service to the public by attempting thus early to review, with the calm temper of a future generation, the history of the great Irish famine of 1847. Unless we are much deceived, posterity will trace up to that famine the commencement of a salutary revolution in the habits of a nation long singularly unfortunate, and will acknowledge that on this, as on many other occasions, Supreme Wisdom has educed permanent good out of transient evil.

— *"The Irish Crisis"*, *Charles E. Trevelyan*, Edinburgh Review, *January 1848*

Whatever You Say, Say Nothing
BY NELL MCCAFFERTY

When Kate Millett came to Dublin in 1980, she expressed surprise that there was no official monument anywhere in Ireland to the Famine. At the time of her visit, there was no official concern either with the IRA hunger strikes then just beginning in British prisons in Northern Ireland. Ms. Millett's speech on international human rights, which referred to both these themes, embarrassed even those who hosted her visit—she came as a guest of the most radical parliamentary group in the Republic, the Labour Party. Its leader was Dick Spring, now *Tánaiste* (Deputy Prime Minister). The woman who introduced her to an invited audience was Senator Mary Robinson, now President. They responded to her astonishment with absolute silence.

In recent times, Ms. Robinson has made Ireland's Famine a motif for appeals to counter famine around the world, and Mr. Spring's government has made common nationalist cause with Sinn Féin, political wing of the IRA. Irish people are just beginning to acknowledge what stunned Ms. Millett all those years ago. The main reason they have kept silent until now has to do with Britain. The Republic of Ireland was under British rule until 1922 and it was difficult before independence to complain about Ireland's greatest disaster without incurring the severe displeasure of Her Majesty's government. Since then, with the six Northern counties still under British rule, it was difficult to mourn without incurring responsibility for the blood of British soldiers, shot by the IRA in the war that continued intermittently there from 1922 to 1994, a war, it seems now, that is not yet over.

The eighteen-month IRA ceasefire that began in September 1994 loosened tongues. No longer afraid to point the political finger at Britain, as the possibility of a blood-free constitutional settlement of the problem loomed in sight, the Irish began to ask what exactly the hell happened in 1845? Kate Millett didn't seem so crazy any more, which was the common opinion offered back in 1980 about the grief she voiced in the course of tracing her Irish roots. (Her refusal, at the time, to take the lithium prescribed for clinical depression stripped a skin off her and made her more empathetic to the sufferings of others. Her international best-seller about that period, *The Loony-Bin Trip*, includes several chapters on her lonely Irish odyssey.)

Part of the hell we have to cope with is the fact that we've lost trace of them, the millions who died and emigrated. Half the population disappeared—just like that. Into graves or off across the ocean. Few records were kept and we who remain don't really know who we are. Further, we have to face that school of thought which accurately points out that we, who remain, represent the survivors—we are descended from those who lived in areas free from blight, who didn't rise up and fight for their neighbours; or from those who profited from the sale of produce to the starving begging rural poor and to the British-government-run work-houses in which they sought relief.

It would be nice to trace oneself back to a selfless great-great-granny who took in the destitute, shared her all with them, and survived only by the saintly grace of God, but it is nigh impossible. Most records, prior to the departure of the British from the Republic, were destroyed in Dublin in the War of Independence and much of what remained was discarded. Since it was the Irish who shelled the relevant government department, the British avoid blame again. On top of that, revisionists point out that little can be retrieved from the oral tradition, since the Famine left the workhouse survivors struck dumb with trauma and their descendants shamed into silence about workhouse origins. Who? Me? Come from people who lived on hand-outs? The modern European nation of Ireland has no defiant Seamus Malcolm X— the British have a veto, just like us, on the current distribution of European Union funds, from which we benefit hugely, and it wouldn't do to upset them.

Christ, it's hard trying to face up to the Famine. Nearly as hard trying to find the places where it happened, in which to confront it face to face. Most traces have been obliterated. In a country with twenty per cent unemployment it would cost a fortune to preserve what little evidence remains. Bit by decaying bit, the physical signs of the Famine that was are fading away.

I went looking for it a couple of times. In 1994, in Northern
Ireland, just before the ceasefire, an amateur dramatic video was
released by a fellow who had become curious about his local graveyard. He saw in it the tombstone of a little girl whose date of death
co-incided with the second year of the dreaded blight. The reasons
why he was able to trace and tell her true story are resonant with
the history of Ireland. The girl's family had the money for a tombstone because they were Protestant peasants, therefore richer than
the norm. Her family, unlike Catholic families to whom education
was denied, were literate and kept correspondence in the family
archives. And since the North escaped the ravages of the War of
Independence, many records of birth and death were preserved.

All the same, the family had suffered the ravages of Famine,
and off our party went to see the documentary-maker, look at his
archives, visit the churchyard, and walk in the family's footsteps
around the townland of Kilrea, in Northern Ireland. We were not
best assured, driving into the village, to note that the pavements
were painted red, white and blue, the traditional signal that "You
are now entering militant, loyalist, British Protestant Ulster." We
were aghast to hear on the car radio that a local policeman had been
shot dead by the IRA, one hour earlier, in the main street. It did not
seem propitious or right to go seeking concrete evidence that per-
nicious Britain had been the cause of the Famine, Ireland's greatest
disaster. We went home and resumed poring over the history books.

Then one day last year, travelling in the west of Ireland, I
saw a newly erected sign in the town of Tuam, in the County of
Galway, directing tourists to the remains of a Famine workhouse.
Astonished, relieved, and pleased that we had started to reclaim
our past, I drove off in the designated direction. I drove round
and round and round, trying to find this place. Few had heard of
it. After two hours in the relatively small town, I finally abandoned
the car and walked through the maze-like streets of a dilapidated
housing estate. There I found the remains of a gable wall on the
edge of a mucky playing field. The workhouse had been knocked
down to provide a green space for the working class young—quite
right in the minds of hard-pressed locals—and the wall bore a
plaque honouring by name those few from the town who died
fighting for independence in 1922. There was no mention of the
thousands who died in the Famine.

There is one place that is relatively evocative of sadness, despair and cruelty living cheek by jowl with fruits of the earth other than the ruined potato. The workhouse in the now prosperous village of Ballyvaughan, Co. Clare, in the West of Ireland, has collapsed in on itself. Nobody has the funds to knock down fully what has become an eyesore in a seaside resort that is trying to capitalise on the tourism boom generated by the ceasefire. Nobody has the funds or the will either to restore the workhouse. Perfectly preserved are the huge stone-cut pillars at the entrance, and the massive iron rings from which gates were once hung. Once those gates closed at night, the late-arriving poor were denied entrance. Ancient stone cottages still stand around three sides of the outer courtyard. Once the dwelling places of workhouse staff and the chaplain, two of the five cottages have been renovated as holiday homes, two are occupied by pensioners, one is the home of the extended family which farms the hinterland; the sixth house, in the corner, much larger than the rest, with its own private vegetable garden in front, is the former dwelling place of the workhouse governor. The farming people who live in the governor's house confirm that drawing plans of the workhouse show that people who had been living and dying on nothing more than the grass they plucked as they crawled towards the gates, had to crawl past the vegetables.

Stables which held the governor's horses and carriage adjoin the workhouse. Hay is kept in their ruined remains now. The workhouse roof and beams have fallen in on the huge dormitories below and it is impossible to penetrate within. You can go by the side of stables though, climbing over debris to get to the orchards, where those of the starving poor who could stand tended and gathered fruit for the governor. The apples have gone sour today, falling unwanted from abandoned trees. The woman now resident in the governor's house refuses to let her family pick the berries which grow in rich abundance around the orchard walls.

"There's blood on them," she claims. Who's to say? Speak quietly or the British neighbours will hear and that would upset bloodless negotiations for an agreed Ireland. People might even remember that there are Irish political prisoners still in British jails. We must decline to mourn too loudly, lest we be plunged into warfare and mourning again. So we go around emotionally

flogging ourselves because our great-grannies survived—somebody has to say sorry in memory of the Famine dead. What
Famine? Sshhh! We'll tell you more when the British have gone.

The Lessons of the Famine for Today

BY TIM PAT COOGAN

During August 1996, a year in which Famine commemorations were being staged world-wide, I attended a dinner at the home of John Silver, the legendary President of Boston University, who was retiring. Another B.U. luminary, sitting at our table, told an Irish joke in my honour. It had apparently been related to him by Sir Patrick Mayhew, the Secretary of State for Northern Ireland. (Boston, it should be noted is an important stopping point for British decision-takers connected with Northern Ireland.)

The "joke" itself was eminently forgettable. But its punch line is instructive for our purposes. It was to the effect that an old "paddy" giving a visitor directions told the visitor that he would find his way by turning right when he came to a "quare-looking green yoke". The "quare-looking" green object was a tree.

In fact the provenance of that story had a direct bearing on the Famine and, by extrapolation, on Sir Patrick's continuing involvement in Irish affairs. It contains, behind a patina of humour, all the tragedy, all the condescending unknowingness which has, and continues to be, the *leit motif* of British involvement in Irish affairs.

Even today, the vast tract of Mayo known as Erris, is one of the most desolate areas in Ireland. In 1847 it is recorded that many of its inhabitants had never seen a living tree larger than a shrub. Poverty had degraded the people beyond our twentieth-century understanding. They lived in low turf caves, seven to ten feet long, cut from the living bog. Richard Webb, a representative of the Central Relief Committee of the Society of Friends, the Quakers, whose humanitarianism during the Famine, shone like a shaft of sunlight on an icy landscape, described them as "quiet harmless persons, terrified of strangers".[1] He recalls that the inn keeper in Achill Sound, in Erris, a man a cut above the average, economically and educationally, told him that when his daughter first left Erris for Westport she was frightened when she first encountered trees, as they neared better land. She expected them to fall on her as the strange things known as branches waved over her head.

Yet somehow on 12 June 1847, two hundred and sixty starving people braved the trees and marched to a workhouse in Ballina some fifty miles away seeking assistance. They were turned away to starve to death, because the workhouse was full. In any case they could not have been helped technically, because the district they came from was so poor that it did not pay rates and therefore they did not qualify for assistance anyhow.

Not surprisingly, by the time the Famine concluded, the state of Erris was such that the landscape looked as though hostile forces had laid waste the fields. It was recorded that in the Erris area seventy-eight townlands did not have either a single inhabitant or a four-footed beast.

Sir Patrick's joke would sound even less funny if told in Erris today than at a table of anglophile sophisticates in Boston.

However Sir Patrick's significance for the purposes of this essay does not lie in his sense of humour. It does so for the fact that his office is still in Ireland as this is being written. It is a part of Ireland that has shown itself to be fractious, violent, and embittered, its problems almost as insoluble as those of the Famine era. Certainly in England it elicits very much the same feelings of angry hopelessness which pre-Famine Ireland, as a whole, did amongst British decision takers.

Moreover Sir Patrick's presence stems from one of the root causes of the Famine – the Act of Union of 1800. The effects of the Act of Union have been almost completely over-looked by historians of all stripes, be they revisionist or otherwise in their assessment of the Famine. But it was the Act of Union which took away Ireland's parliament and created the situation whereby when the Famine struck, its handling was entrusted to a handful of British civil servants, chiefly the head of the Treasury, Sir Charles Trevelyan.

Let us now ask ourselves a simple question concerning another disaster which originated in Ireland, the sinking of the Belfast-built liner, the Titanic. What caused the huge death toll? Was it the impact with the iceberg, or was it the failure of rescue ships to get to the scene on time, coupled with the inadequate provision of life-boats?

The Titanic, as we know, stayed afloat for a long time after the impact, but no help came in those vital hours. Neither did it come to Ireland, and she did not possess social and political life-boats which would have reduced the impact of the potato failure either.

The central fact is that Ireland did not have a government of its own. It was administered from London—as basically is Sir Patrick's fifedom today—not by duly elected Irish Cabinets responsive both to their own constituents and the evidence of their own eyes. Given the scale of what was happening in Ireland during the Famine years one would have expected British political heads to roll. Not so. In real terms Ireland, although legislatively linked to England, insofar as English public opinion was concerned, was a strange, dangerous, foreign and incomprehensible place. British MPs, or Ministers, probably came under less pressure from public opinion to do something about the Famine than the minuscule amount they undergo today because of the Irish peace process.

Suffice to say that, though linked by a long and often horrific history, Ireland and England have their own separate interests, compulsions and methods of dealing with crisis. In the mid-nineteenth century Ireland had no such methods available to it. And the writing of history of the Famine continually overlooks the root cause of this.

Roy Foster, in his book *Modern Ireland 1600–1972*, which for a time became the bible of revisionists, says:

> Traditionally historians used to interpret the effects of the Famine as equally cataclysmic: it was seen as a watershed in Irish history creating new conditions of demographic decline, large scale emigration, altered farming structures and new economic policies, not to mention an institutionalised anglophobia amongst the Irish at home and abroad.[2]

Foster goes on to quarrel with this assessment:

> As a literal analysis this does not stand up, at least insofar as economic consequences are concerned. All the processes just mentioned can be traced to well before the Famine, even if the disaster elevated them to a

level where they became qualitatively different. If
there is a watershed year in Irish social and economic
history it is not 1846, but 1815, with the agricultural
disruption following the end of the French wars. Some
contemporaries at least recognised this. As one witness
to a parliamentary commission on Irish poverty
sighed, "It would have been better for the Irish farmer
if Bonaparte never lived or never died."[3]

Foster does state "unequivocally" that the potato was a
dietary staple by the 1840s and sketches out, very fully, what this
meant in terms of subsistence living to a large section of the Irish
population. However neither in Foster's often quite masterly
analysis of the catastrophe, nor in that of others will one find any
serious reference to the impact on Ireland of having so much of
the country's vital interests in the hands of people who showed
little or nothing in the way of either affection or insight for the
country.

In fact Foster, while discussing the Act of Union, when it
occurred, not in terms of its impact on the Famine, states cate-
gorically that "the Union was a crude political reform act disenfranchising eighty boroughs and reducing thirty-two to one
member. But what it did not do was cause economic decline as so
often subsequently stated".[4]

While respecting Foster's research I disagree strongly with
this judgment. It makes no allowance for the destruction of what
might be termed the initiative quotient in Irish political, economic,
and indeed social and cultural life which followed the Union. From
being a glittering capital where artistic life flourished, Dublin fell
into a long period of decay and somnolence, from which indeed it
could be argued it is only now indeed fully recovering.

When the decision-takers moved to London and the new seat
of power, the House of Commons, wherein the Irish MPs were easily out-voted and rendered powerless, the move did not merely
constitute a flight of politicians. Artists, artisans, tailors, writers,
landlords, merchants all followed. It can be validly argued that
"Grattan's" parliament had been, like Grattan himself, representative of the interests of Ascendancy Protestantism. Nevertheless,
Grattan himself had argued, very much against the prevailing
theories of the time, that an MP's duty was to his constituents,

rather than the general "squire-archical" assumption that it should be the other way round.

People like Grattan, in situ in Ireland, with a hands on capability, would have been far more effective in dealing with matters which affected them directly and very keenly, than were either civil servants or absentee landlords living in another society, the "United Kingdom Mainland" as it is sometimes, significantly, referred to. These were London orientated and dependent on agents and third parties, not alone for their rents, but even for news of what was happening in the "United Kingdom Overseas". The British policy makers on the "mainland" simply did not share common interests with, nor understanding for, its subjects "overseas"; such foreign peoples were not treated with the same respect as their own citizens on the "mainland". For example, though it would take us too far from our subject to describe the situation in detail, it should be noted that in the period under review, Scotland too suffered a famine. But the London government ensured that nothing remotely like what occurred in Ireland befell the "UK Mainland".

Nearly half a century elapsed between the passing of the Act of Union and "black '47". Who can say how an independent parliament in Ireland would have evolved in that time had it not been bribed and threatened out of existence? Does the mere fact that London had to go to such lengths to destroy the Irish legislature not indicate that it had a potential for strength which British statecraft found dangerous?

I would submit that we can find some guidance in answering those questions by examining a partial breach of the Union, in twenty-six of Ireland's thirty-two counties if we look at how an independent Irish Republic evolved in a similar space of time, despite the evil effects of a destructive civil war, emigration, partition, an economic war with England in the thirties, and the stagnation caused by isolation during the years of World War II and its aftermath. The comparison may not be exact but it is far from being irrelevant.

There will always be an element of backyardism in the relationship of a big country to a small one. Look at America and Cuba for example. But it was the particular misfortune of Ireland to be helplessly dependent on British political will at the time of the Corn Laws debate, one of the two great controversies which almost threatened to split the Conservative party.

Ironically, the second, which also had and is having, a profoundly harmful effect on Ireland, occurred, on the Famine's anniversary: the division amongst the Conservative Tories over Europe.

Briefly, the Corn Laws debate centred around the fact that Sir Robert Peel, the Conservative British Prime Minister, had decided to repeal the Corn Laws which placed a tariff on imported corn. British grain producers benefitted from this arrangement. But the poor, and particularly the increasing urban proletariat thronging into the great industrial cities then growing up in England, paid for this benefit through unfairly high bread prices.

Peel, although a staunch Unionist of such orange hue that Daniel O'Connell dubbed him "Orange Peel", was conscious of his responsibilities to those he ruled over. He instituted various Irish relief schemes, including one whereby maize was purchased in America for distribution in Ireland whenever prices rose unduly, so as to regulate the market. But, apart from the fact that this strategy ran contrary to the *laissez faire* theories of political economy then current (these frowned on government intervention), Ireland and the Famine also became directly involved in the Corn Laws debate.

Peel had argued that it was not possible to feed with grain the millions of Irish who lived on potatoes without repealing the Corn Laws so that the said grain could be imported un-checked. This self-evident proposition however had the effect that those who opposed repeal included in their quiver of arguments the assertion that the extent of starvation in Ireland was greatly exaggerated.

The debate was one of the most bitter in British political history, dividing the country from top to bottom. Peel resigned over the issue, but then had to be invited back by Queen Victoria, because a Cabinet could not be formed without him. Repeal was carried, but ironically on the very day that the measure passed into law, 25 June 1846, Peel's enemies managed to turn him out of office—over Ireland.

The specific issue was an Irish Coercion Bill, which Peel had introduced under his "Orange Peel" hat the previous February.

Understandably, in light of the catastrophe which was then unfolding, Ireland was in a state of considerable disarray. The bill can be seen as part of the traditional British "carrot and stick" approach to Irish affairs. A measure which bestowed a carrot, such as Corn Law repeal on the country, tended to bring forth a stick like the increased repression envisaged by the Coercion Bill. But Ireland *per se* was of such disinterest to the House that hitherto it had been invariably almost empty as the Bill passed through its various readings.

However when the House divided on the Bill's Second Reading, a few hours after the Corn Law measure was enacted, Peel was ambushed by a combination of the opposition Whigs and his own anti-Corn Laws Conservatives. His measure was defeated by some 73 votes, which, as a perusal of Hansard will swiftly demonstrate, represents considerably more manpower than had ever been present in the House during the Bill's earlier stages. In the words of an observer of the time the anti-Peel majority had "as much to do with Ireland as Kamschatka".[5] His resignation as Prime Minister was announced on 29 June.

What exactly this meant for Ireland is soon and sadly told.[6] The previous October a group of distinguished personages had met the Lord-Lieutenant of Ireland, Lord Heytesbury in Dublin to urge on him a scheme of Famine relief drawn up by Daniel O'Connell. The delegation included the Duke of Leinster, Lord Cloncurry, Henry Grattan, a son of the father of the ill-fated Irish Parliament, and many others of similar standing.

O'Connell's proposals for dealing with the accelerating catastrophe befalling Ireland included the following:

> The export of corn and food from Ireland was to be banned, as was distilling of grain. The free importation of corn, food and rice should be permitted. Relief measures, and food stores were to be set up in every part of the country. A loan of £1,500,000 was to be raised against the security of the Irish forests. And taxes were to be levied on landlords, ten per cent on those resident in the country, twenty to fifty on absentees.

This was the programme which the most knowledgeable men in Ireland deemed necessary to save their people from Famine. But what did the British decision-takers do with O'Connell's proposals? The answer was foreshadowed by Heytesbury's reception of the scheme. He received plan and deputation "very coldly" and had his visitors speedily ushered out of his office.

The new Chancellor of the Exchequer, Charles Wood, was a very different man to Peel. He opposed new taxation, in fact new expenditures of any sort, and was as firm in his upholding of *laissez faire* principles as was his head of the Treasury, Trevelyan. Delighted with his new boss, who soon came under his influence, Trevelyan displayed his attitude to Irish Famine relief just ten days after Peel's fall. On 9 July, he cancelled a shipment of American maize, destined for starving Irish, aboard the *Sorcière*. He said it "was not wanted".[7] From then on there was no more talk of O'Connell's proposals that food exports should be halted or taxes raised. Relief measures were something less than minimalist, and food in large quantities continued to be exported all through the Famine. There was never a shortage of food in Ireland. There was a failure of the potato crop only.

O'Connell's last appearance in the British House of Commons was a paradigm of the tragedy that had befallen him and his country. A broken man, his once splendid presence (and voice) gone, he spoke with such difficulty that he could only be heard by those in his immediate vicinity. "Ireland," he husked, "is in your power. If you do not save her, she cannot save herself. I solemnly call on you to recollect that I predict with the sincerest conviction that a quarter of her population will perish unless you come to her relief."[8]

O'Connell's words were received with respect and sympathy. But insofar as meaningful action on Ireland was concerned, the reaction of those with influence to bring about change could be summed up by that of Disraeli, the architect of the plot to use the Coercion Bill to dethrone Peel. He said of O'Connell's last appearance that he saw only "a feeble old man muttering before a table".[9] O'Connell died three months later. As he prophesied, between starvation and emigration, the Famine did cost Ireland over a quarter of its population.

The Corn Laws and the Conservative divisions over Europe were of course far from being the only occasions in which a British parliament acted harmfully towards Ireland because of party considerations. Another right-angled turning point, and an especially disastrous one at that, occurred in 1970, eerily recalling the transition from the policy of Peel to that of Trevelyan. It too occurred between the months of June and July. On 20 June a general election put the Labour government out of power, returning the Conservatives to office.

On 3-5 July 1970, the Conservatives, then as now, the allies of the unionists, sanctioned an arms search in the nationalist Falls Road district of Belfast.[10] Hitherto, the Labour decision-takers had reigned in the army and had treated the complaints of the unionists on their merits, not as dogma. Now, however, the army were let off the leash to ransack the area. Many were injured in savage hand-to-hand fighting which caused at least five deaths, if not more. Houses were wrecked, Catholic religious objects destroyed by Protestant Scottish soldiers. The area was curfewed and saturated with CS gas. A relatively small arms cache was discovered. However no searches took place in Loyalist areas, which, according to Hansard, the British parliamentary record, contained at least 110,000 licensed weapons. To these must be added an unguessable toll of unlicensed weapons and explosives. Some of these weapons had been used to kill Catholics, or to intimidate them out of their homes.

The Provisional IRA had only been formed the previous January and did not kill a British soldier until the following February 1971. However the "rape of the Falls" as it is known in Republican folklore, combined with the bitterness caused by the absence of searches in Loyalist areas, sent a tidal wave of recruitment into the ranks of the Provisionals. The IRA, the manifestation of the physical force tradition in Irish history, took its rise from the change in British governmental policy between June and July of 1970. Twenty-five years of death, violence and destruction later, there arose a golden opportunity to remove the physical force tradition from Irish life once and for all.

A combination of new faces and new circumstances created a situation in Ireland, wherein with the help of America, and the behind-the-scenes approval of the British, the IRA was induced to declare a ceasefire on 31 August 1994.[11] The news was greeted with euphoria. The Irish Taoiseach (Prime Minister), Albert Reynolds, who had played a major role in the negotiations which had brought about the cessation of violence, immediately put in train a series of confidence-building measures to ensure the cease-fire held. IRA prisoners were released, the broadcasting ban on Sinn Féin appearing on the national airwaves was lifted, and Gerry Adams was welcomed at Government Buildings, and in the White House—but not in the House of Commons.

Again, as during the Famine period, the Conservative party was deeply riven, to the point of splitting almost. Indeed it became commonplace for commentators to observe that the European issue had become the most divisive to confront the Tories since the Corn Laws controversy. Again the Irish situation became embroiled in domestic British politics. The votes of the unionist block at Westminster became crucial to the Conservatives' survival. The unionists and the Conservative Right made common cause and the peace process was stalled on the issue of "de-commissioning". This was a unionist-inspired demand, not made during the pre-ceasefire negotiations, during which John Major had been kept fully briefed by Reynolds. It meant in effect that the IRA should surrender, and give up their arms in advance of any talks being held.

The IRA rejected this and for close on a year and a half the sands ran out steadily on the peace process. Throughout Ireland, depression replaced euphoria. Then, late in 1995, President Clinton paid a visit to Ireland which resulted in a Commission being set up, under the Chairmanship of the former Senate Majority Leader, George Mitchell, to make recommendations to resolve the rapidly building crisis. Mitchell and his team came to Ireland, took submissions in a painstaking, sympathetic fashion which impressed everyone who contributed to the Commission (including the present author) and worked over Christmas to produce a compromise in January 1996. The compromise, the so-called "Mitchell principles" which stipulated that participants to all-party peace talks should sign up to a set of non-violent, democratic principles, was accepted by the Irish government.

The Irish Taoiseach, John Bruton, had had a thirty-five minute phone conversation with John Major on the night before he stood up in the Dáil (the Irish parliament) to welcome the Mitchell report, confident, on the basis of the phone call, that Major was going to do the same thing later in the day. However,

unknown to Bruton, Major was being savaged by his Right wing
at a private parliamentary party meeting in the House of Commons,
as Bruton spoke. The unionists' allies were sticking out for "de-commissioning". Accordingly, that afternoon Major in effect rejected the
Mitchell principles, and adopted instead a scheme put forward by
the unionist leader, David Trimble, that elections be held to a new
North of Ireland Assembly.

John Hume, the leader of the constitutional nationalist
Party, the SDLP, who had done more than most to bring about,
and hold, the ceasefire, jumped to his feet as soon as Major had
finished speaking to point out, with un-characteristic anger, that
the lives of innocent civilians on the streets of Belfast were being
put at risk. To no avail: Hume was treated with the same incomprehension and contempt as was O'Connell before him. The IRA
ended the ceasefire with the Canary Wharf bombing in London a
few days later, on 9 February. Again American intervention helped
to restore relationships between Dublin and London. A kind of *de
facto* IRA ceasefire came into being. The Assembly elections went
ahead, but the decommissioning demand remained, effectively
excluding Sinn Féin from the negotiating process. In the event,
peace talks without Sinn Féin proved to be Hamlet, not alone
without the Prince, but without Shakespeare.

In the absence of any form of viable native government
acceptable to the people of Northern Ireland, Irish national interests had once more, catastrophically fallen victim to British political concerns as they had during the Famine period. It is not
suggested that there were no Irish evil doers during the Famine.
There were. Who for example grew much of the food that was
exported during the Famine, having first been transported past
starving people? The answer of course is Catholic Irish farmers.
Who frequently profitted from the Famine, to indulge in land-
grabbing or other misdemeanours? Again, regrettably, the answer
is Irish Catholics, as the following only too clearly illustrates. It is
the story of Bridget O'Donnell of Clare, which incidentally was
set down in 1849, a date by which most people would have imagined the Famine to have passed:

> . . .we were put out last November. . .As soon as it
> [corn] was stacked one "Blake" on the farm who was
> paid to watch it, took it away to his own haggard keep

and kept it there for a fortnight by Dan Sheedy's
orders. They then thrashed it. . .I was at this time lying
in fever. Dan Sheedy and five or six men came to tum-
ble my house. . .within two months of my confine-
ment. . .they commenced knocking down the house
and had half of it knocked out. . .Father Meehan
anointed me. I was carried into a cabin and lay there
for eight days, when I had the creature [baby], born
dead. . .I lay for three weeks after that. The whole of
my family got the fever, one boy, thirteen years old
died. . .Dan Sheedy and Blake took the corn into
Kilrush and sold it. I had not a bit for my children to
eat when they took it from me.[12]

Bridget and her remaining two children apparently perished
in a workhouse, not long after telling her story. The O'Donnells
were examples of un-restrained *laissez faire* economics in operation
during a time of Famine. There will always be Sheedys and Blakes,
people who will take advantage of such conditions, be they from
Ireland, England or Somalia. But, as Daniel O'Connell and his deputation made clear, it was the will of thinking Irish people that
restraint, humanity and initiative be exercised. In the absence of an
Irish government these qualities were not forthcoming. The parliament in London chose to exercise its authority but not its
responsibility. That is what made the Famine so grievous. That is
why the lessons of those days should be applied to today's Anglo-
Irish relationships. History should be learned from—not replicated.

NOTES

1 Cecil Woodham-Smith, *The Great Hunger*, (London: Penguin, 1991), p.311.

2 Roy Foster, *Modern Ireland 1600-1972*, (London: Penguin, 1988), p.318.

3 Ibid.

4 Ibid., p.284.

5 *The Croker Papers. The Correspondence and Diaries of John Croker*, (Vol III,
1884), p.51.

6 The period is well covered in either the *Freeman's Journal*, or by O Rourke,
History of the Great Irish Famine (1845), pp.53-59.

7 Woodham-Smith, op.cit., p.87.

8 Hansard, Vol. 89, Feb 1847, pp.994-5.

9 Benjamin Disraeli, *Life of Lord George Bentinck*, 1852, p.159.

10 Described in Tim Pat Coogan, *The IRA*, (London: Harper Collins, USA: Roberts Rinehart, 1996).

11 The ceasefire and the course of the ensuing peace process are described in Tim Pat Coogan, *The Troubles*, (London: Hutchinson, 1995, USA: Roberts Rinehart, 1996).

12 *Illustrated London News*, 22 December 1849.

Funeral at Skibbereen, Co. Cork (Illustrated London News, *30
January 1847; courtesy of the National Library of Ireland.*)

CHAPTER EIGHT

Transgenerational Shame

A man had died from hunger, and his widow had gone into the ploughed field of her landlord to try to pick a few potatoes in the ridges which might be remaining since the harvest; she found a few—the landlord saw her—sent a magistrate to the cabin who found three children in a state of starvation and nothing in the cabin but the pot, which was over the fire. He demanded of her to show him the potatoes— she hesitated; he inquired what she had in the pot—she was silent; he looked in, and saw a dog, with the handful of potatoes she had gathered from the field. The sight of the wretched cabin, and still more, the despairing looks of the poor silent mother and the famished children, crouched in fear in a dark corner, so touched the heart of the magistrate, that he took the pot from the fire, bade the woman to follow him, and they went to the court-room together. He presented the pot, containing the dog and potatoes, to the astonished judge. He called the woman—interrogated her kindly. She told him they sat in their desolate cabin two entire days, without eating, before she killed the half-famished dog; that she did not think she was stealing, to glean after the harvest was gathered. The judge gave her three pounds from his own purse; told her when she had used that to come again to him.

. . . *A cabin was seen closed one day a little out of
the town, when a man had the curiosity to open it, and
in a dark corner he found a family of the father,
mother, and two children, lying in close compact. The
father was considerably decomposed; the mother, it
appeared, had died last, and probably fastened the
door, which was always the custom when all hope was
extinguished, to get into the darkest corner and die,
where passers-by could not see them. Such family scenes
were quite common, and the cabin was generally pulled
down upon them for a grave.*

— *Asenath Nicholson in Mayo,* Lights and Shades of Ireland, *1850*

A Nightmare Revisited
BY SEAN KENNY

*And these, Turlough reminded himself, were the lucky
ones, given food and shelter. But to look at them was
almost to agree with Trevelyan, for this legislated charity would not save them, would only prolong their sentence on this earth. Those few who might emerge with
some semblance of their health in the spring would suffer the same nightmare again. They would go and
plant potatoes and again their crop would be totally
blighted.*

*Even if he could have held it at arm's length, it was
apocalyptic, beyond all rationalisation. Not even the
coldest application of logic could ever explain it. He was
glad of the tears that streamed down, glad because they
blurred his view, the only respite available to him. He
stumbled through yet another room of the half-dead,
wiped his eyes, focused one more time, and saw him!*

When first approached about writing an essay for this volume I thought the task would be very simple. After all,
I had a hard disk filled with ruminations on the Irish
past in general, and on the Great Famine in particular. And when
it was specifically suggested I write about where I got the idea for
my novel *The Hungry Earth*, quoted above, my confidence rose
yet another notch. But, if the creative process itself is difficult and
elusive, to describe what might motivate anyone to spin a tale
around such a horrific theme as the starvation of a million or more
people, I now see, is all but impossible.

And yet, so many Irish people who have read the story seem
either to have failed altogether to see what was behind it or, worse,
to have understood and then utterly dismissed the underlying
premise—which is that we remain traumatised today by this cataclysm one hundred and fifty years ago—that I am compelled to
explain myself here once again.

Ireland's past certainly does not want for barbaric incident. No century has been without its wars, revolution, invasion or change in the method of government. As a small island nation repeatedly pummelled by outside forces, one would have expected the Irish to have long since coalesced into an immutable people, motivated to defend their continuous shore against the outside world, and yet nothing could be further from the Irish experience. From the dawn of time, there has not yet been a successful attempt by the Irish to establish a single government of the whole island and all its people.

Indeed, it is this very confusion, this doubt about the essence of what it is to be Irish, that seems to me to be the driving force behind so much of what we would call Irish culture. Do we not mythicise the characters of our history—Brian Boru, The Great O'Neill, Sarsfield, Wolfe Tone, Robert Emmet, Michael Dwyer, Pádraig Pearse, James Connolly, and now Michael Collins, to name just a few—because we so desperately need to fill this void, to give substance to this elusive, intangible civilisation of which we feel we are a part?

Other nations seem so much more sure of themselves—no matter what atrocities their past empires perpetrated. Yet we, the Irish, who conquered no one, whose missionaries will probably be remembered as the only Western influence not driven by pure greed, and whose contribution to music and literature remains a source of astonishment to those with the attention span to comprehend it all, seem beset, and incurably so, by a frame of mind that holds us back and stops us from ever achieving our individual and our collective potential.

What is this unseen force? And why is it so pervasive? And it is: one has only to live outside of Ireland for a few years to realise the extent to which the Irish are so different from others and to see with *plein-air* clarity that there is a common theme running through the thought processes of Irish people. I don't mean to imply here that we're all shuffling around like morbid clones of one another, but rather that Irish people of widely varying social backgrounds, education and intelligence all share, to some degree, common emotional characteristics which seem to be unique to us.

This point was driven home to me a few years ago when I attended a weekend workshop by Dr. Garrett O'Connor, an Irish professor of psychiatry in Los Angeles. At that time I had already made the decision to leave the corporate world and concentrate on my writing full time. I had finished one novel, set in ancient Ireland, and drafted a second one, set in the present day. The first was an attempt to understand the stories behind the origins of the stone mounds and ring forts dotted around Ireland that have always arrested me; the second my initial pass at demystifying the uneasiness I had always felt as a business executive.

But it was only when I stirred Dr. O'Connor's ideas into the murky cauldron in my head that it occurred to me that there might in fact be a very real connection between the two. What he had successfully demonstrated was the way in which the events of our time—the experiences foisted on us by society, by the history in the making around us—leave us with an emotional construct which we unwittingly pass on to our children, and they to theirs. And in the case of the Irish people, when you step through all the defeats, the ignominy, the poverty, the dispossession and, finally, the exile, a very clear picture emerges.

Dr. O'Connor aptly dubbed this condition "malignant shame". Leaving aside any precise clinical definition, I would say this means a lingering, unhealthy and deeply troubling sense that we are unworthy, that it is wrong to be happy and prosperous, that pleasure itself is in some way forbidden to us.

How can this have come about? Well, consider a few facts. In the early part of the nineteenth century, the western seaboard was the most densely populated part of Ireland. Even fifty years after the depopulation that followed the Great Famine it was necessary to set up the Congested Districts Board to deal with the over-crowding which persisted into the early twentieth century. Yet today, western Ireland has the lowest population density in Europe.

All of these people didn't simply vanish, any more than the tenant farmers throughout the rest of the country. They moved into towns, or emigrated. And their residue is still to be found— old men in pubs all across Ireland. We are, as it turns out, the children of the dispossessed and the legacy of this mass migration can only be one of loss and of confusion.

No perpetrator has ever come forward, been accused and found guilty. For every voice that lays the blame at Britain's door there is some Irish apologist to say we did it to ourselves.

And the final irony is that even those few who don't fall
into this category, those who became the new possessing class
can hardly have feelings that are much different. Somewhere
beneath the surface there has to be an awareness of some compromise, some sleight of hand, that gnaws away and sets up the
very same feelings.

The more I thought about it, the more convinced I
became that Dr. O'Connor's ideas were very accurate, that what
has since become known as transgenerational shame really does
exist, that it is pervasive in Irish society. And I felt that I ought
to be able to come up with a novel that would demonstrate this
to the world at large. But for a long time no idea crystallised into
a story for me.

I studied various periods of Irish history, quickly dismissing
the Troubles as being too complex, mulling over 1798 as being a
perfect example of the Irish obscenely slaughtering each other,
finding earlier events to be too difficult to relate to the present,
and finally roamed up and down the nineteenth century until I
took to re-reading Cecil Woodham Smith's *The Great Hunger*.

Yes. This was it. Here was one of the greatest catastrophes
in human history: millions dying in a small area in a short space of
time. This was the device I would use to make my point. The story
itself was easy enough: a present day Irish businessman inherits a
small piece of land, and as events unfold he becomes increasingly
aware of how this property came into his family, which as it happens is because he's descended from a cannibal, who ate his neighbours to survive the Famine.

So, using Turlough, my protagonist, to symbolise today's
vacuous and morally bankrupt Irish society I set about finessing
my way through a series of timeslip sequences wherein he actually
finds himself back at the time of the Great Famine. After all, Garcia
Marquez had legitimised magical realism, it's the "in" literary
genre, so why not an Irish version?

How innocently it all begins. And yet I should have known
better: I had done enough writing to know that there is no way to
create the experience for the reader without being there myself, in
the midst of the excitement, the love, the betrayal, or whatever
sensation the story must elicit. And so, as the weeks went by and
Turlough became more and more immersed in the horror of what

transpired between 1846 and 1848, I began to see it all far, far too clearly myself.

Like everyone in Ireland, I had been brought up to see the Famine as simply one more calamity in the Irish past. It was something that had happened to people not like me—these were unwashed, illiterate, barefoot peasants who had not the wit to buy a fishing rod to save themselves. They were like those scruffy, thieving tinkers that are still around today, whom you wouldn't want to let near you for fear you might catch lice from them.

Yet these half-baked prejudices are no more than elaborate ploys, concocted by earlier generations, and passed on to us, as a defence against the truly terrifying images of our own ancestors dying the way they did. And in our well meant attempts to block out this appalling past we have left a piece of ourselves crumpled up, unknown, and all but inaccessible.

I realised, as I moved on through this story, just how like the character Turlough I was—or at least was capable of becoming. And I couldn't be like that, not for long anyway, and the work became an ever more desperate search for a way out.

After the Great Famine, vast numbers of Irish people turned to religion and what is pejoratively described as a "devotional revolution" took place. In my view, this was a very real spiritual revolution, a heartbroken people, turning to God, desperate for a higher power that would make sense of it all. Priests, nuns, monks, brothers multiplied in number from then on, redefining Irish society—and assumed the task of atoning for the sorrow and the shame of the many. But now, in an increasingly secular world, they and the religion they espoused have wound up as confused as the rest of us.

And confused we are, and will remain. Although my novel has been praised for the story and the writing, as I said earlier, the ideas on which it is based have met with, at best, controversy. On Irish national radio, I've been challenged as to whether, as an engineer, a man of science, I could possibly believe that in some way the ghosts of the Famine could bother us in the present day. Reviewers have pushed aside the transgenerational shame idea as a publicity angle and friends have pointed out to me, some quietly, some less so, that if I'm crazy enough to blame the Famine for everything that's wrong in my own life, well, my wife has their sympathies. They, however, are not about to have this notion rammed down their throats by me or by anyone.

Irish people have the highest level of dialectic tension of any nation I've encountered. No matter what you say they will argue with you. Challenge and conflict seem to be at the heart of Celtic culture, a state of mind that goes back not centuries, but millennia. And the ideas behind this story are not the kind to pervade easily even the most willing consciousness without a significant effort. Perhaps the very enormity of the burden of the past is still beyond any of our imaginations. Perhaps it will take generations of Garret O'Connors to complete fully the jigsaw puzzle of how to heal the Irish psyche.

Yet I feel the better for having encountered in my heart what it must have been like to live through that hell. And I think I understand more of my own Irishness for having confronted that time. When I drive around the west of Ireland now I see very clearly the lazy-beds where people once grew potatoes: flat topped ridges wide enough to grow a single row of tubers, with narrow furrows for drainage in between. They are still there, on impossible boggy mountainsides, witness to the time when every arable square inch that was available to the people was cultivated. And I feel that at last I have some sense of the suffering that these people, my people, endured.

We should not underestimate the significance of re-awakening memories of that time, especially in America. It is often said that those who ignore the lessons of history are doomed to repeat them, and while it is highly unlikely that the Irish-American diaspora will experience real hunger ever again, it is certain that the dislocation of exile will remain a force shaping American society until all the different origins, the roots from which it has grown are understood by its people.

The search for myths of origin, a universal need in all of us, is leading Irish America to look to the Great Famine as the source of who they are and why they are here. And while admittedly there were already many Irish here before the 1840s, it is indisputable that the post-Famine influx vastly outnumbers what came before. It is the overwhelming point of departure for the evolution of the Irish-American psyche.

These people came with very little education, ill-prepared to assimilate what they would find, but they brought with them a race memory that, in ways that are perhaps not yet apparent, has shaped America ever since.

The Irish believed, long before the discovery of the New World, in mythical realms beyond the Atlantic horizon. Oisín, last of the Fianna, is enticed there by a beautiful princess who says to him:

> I put on you the bonds of a true hero, you to come away with me now to the country of the young. It is the most delightful of all that are under the sun; the trees are stooping down with fruit and with leaves and with blossom. Honey and wine are plentiful there, and everything the eye has ever seen; no wasting will come on you with the wasting away of time; you will never see death or lessening.

This is from the 1904 translation of Irish myths, *Gods and Fighting Men*, by Lady Augusta Gregory, but the story itself is an ancient one and, to prove that point, Oisín, lonely for the other warriors, returns from the West, without having aged a day, though centuries have elapsed in Ireland, and is confronted by Saint Patrick.

It is a staple of Celtic literature that heaven and immortality lie to the West, and not in the sky. King Arthur, and Tolkien's hobbits, all sail into the West as they leave this world. And the voyage of Saint Brendan, a significant legend throughout Medieval Europe, describes an Irish monk and his followers sailing to one other-worldly island after another somewhere beyond the edge of the known world.

So these post-Famine immigrants arrived, optimistic, fortified by these beliefs, only to find more hardship. The industrial revolution was underway in the eastern US, swallowing up the poor in coal-mining, manufacturing and the construction of cities and railroads. But still, in the Irish mind, somewhere in the West lay the promised land, and so the Irish pressed on, at the forefront of the Indian wars and the claiming of this new land.

It is those actions, that spirit of manifest destiny, that has given us the America we experience today. No group, of course, is about to come forward and proudly claim ownership for such a discredited idea as manifest destiny, used to annihilate an entire native people, but the Irish of that time did not foresee the dark side of their dream, nor were these people in any way in a position of political leadership, and no one foresaw that what was taking shape in the United States then would cause it to emerge as by far the wealthiest, most powerful and most influential nation on earth a century later.

Is it not a stunning irony that the people who suffered most from a new world discovery—the potato—returned to redefine that place to their own liking? But there was and is no Tír na nÓg (Land of the Young), other than in the Irish mind. The Irish gave that myth to the United States, and neither we nor this country have ever let it go. The descendants of those people are now a driving force in American politics.

No group that has become aware of the iniquity of its position in America has remained silent for long—or failed to influence the views of others. And I believe that the Irish Americans, increasingly aware of their effect on the course of history here, can have a profound effect on the arrogance that prevails today, on the self-imposed mediocrity of a homogenised country, on the lack of willingness by the middle-class majority to accept responsibility, and the burden of humane action that goes with it, for the poverty and violence that are the real theme parks in American cities today.

There is one other twist to all of this. My novel concerns itself with the awakening of an Irish person to the traumatic legacy with which Irish society must wrestle. But there simply aren't many Irish people who are likely to go down that path. The numerical odds are stacked in favour of the status quo in Ireland itself. Everyone has benefitted along the way from working the system. "The Poor Mouth" is alive and well, and the labyrinth of dole, grants, subsidies and entitlements keeps the population well rehearsed at deceiving each other and, ultimately, themselves too.

Education in Ireland is a highly competitive environment, centred on training children for secure employment, with little emphasis on history in the curriculum. Yet, paradoxically, to grow up in Ireland is to be surrounded by history: as a child I had to walk past a sixth century round tower every day on my way to school, its original roof still intact. So many photographs of an Irish landscape will reveal a Norman tower-house, ruined church or hilltop kern. Strangely, this proximity to the past seems to make us less compelled to study it, or, more accurately, less driven to seek out our own relationship to it all and to the ancestors who left behind all these clues as to who they were and what they were about.

Now the diaspora, and particularly the forty-five million or so here in America, have created a very different situation. There is a whole industry in heraldic crests, Gaelic name family videos, and images of the architectural icons of Ireland's past, built up on the desires of this group. What this points to is a need to be immersed in the past as the people who live in Ireland always have been, to try to fill the void that is the price of exile. And in the face of the overwhelming transgenerational resilience of the human unconscious, it matters little whether this life of exile started in this generation or six generations ago.

There is a triangle of relations here: the apex is the Famine, one hundred and fifty years ago, and the other two corners are Ireland and Irish America today. Both societies are products of that event. But the Irish who left have both a greater need to become aware of it all, and less internal resistance to overcome. For them there are no compromises, they were dispossessed, and they did not re-emerge as what Professor Joseph Lee calls the new possessing class back in Ireland. For the diaspora, dealing with transgenerational shame does not involve any reconciliation of how they came to survive when others perished. As far as their relationship with Ireland is concerned they made the supreme sacrifice: they left. They are, in fact, on very high moral ground.

Studies of the Famine are making their way onto the American school curriculum. Now, for the first time since they were obliged to blend in, the Irish will stand out again, just as blacks, Jews, Hispanics and Chinese do. That will further drive them to understand themselves and, with any luck, the current trickle of Famine literature will become a torrent.

Discomforting questions are being asked again: why did so many people die? Would this disaster have run its course if the nation were governed from Dublin and not from London, whose politicians were saved from the wrath of the people by a hundred-mile-wide moat? Was this a final solution, unfolding more slowly than in Nazi Germany, but welcomed and abetted by unfeeling economic powers who approved of the labelling of the Irish as lazy and immoral?

And as we strengthen one side of this triangle, we surely affect the others as well. Only good can come of this. Burying the past is a deceit, with a high psychic price, higher than any of us can afford to pay, and opens the door to the kind of confusion mentioned earlier. That reliving the past may be almost too painful to bear was James Joyce's nightmare from which he was always trying to awake, but, as in our individual lives, if our society is to get well, and move on, and flourish again, we have no other choice.

So then, what will happen when every American schoolchild learns about this Irish potato famine, and some of them go on to be tomorrow's shakers and movers? Will the coming generation vanish into the ever more ubiquitous cyber-culture, their awareness doled out to them in Hallmark holidays? Or will they re-evaluate who they are, where they came from and their feelings about the society they have inherited?

The Great Famine is just one of the appalling traumas suffered by the Irish people, and the Irish are just one of the ethnic roots of modern America. Our real shame is that we have allowed it to slip out of memory and into our unconscious, and this we can heal. Let's hope that we are fanning the flames kept burning by those who have popularised Irish dancing and Irish music again in recent years.

Restoring our memory of the Famine, by every means available to us, will position us to pursue the many other themes that make us what we are and inspire others to do likewise. Strengthening the ties between Ireland and Irish America, piecing together the fragments of the past that now lie on both sides of the Atlantic, can only be good for all of us.

My Famine

BY RAY YEATES

M any acting teachers speak of their classes as "a safe place to fail", where students can make fools of themselves without judgment. I wonder is it possible to create such a safe place for me to write about the Irish Famine? I dreamt recently that I, along with the audience in a theatre, built a circle of interlocking white stones like the walls separating fields in the West of Ireland (although they are grey, not white). I think the dream was something to do with the phenomenon of "fairy forts", strange circles of bushes in fields in Ireland inside which the fairies are said to gather and which no farmer will disturb for fear of the bad luck said to visit any who dare to. The result of this communal building was that I was walled in by a knee-height circle of stones. Inside this circle I declared myself to be safe. And this is what I have to say.

It is, I think, about 1952, very dark, the kind of dark that people always tell you it never gets in cities. So dark you can only see vague shapes and hear animal sounds, some pretty scary rustling sounds actually. It's cold, damp Irish country cold. I am wearing the new coat I have just bought in New York for eighty bucks. It's like wearing a sleeping bag. I am going to need it if I am to get through this. I am standing in shoulder-high dew-wet grass outside the door of a broken down one-storied cottage in Balinafid near the village of Multyfarnham seven miles from the town of Mullingar, County Westmeath. It's seven years before my birth. I can assure you it is happening now.

I hear sounds different from the ones I have gotten used to and I push my way out from the overgrown house to the tied up metal gate by the narrow road. I look down to my left in the direction of the main road and the sounds are recognisable now. It is two bikes, one with a bobbing battery-powered lamp on the front about a hundred yards away. It is my mother and grandmother, silent, looking for this house, stopping to look at other ones. Whispered words reach me, and they set off again. They cycle right by me. They can't see the house. It's

*too overgrown. Or maybe they do not want to believe that this is the
house they have been given by the County Council. Maybe a bit of
both. I can hardly see them as they cycle past sweating, intent, puff-
ing up the incline.*

But I know I won't have long to wait for their return.

I am afraid of the Irish Famine. It is a combination of ideas,
facts, history and images from my imagination which echoes
strongly in the close personal history of my family and more frighteningly in my recent experiences. Irish and hungry, Irish and poor,
Irish and emigrated, Irish and dead. A fate from which our noble
history could not protect us, centuries of endurance and all for
nothing. I have always been afraid that I would never have
enough, and not just enough food but talent, knowledge, character, and indeed everything that is thought to be essential for life.
I have always felt there was something wrong with me and I have
come to learn that because of this fear much has gone wrong
around me.

My parents whose grandparents could remember the Great
Famine were themselves both very poor in their youth. My mother
comes from a family of twelve children in rural Ireland and her
father, my grandfather, was invalided very young. My father lost
his mother as a child, and his father remarried. His new wife had
the first family of children placed in an orphanage. I am told that
this was not at all uncommon at the time. My mother's stories of
begging, walking barefoot in the snow, and living on porridge,
coupled with my father's obvious hatred for his father, and later
the horror of my own father's alcoholism, have left me with a fear
of poverty and a distrust of family (which is of course a distrust of
oneself) that led to an emotional roller coaster of a life. Added to
this are my own mistakes, above all an inability to tell the truth,
which has caused me finally to leave Ireland, and my famine and
family behind.

*My mother and grandmother are coming back. God, they had
to climb that awful hill at the end of the road before they came into
the village of Multy' almost a mile from where I stand before they
realise that they have gone right by the house. They are free wheeling
down the hill towards me now, iron brakes groaning. They dismount
cautiously a short distance away and push their bikes slowly, the slow
clacking of their spokes the only sound, getting even slower as they*

come to a stop right in front of me, looking right through me at the
house that barely peeps in places through the grass. My grandmother's
lined slightly Slavic face is masked to whatever it takes to get her fam-
ily a home. My mother looks nervously up at her, learning another les-
son in the war against poverty. Now the first words my grandmother
says, "This is it, Bridie"; and starts to undo the wire fastening on the
gate.

Despite my parents' early poverty I come from a comfortable middle-class background. I went to university and now work
as an acting teacher and theatre director. I am privileged and
should count my blessings. One of my greatest blessings was to
make some terrible mistakes, mistakes for which I could not make
excuses, mistakes which caused harm to myself and others. In
order to be able even to get out of bed I had to search for the
answers, or at least better questions as to their causes. I am not
about to make a case that one of these causes is the Irish Famine.
But I will say from my own experience that the difficulties of the
previous generations of my family continue to be lived out now,
not least because this is often the only way that we can be close to
them (as my own bouts with addiction brought me closer to my
father).

I have never really discussed any of these things with my
mother (my father died thirteen years ago). My only other sibling,
my brother, and I have gained more and more insight as the years
have gone by but the circle has not been completed by the three
of us sitting down together. I know that we have all confided many
times in other people about ourselves and each other, but the truth
sits between us and makes us silent or is acted out in kindness or
lack of contact. It is always, as my mother says, "either a feast or a
famine". I see reflected in my family the deeply fierce and protective pride that Irish people have for each other, coupled with a
deep distrust. Deprivation has that effect.

Through the overgrown yard up to and through the front
door, struggling with its stiffness, they enter and survey the house.
They light a lamp they have brought and my Grandma lights a
Woodbine cigarette, forcing my mother to take a puff to ward off
germs. They rest for a little while and talk. Grandma lays out the
work that needs to be done to get these deserted three bedrooms and
a kitchen ready for the ten children who are waiting for them in

*temporary accommodation in Mullingar. She speaks softly, making
the work seem possible, even easy. Bridie, looking around the kitchen
where animals have nested and nature virtually surrounded, cannot yet imagine that anyone could live there. But live there they did,
and images from their future are mixing around them now as they
begin their work to make the future happen.*

Today is my son's fifth birthday. His voice was on my
answering machine this morning: "Daddy, someday will you come
home?" This is the reality of emigration and no language can
express its loss. Individual stories are lost. I know I cannot compare my experience to those of the millions of my countrymen and
women who came to this country with no hope of return. I can
only say that forced economic emigration continues in Ireland one
hundred and fifty years later with no real end in sight. Many people are writing about the causes of the Famine. There is no doubt
that Britain directly and indirectly caused the deaths of upwards of
a million people and the displacement of many millions more.
Britain's oppression of Ireland is a fact. All survivors of a difficult
past have a common heritage and common difficulties.

As a child I escaped into my imagination, daydreaming
romanticism and idealised fiction. I eventually discovered that I had
a talent for the theatre. Today I watch my students do the very
same, seeking in the difficulties of the characters they play, an
expression of their own difficulties. Much of this "acting out" is
unconscious and provides only temporary relief. Attempting to
make a career in the arts or any field requires real engagement in
the world through consistency, commerce, and personal stability.
Irish artists have historically possessed a talent far beyond their ability to exploit it and become successful. I am no different. My talent for theatrical ability has been a curse and a blessing. A blessing
because it does allow me to express myself. A curse because I have
deluded myself that my talent was enough and I did not need to
face the pain which brought it into being, indeed often believing
that growing up and taking personal responsibility would cause my
talent to disappear. The enormous literary and artistic achievements
of the Irish people combined with a romanticisation of a glorious
pre-Famine pre-British past have greatly obscured the truth.

*Drawing water from the pump in their one bucket five-minutes-
-walk away, they work through the night. Bringing in kindling, they*

open and clean out the old iron range, boil water and wash every sur-
face of years of neglect. They find it hard to speak loudly in the house as
it is not yet theirs and they really feel, like all the poor on welfare, that
they are stealing it from someone, that the owners are listening nearby,
ready to run in and catch them. My grandmother therefore keeps up a
steady murmured stream of orders and encouragement to her eldest
daughter, deputy Mother. Slowly, in the lamplight, clean space becomes
visible. I follow them into every room wondering how they will afford
beds, furniture, linen and, more interestingly, how they will get the
children and their belongings out here. I know they have no money.

I want to write about the British and how I feel about them.
A memory keeps coming back as I do. I am nine years of age and
sitting in a darkened auditorium at the end-of-year school play.
Our school was special, being the only one in Dublin at the time
which taught its subjects through the medium of the Irish language. It is coming to the climax of the play and suddenly a group
of seniors bursts through the front door of the theatre dressed as
"pikemen", the great Irish heroes of the rebellion against the
British in 1798. They run up through the audience and stand, one
on each ascending step, from the stage to the back. They hold
their pikes proudly in front of them as a patriotic song of their
heroism is sung. I wanted then, and for a long time afterwards
more than anything, to die for Ireland.

This memory sums up how Irish history was taught at my
school. We were glorious failures, not to blame for any of our
faults, fiercely ready to defend ourselves, not just against the
British but indeed against any criticism of Ireland from any quarters. There was very little talk about the despair of defeat, the powerlessness of overwhelming odds, the generations of Irish people
who never rose against the British. Deep down, however, I think
I have always known that to be Irish meant to be a lovable loser.

Almost twenty years later, I was in Belfast at the height of
the "Troubles". I was directing Peter Sheridan's fine play, *Diary
of a Hunger Striker*. The play was to be performed to an audience
who would have direct experience of the events of the 1981
hunger strike by IRA prisoners at the notorious H-Blocks, as a
result of which ten men starved to death, the first and most famous
being Bobby Sands. One former H-Block prisoner came to talk to
us about what it was like in the jail during the hunger strike. It

became obvious to me from the way he spoke and the way he was treated that he was still an active member of the IRA, that I was face to face with a bomber. The man was held in the cell next to Bobby Sands and, when Bobby was unable to leave his bed, would help to clean his cell every morning. We spoke at length about the events of the time but that is not why I remember him. He told me of the brutality of the prison system and I had no reason to doubt him. It was a daily routine of beatings, strip searches and taunting. The IRA and loyalist prisoners keep their own military discipline while in prison with a military command structure and their own organised activities. The republicans are kept separated and each night when the prison officers leave the block they begin by shouting to each other from cell to cell a range of classes in the Irish language, Irish history and general debates about the struggle (as they call it) which had brought them to prison.

This man told me, and it was not hard to believe, that the prison officers were hated by many of the prisoners, who held forth the view in these debates that these officers were "war criminals" who should be brought to republican justice once the prisoners' struggle had been won. But, he also told me, and I found it difficult to believe, that this view was never supported by the majority of prisoners, that the argument which won out in all of these nightly debates was for reconciliation and forgiveness. I pressed him further to explain what he meant by forgiveness.

Many prisoners, it seems, when they were first brought in, resisted the prison officers' brutality. This of course only made their treatment worse and all resistance was useless. Some could not live with this and were removed to the hospital wing in a straitjacket. The only option, according to this ex-prisoner, was to forgive the prison officers and preserve your sanity. "Everybody," he said "at some stage in their lives must forgive the people who have harmed them. In the H-Block we had to do it on the first day." Bertie Ahern, now leader of Fianna Fáil, has called on Britain to apologise to Ireland for the Famine. It would, I think, be much more valuable, but just as unlikely, for Irish people everywhere collectively to forgive Britain for all their mistreatment of the Irish and move on into the future.

It is hard to believe the amount of work these two tiny women have done. But now they face an old, old, ever-present problem. They

are hungry. The young teenager has daydreamed many times about
what it would be like not to feel hungry. Not about food, mind you,
but just about the absence of hunger. Her mother has rolled the prob-
lem around as she worked. Exhausted, they will have to stay the night,
returning to the family by daylight but her child will eat, whatever
the consequences. She takes her bicycle lamp, opens the door and tells
her daughter to follow her out again onto the road and down three
fields' length to the gate of an adjoining farmer's land.

In the years before he died my father somehow managed
after each night of drunkenness, followed by what must have been
terrible hangovers, to leave for work the next day at 7 a.m. I have
a memory of him on those miserable dark wet Irish winter morn-
ings walking miserably away from our house. He had a lot to say
when drunk but what struck me about him sober was his silence.
Irish people have a language for everything except their feelings.
They embarrass us.

What strikes me most about my memories concerning the
Famine is the absence of any real discussion of it. Was it the
Famine itself that made my people so eloquent, so ready to identify with suffering everywhere and yet so unable to tell this part of
their story? It is understandable that before its real horror there is
only silence, but this is all the more reason to speak. I cannot
express my love for my children but I will always try. Art and literature attempt to name the unnamable and the attempts are what
matter. Success is not expected. The Irish Famine was the chief
cause of the decline of the Irish language. Early Irish literature
seems to indicate that Irish people then were different, openly sen-
sual, wise and proud. With the decline of this language and culture, only strains of these qualities remain, often in conflict with
other imported ideas of morality. Perhaps they would have vanished in a modern world in any event, but with the loss of language itself, Irish people have surely lost the key to another way
of thinking.

I know why Irish people do not talk about the Famine. It is
the same reason I found this article so difficult to write. To talk of
certain things in our past will lead to talk of other, closer, more
painful events in the present. I have a strong internal scaffolding
system. It's called my personality. I do not know what will happen
if even one support is removed. Irish people are proud survivors.

Talk of those who died, as opposed to those who were martyred, (for they have never died) threatens uncomfortably the confidence of that survival. To be a crushed helpless tiny backward backwater of Europe dwarfed by our neighbouring island, considered to be less than human, and universally patted on the head is as much a legacy of being Irish as the songs our fathers sang. It is really time to stop the patronising celebration and to speak of our sadness. It does not matter that our hardship was not our fault. That has been the convenient way of denying its existence and excusing our part in its continuation.

"Say nothing now, Bridie," my Grandma whispers, "and follow me in here. Be quiet now." The farmer's yard one field away is dark. His dog barks, but not for long, and they unfreeze themselves and move on into the field. My mother knows what is going to happen but still does not believe it. Switching the battery-powered lamp on and off to avoid detection, my grandmother searches the field. She falls once and stings her legs on the nettles but does not cry out. My mother retrieves the lamp and they continue. Shortly afterwards their light shines on the straw covering a potato pit.

During a conversation with a friend who is a psychotherapist, he spoke of the dominant clinical characteristics of the children of alcoholics. "Oh yes," he said "they are usually found in the communication industry or the arts. They are afraid of intimacy and terrified of success." How well this describes me and many Irish people I have known. The Irish resentment of success has been well documented and is continually spoken of by Irish emigrants in America. The ambiguity of forced emigration is the freedom it has brought, freedom to succeed, freedom to enjoy, to criticise positively, to see things differently without fear of taking sides, above all, the freedom to love without embarrassment. Life, liberty and the pursuit of happiness is an unthinkable sentence in the Irish Constitution. It is as if, having had our hearts broken so many times, we expect them to break again at any moment and have decided for generations to remain half-hearted—less to break, less to lose, less to achieve. I cannot tell anyone to do anything, but I for one want to remember the Famine and never to forget it. Thus it can become a personal source of inspiration for the achievement of abundance without oppression which is the right of all Irish people everywhere.

Grandmother and daughter are on their knees now digging the pit for potatoes. They are not fully grown and my grandmother wraps the best of them in her apron, indicating to the child to do the same. But she is crying and beginning to make noise. "It's a sin, Mammy," she breathes out with difficulty, "a sin!" Fiercely, more to shut her up than anything, her mother grips her cardigan and says, "It is not a sin for you. It is a sin for me."

I am told that forty million Americans claim Irish descent, many millions more worldwide, I am sure. Forty million people who want to be like me (well sort of). This could not have happened without the Famine. It is as if to be Irish is an international passport to friendship. You are Irish now if you say you are and that is how the good things in life should be, available to all who ask for them. We lost half our family to gain the world. It is a nice thought and beginning to bear economic fruit in Ireland as foreign companies come home. I have just returned to New York after Christmas in Ireland. I think it is safe to say after so many false starts that Ireland is doing well economically and culturally, and that the recent ceasefire and ongoing peace process have increased Irish people's self-confidence. A new generation of highly educated young people are enjoying themselves in Dublin, the authoritarianism of the Church is on the wane, the old two-party political system is no more, and it is possible to debate and discuss many issues which hitherto seemed impossible, for instance the divorce referendum in November 1995.

The Famine cannot be celebrated like the successes of the Irish football team. Yet, it is perhaps only now, one hundred and fifty years later, with the sacramental fires of loss finally dying, that a proper ritual might be enacted to honour the Famine dead. I would like to make a suggestion as to what this might be. But before I do, I really hope that the new powerful Irish society in the making will above all be a just one. That is only possible if we continue to remember.

My suggested ritual of honour would involve an African, as the representative of ongoing Famine, a native American, as a traditional symbol of oppression involving hunger in the most powerful country in the world, and an Irishman or woman. They meet and tell each other the stories of the hunger of their people. They sing their songs of loss, each accompanying the other. They admit how they may have added to their difficulties through lack of unity or by imitating all that was bad from their old masters. They do this through rhyme and playlet. They tell also how, ironically, they may have gained from oppression. They use their ancient languages with simultaneous technological translation and rededicate themselves to keeping them alive. They use and accept technology as their friend, information as their new currency, and power as their right. They show each other sacred native foodstuffs. (I know what I would bring, Tayto crisps, Jacob's fig rolls and rashers!) Finally, they deliver a warning that these events cannot and will not be allowed to continue. They do this by showing their own capacity for power, war and oppression. They show the murderer within themselves. They sing a song of mercy. They thank the past for its richness, mourn its unnecessary waste and declare that, although it will never be forgotten, it is the past and should remain the past. They live in the present and look forward to the future.

At the beginning of another new year I have returned to New York. America still holds for me the boundless possibilities that it did for so many of my ancestors. Although so many died, many more reached the new world and made it theirs. It is hard to forgive them that they did not tell their children of the horror they left behind. They after all had survived and perhaps thought they should not have. They joined many more who were trying to forget and perhaps with some wisdom left it to others to remember. I have enjoyed writing this short piece because it has reminded me at a critical time in my own self development how I must let my past, present and future flow into each other.

One final thought: I would like to see the names of all those who died, either directly or indirectly as a result of the Irish Famine, gathered, recorded, published, and read out. To make the Famine real to the surviving Irish people of today would seem to me to be of the greatest importance. The Great Hunger was followed by the Great Self-Imposed Silence. I am grateful for this opportunity to break mine.

The Day after the Ejectment (Illustrated London News, *16 December
1848; courtesy of the National Library of Ireland.*)

CHAPTER NINE
Making History

Return
BY SEAMUS DEANE

The train shot through the dark.
Hedges leapt across the window-pane.
Trees belled in foliage were stranded,
Inarticulate with rain.
A blur of lighted farm implied
The evacuated countryside.

I am appalled by its emptiness.
Each valley grows with pain
As we run like a current through;
Then the memories darken again.
In the Irish past I dwell
Like sound implicit in a bell.

The train curves round a river,
And how tenderly its gouts of steam
Contemplate the nodding moon
The waters from the clouds redeem.
Two hours from Belfast
I am snared in my past.

Crusts of light lie pulsing
Diamanté with the rain

At the track's end. Amazing!
I am in Derry once again.
Once more I turn to greet
Ground that flees from my feet.

The Shawl of Grief

BY JAMES CARROLL

A boy of fourteen peers over the rail of a ship. Out of the mist, a landmass looms. The moisture-laden air muffles the shrieks of gulls. The shape of the land emerges. There are hills, the silhouette of houses, the pilings of a harbour. Tending craft approach, with the sound of motors, sailors hailing-ho. The sea is grey, but colour comes into the landscape now—green. The hills are green. The trees are green. The very boulders on the shore are green to him. This is his first sight of Ireland, and yes, the island is green to him.

That boy is me. The ship is the *S. S. America*. The year is 1957. When I look up at my mother next to me at the rail, it seems right that she is weeping. She squeezes my shoulder expressing both her affection and her sorrows. I know that I am near the age her own father was when he pulled away from this very shore—Cobh, the harbour at Cork—nearly seventy years before. I see Ireland for the first time through her eyes, and I see as well the mist-shrouded shape of a mystery of which she has never spoken and almost never will. It has taken me all these years to speak of it myself.

Seeing Ireland first through my mother's eyes means I didn't see Ireland, really, at all. I saw the green figment, the Irish-American dream, the primordial memory, the sentimental illusion. My grandparents and great-grandparents never identified themselves as such, but they were the sons and daughters of the Great Hunger. They were forced by that legacy to emigrate, and had little to take with them but their hopes. When America proved to be hospitable only to a point, they nurtured, particularly in their children, the invented memory of a place in which they had been at home, in which their religion, their accent, their lack of polish, their love of talk, and their inbred suspicion of authority had not kept them on the margins, permanently apart and, inside themselves at least, inferior.

They remembered an Ireland of extraordinary beauty—the hills of Wicklow, the cliffs of Moher, the stark rock of Connemara, and the lakes of Killarney were always featured. They remembered the sod when it had been theirs, and not the landlord's. They remembered an Ireland blessed with rare human virtues—the courage of the Irish patriots, the conviviality of the pubs, the holiness of saints and the friendliness of strangers were always featured. The Catholic faith in this memory was salvation pure, and not also a shackling to that other great colonial power in the Irish story: Rome. With a handful of songs our grandparents and parents indulged the sweet nostalgia. There might have been frantic jigs and reels at their old country weddings, but the ballads they crooned in America were all lullabies. They survived, then thrived because they could rock their children to sleep with the bittersweet music of dreams of a place that never was. They were not like other immigrants, for even as they built an American future they harkened to an Irish past that never faded quite away.

But neither did that past ever come quite into focus. What we Irish-Americans have yet to confront in any real way is the fact that our fond mythology of Ireland's yesteryear—what we learned in our mother's arms: toora, loora, loora—lies in the apparently intractable tragedy of her present. As I write this in the summer of 1996, the long-awaited Belfast peace talks are off track as the IRA clings to its savage strategy of bombing, and Paisleyite Protestants reject the talks' convener, the staid George Mitchell, as a biased Irish-American. It is as if that small country cannot relinquish the chaos and pain and bitterness of this ancient war, though its practical meaning has long since been lost to all but a few fanatics. Every character in the Irish story, from London to Belfast to Dublin to Derry to Brooklyn to Boston to Vatican City—to the hidden bomb assembly rooms of Active Service Units—has made an idol of his own image of that island. Yet in every case, the image is shrouded in what Conor Cruise O'Brien long ago called the green fog—the green fog of sentiment, of nostalgia, of nursed wounds, of noble violence, of old enmities, of unquestioned truths.

What is the block that keeps the Irish people—including Irish-Americans—from re-examining Ireland's authentic past, or re-imagining the island's real future? That political question suggests a psychological one: what is the block that keeps the Irish person from ever settling into true self-acceptance or a mutuality that allows for disagreement? What are the dark feelings that lick up at us, seemingly from nowhere? What are these claws that drag us back into the primeval bog of depression, self-doubt—or only drink? Who were those stalwart exiles of Ireland's great Diaspora, and what happened to them? And what was the secret of their silence? A savage war refuses to end because of this mystery. A curse of personality—that jibe sheathed in the job—will not be lifted. Why?

The green fog in which our beloved island is permanently cloaked really amounts to an uncalculated, yet willed, act of forgetfulness. The common memory that I have from my parents and grandparents is in fact selective, and what matters most, of course, is what has been selected out. My mother loved to tell me about her uncle Jim, her father's younger brother who remained behind in Tipperary. He died in 1916, she told me, a martyr to the cause. Years later, I found his grave in an abandoned cemetery on a remote hillside above the village of Four Mile Water, ten miles from Clonmel. There it was, a stone inscribed as she had heard: James Morrissey, it said. The year was 1916 all right. But the tombstone was emblazoned with a seal; "Rule Britannia," I read, realising this was the marker of a British soldier. Instead of in the Easter Rising or its aftermath, my great uncle died in France, wearing khaki. While two hundred and fifty Irish rebels seized the General Post Office in Dublin on Easter Monday, 250,000 Irishmen were wearing British uniforms fighting the Hun. Why do we know nothing about them? The island is awash in secrets, blanketed in shadows, in the shades of unnamed men whose ghosts have yet to sleep. We know nothing. Nothing.

Wendell Berry describes the way in which the American nation is still undermined—morally, politically, socially—by the unfinished business of its "hidden wound"—the crime of slavery. In America, the white man's secret begins with Christopher Columbus, and continues today with white racist hatred of people of colour whose existence lays the secret bare. Even despite the witness of Martin Luther King Jr. and others, the real meaning of one man's claim to own another, and the real bite of slavery's permanent consequences, have been selected out of American memory. "Forgetfulness is the way to exile," an inscription reads at Yad Vashem, the Jerusalem memorial to the Six Million, "Remembrance is the way to redemption." The point of this book is to suggest that the business of Ireland, and of the Irish everywhere, will remain unfinished—experience unredeemed—until the hidden wound of

the Hunger, the Irish holocaust, is openly acknowledged, politically
and personally.

Firstly, politics. The public consequences of the long denial
of the Hunger's meaning are evident in the slow, at times stalled
nature of the peace process. An act of remembrance that vividly
includes Ireland's largest event of the nineteenth century, which
afterall was our grandparents' century, could liberate for starters,
a political imagination for the twenty-first century, which belongs
to our children. If we took, for example, a fresh look at the very
geography of the place, the ground might shift under some of our
certainties. Until the era of modern road building, Ulster was cut
off from the south of Ireland by mountainous terrain, while a gap
of only thirteen miles of water separates the province from
Scotland. Can an Irish Catholic ask if the centuries-old orientation
of the North to Britain is geographically appropriate? Sinn Féin
("Ourselves Alone") nationalism depends on the island character
of Ireland; the goal of a "free and united" Ireland always comes
back to this geographical notion. But in the wired new world of
information technology, what is an island? It remains a landmass
that was formed by rising sea levels 8,000 years ago, when the
glaciers melted, but the isolation of this particular island, even
from England, has melted in the rise of the New Europe. Why are
die-hard nationalists so slow to grasp the dimensions of this radi-
cally changed situation?

History looked at freshly can be even more instructive—and
unsettling of old certainties—than geography. The Irish resentment of the English rests on the indisputable fact that the English
came to the island as invaders. But so did the Irish themselves,
before the English. The population of aborigines, whose magnificent ruins stand as an eerie rebuke at Dún Aengus on the Aran
Islands and elsewhere, did not survive the coming of warlike Gaels.
Of course, the main fact of human history everywhere is that
native and foreign elements constantly combine through conquest
and migration to form new cultures.

What we think of as Irish is no doubt Gaelic, but it is also
Roman, Druid, Viking, Norman and yes, English. The word
"Ireland" itself has a Norse origin. The most famous Irishman,
Saint Patrick, was from Britain. The most famous Irish artifact, the
books of Kells, was transcribed probably on Iona, off the coast of

Scotland. We date the occupation of Ireland by England to Henry
II's invasion in 1155, but can we imagine that Henry II, King of
England, was a Frenchman? He put an end to the Gaelic hegemony over Ireland, but what sense does it make in our present set
of fog-bound definitions that he did so acting as an agent of the
Pope, who considered Irish Catholics lax in their attachment to
the creed? Or, for that matter, that the Pope, Adrian IV, was himself an Englishman? Since the Reformation, the Irish wars have
been famously between Protestants and Catholics, a structure of
conflict that continues to this day. Yet where is the sense in that,
given the long litany of Protestant names in the roll call of the Irish
resistance from Wolfe Tone to Charles Parnell, Maude Gonne,
Roger Casement and Erskine Childers?

All of this is well known, yet curiously unremembered. Why?
There are other mysteries. Why is England so ambivalent about
Ireland, unable to bring the bedeviling question to full resolution
either through conquest, as in Scotland's case, or through a relinquishing of sovereignty, as in India's? Why have the Gaels persisted
in a rejection of the Anglo-Irish as allies against London, despite
the commitment of Anglo-Irish politicians like those named
above, as well as the cultural resistance of Anglo-Irish figures like
W. B. Yeats, J. M. Synge, Lady Gregory, George Moore, Oliver
St. John Gogarty and Sean O'Casey?

No matter how the Irish puzzle is put together, a piece is
always missing. On the intensely personal level, every Irish family
knows what it is to feel a shadow falling across what should have
been a happy table, the father's fist banging down, the bottle
upended once too often, the mother rolling her eyes in a silent
offering for poor souls somewhere else. What about the poor souls
here? Once Irish men and women typically married each other at
a young age. Then something happened, and they became noted
for marrying late. Once the Irish were famous for a simple jovial-
ity. Then that changed, and humour became a weapon. Once the
Irish spoke their own language. Then, within a generation, their
language largely disappeared. Once the Irish took their religious
faith with a grain of salt; then they became obsessively devotional.
Once priests were few and far between; then they were everywhere. The Irish always had their enemies, but then they began to
turn against each other, making enemies of themselves. Each of

these turns in the Irish story was caused by the same large reversal of fate, which was an act of Parliament, politics, nature and
God—all at once. A shadow fell over the people, never to lift and
never to be named.

The psychologist Carol Gilligan describes how human
beings, in response to stress, "learn not to know" what they in fact
know very well. The Irish learned not to know what had happened
to them. In his magisterial *Modern Ireland 1600–1972*, R. F.
Foster cites "a senior economic historian" to say, "Discussion
about whether the Famine constituted a watershed often seems to
take for granted that we know what happened during the Famine.
We don't." We know that between the years 1845 to 1851, the
population of Ireland fell by 2,225,000; that from a population of
8,200,000 in 1840, the number by the year of my mother's birth,
1911, was half that. But what else do we know?

Where are the searing memories of the starving, disease-
ridden boys and girls who were the brothers and sisters, aunts and
uncles, if not mothers and fathers, of our own grandparents?
Where are the full accounts of overseers and landlords harvesting
grain for export, while their potato-dependent tenants starved?
What sermons did the Anglican vicars preach? What did the fine
ladies wear when their servant girls disappeared? Who mucked out
the thoroughbreds' stalls when the grooms fell ill? Where are the
stories of dirges, funeral pyres, rotted corpses, coffin ships? What
about the bloated bellies, the sunken eyes, the recourse to eating
dirt, or even human flesh? What about the secret suicides? Recall
the famous coroner's verdict: "Accidentally shot himself while
cleaning the barrel of his gun with his tongue." Denial. Denial
everywhere. What about the curses hurled at God? What about the
year after year of prayers unanswered, or hatred calcifying in the
bone, of despair?

In or around 1890, my grandfather Tom Morrissey, whose
brother Jim would later die in France, left the village of Four Mile
Water and made his way to America, unaccompanied. He was
about twelve years of age. What drove him to that? What drove his
parents to permit it? My mother never said. In my family we never
bothered to ask—or was it that we never dared? And having abandoned childhood, why shouldn't Tom Morrissey, then, forty years
later, brought low by booze and, I believe, by the curse of this very

silence, have abandoned his own children? Because he did so, my
mother quit school in the eighth grade to take his place as bread
winner for her young sister and brothers. Years later, when I was
perhaps twelve, I found my mother weeping. I asked her why? She
told me she had just had news of her father's death, which stunned
me. I had not known he was alive. Denial everywhere. And who
says the shadow is not on me?

Occasionally a ghost of these memories appears, flickering
up out of the willfully forgotten darkness. Once, at the dinner
table, I asked my Air Force father why his new Pentagon boss, an
Irishman named Robert S. McNamara, was not a Catholic? Before
my father could answer, my mother said, "He's a souper." "A
what?" "Someone in his family took the soup," she said, then
explained that during the Famine the British government offered
relief to the starving peasants at soup kitchens set up at the
Protestant churches. In order to get the soup, a villager had to
convert to Protestantism. Those who did so left a curse upon their
village—a curse that made me shudder at my mother's mention of
it. "Now, Mary," my father said, ending the discussion. This was
years before we recognised that if ever a cursed man walked the
earth, it was McNamara.

In their determination to put the savage experience behind
them, the survivors of the Famine denied its relevance. Those who
emigrated began thinking of Ireland as a mythic place, and their
children and grandchildren learned to think of it as a kind of lost
paradise. Blarney-struck American entertainers and politicians
exploited the fantasy; Irish-Americans, wearing the green and kiss-
ing the colleens, barely noticed that the real Ireland had little or
nothing to do with their fantasy of it. In truth, the Irish past is a
gnarled scar, encrusted around a still unhealed wound, a nightmare around a horror as yet unnamed. The English past, of course
and equally, is a leprous conscience festering around an unadjudi-
cated crime. The past is no paradise for any people, but for the
Irish it is a true abyss. Nietzsche said that if we stare into the abyss
too long, it begins to stare back. Perhaps. But he never told us
what happens when, though the abyss exists at the dead centre of
our selves, and our nation, we hardly glance toward it at all. What
would we see, peering through the shroud of green fog, the shawl
of grief, if we did?

Famine Roads

BY EAVAN BOLAND

When I was seventeen my mother told me a story. My mother almost never told stories. She did many other things. She spent time with me when she had it. She listened with surprising intentness to my teenage conversation. She loved sunny weather and turkey eggs and a whole range of items which I only learned to look at because of her. Odd items. In fact, by the time she told me the story I was beginning to question those attachments of hers. Not because they seemed false or unlikely, but because they might be clues to some part of her I was only just beginning to realise was hidden. She loved the appearance of snow falling in old movies for instance, so much so that she looked for it and pointed it out to me whenever those films were re-run on television.

What did she see there I wondered? What old magic did that represent—the grainy output of a Hollywood snow machine falling on a stage set? I may not have answered the question but its existence said something about our relationship. She side-tracked me out of a self-important and doubting adolescence into elements of surprise and revelation.

For those and other reasons I never noticed the absence of story-telling. Then one summer night we both happened to be in a back room in a flat in Dublin. That in itself was unusual. My mother was rarely in Dublin for the late summer. She lived in New York at that time with my father. The window of the room looked out on a mixture of humid light and soft distance which is typical of an Irish summer. There was still brightness outside but the trees were beginning to be dark outlines. The narrow garden was damp with river air. There was already a heavy dew.

Out of nowhere my mother began her story. It was about the Famine or, more accurately, about its aftermath. It was not a precise narrative. There were no names in it for instance. It had something to do with two sisters and the city of New York. Incongruously, there was a laundry in it in which one of them had worked. And there the particular details fade and the generic ones intrude. I could say it was about waiting, and separation and finally death. I could fill in the story now with additional information—letters arriving after months, money saved up for passage, a bitter, futile homesickness—but if I did I would be telling the generic story and not the real one. And this was a particular story. My mother told it to me as someone had once told it to her, her voice full of detail and emotion and anxiety.

But the story within this story is about myself, or at least my forgetfulness. I can remember the room. I can remember the abstract regret her words gradually filled it with. I can see the tree, the granite windowsill. I can be exact about the curtains that were tied back and the new carpet we had just put down. But when I next turned to that story—was it months or years later?—it was gone. Gone from my memory and understanding, despite the fact that some vivid ghost remained of the impression it had made. The single circumstance that I had forgotten a story would mean little enough—would indeed be an odd and inappropriate place to begin—were it not for the fact that even then I knew the story was unforgettable.

This piece is about an event which happened long ago and in another country. It is not an exact account. I will not be writing about crop disease or the policies of a government, but about something smaller and more personal. I will be trying to describe here how the meaning of the Famine influenced and directed me in the way I thought about my country, my nationality, my poetry. Even within this fenced-off and fragmented part of the subject I have to add a caution: I am a poet—not an historian, not a sociologist. The past does not seem an exact science to me, but a collage put together by two fiction-makers: the need to remember and the need to forget. I am writing about an event I never witnessed, never studied, never discussed with friends, never heard about from family, which nevertheless became imaginatively important to me. In a way I wish that what I have to offer here could be more precise and clear-cut.

But since the Famine seems to me an event that happened in history but whose effect—in terms of silences and avoidances—continues to happen outside it, then any account of that effect must in turn be shaped by those silences. And so this piece is not

about a product of history but about the process of remembering
it, of trying to recover something outside the bounds of sanctioned recall. Since I am not a scholar, the only text I have is my
own flawed approach to the subject. My own insight, such as it is,
into the Irish methodology of memory.

The method by which the Famine is, and has been, encountered remains a crucial part of the event and its meaning. I am not
speaking about history books or historical controversy here but
about something that both are likely to exclude: the untidy and
wounded strategies by which a later generation struggled to
recover an event that an earlier one wanted to forget.

I was born in Ireland and spent my childhood outside it. I
came back to pick up the story of my country through fits and starts
of discovery. In many ways, throughout my late teens, I was struggling to absorb a text that had no context. And so, ironically, the
way the Famine unfolded in my mind, for all the confusion of the
process, is an inverse, and possibly accurate, image of its cultural
suppression in a wider society. Just as an act of cultural silencing—
and there was certainly one in this case—takes a narrative and
hushes it until there is nothing left except hints and codes and symbols, so the Famine arrived in my consciousness the other way
around. It began as images, fragments of language and retrospect.
Gradually these broken pieces of meaning beckoned to a more
coherent narrative. The narrative began in a fragment. The fragment began in images. Gradually, not without difficulty, I came on
the whole, heart-broken story. In the hope that the process of discovery I went through, even though personal and full of less than
relevant detail, is also representative, I will try to set it out here.

I spent nine years of my childhood outside Ireland. My
father was a diplomat and part of his time abroad was spent in
England. In our house the word Ireland was a common occurrence. I learned to listen for it. Irish. Ireland. It came without
details and in a rush of images, some inauthentic and some not. I
went to an English school. I knew no Irish history. I knew little
enough about my own background. Strangeness had become a
norm: strange vowels, an unfamiliar countryside. If I had been
more aware I would have known that I came from a country I
could barely remember and lived in a country which would not
help me do so.

In the evening my father climbed the stairs to our playroom. He was a good pianist and he liked to play. Mostly he played ragtime—the songs and tunes he had picked up as a graduate at Harvard during the 1920s. But I learned to listen for a change of tone and pace. Then the slow lilts and melodies of Tom Moore would begin. *The Minstrel Boy. Oft in the Stilly Night.* An Ireland that turned into liquid syllables in our playroom at dusk, high over the squares and trees of London, just as it had once turned to wishes and melodies in the British drawing rooms of the early nineteenth century. I listened to them and learned something from them: that there was a glamorous, unpainful, irresponsible way of thinking about a country. That it could even be beautiful.

I went to Trinity College shortly after my eighteenth birthday. My father had gone there and had spoken about it so it should not have been unfamiliar. But when I finally went there as an enrolled student it seemed strange. A dark, enclosed place where it was possible—in some poorly articulated way—to feel actually homesick for the city outside. Having spent part of my childhood in what had increasingly seemed an exile from my own country, I was alert to the registers of exclusion. Here among the statues and windows, the graceful squares and intact eighteenth century ceilings, I felt it again. Something here resisted any act of imaginative ownership on my part. In any case, I was not about to make one.

In my second year I sat for the scholarship exams. They happened just after Easter. A few weeks before the date I went to Achill in County Mayo to study. I was not there for more than two or three days. It was biting spring weather and the friend's cottage I had borrowed looked west to a cold ocean. In the evening time an old woman came up to the cottage and once or twice in the morning as well. She pointed out the cliffs and the hillside with its broken cottage walls. She spoke readily and easily about the Famine. Years later I would go back over those conversations and try to strip them back to their modest details. What was it about them that made them so important to me later? After all, I remember only one sentence clearly, with its hesitancy and emphasis. We were standing inside the cottage I was staying in. It was a typical interior—a single room which had once had a space at one end for animals and a wide fireplace. The window at the other end looked out to the cliffs and the ocean. We were at an angle to the light and the view. She may have been naming the cliff or the actual village of Keel at the bottom of it. And then she said *they were a great people, the people in the Famine.*

I can remember exactly where I was when I came across the printed term *famine road.* Something in the fact of a book naming it and a historian describing it made it seem especially chilling, although I had seen a famine road in real life only a short time before.

I was sprawled across a bed reading a book of Irish history. I had been married for almost a year and we lived in a flat in Dublin. It was not ideal. The top edge of the ceilings had a damp stain. The kitchen was cupboard-sized and the bath was a stubborn green colour. But the rooms were large and airy, the rent was reasonable and we were lucky to be within walking distance of Grafton Street.

The bedroom I was reading in looked out on rowan trees and wide pavements. And there I was, leafing through the book in a sideways fashion. Suddenly I came on the term—and the explanation for it. Famine road. These were the roads that the relief committees had assigned to the victims of Famine in 1847 and 1848. Who had started to build them and then, as their strength gave out, had died building them. The bleakness hit me there and then in a way the statistics never had. Almost more than when I had seen the famine roads in reality with my new husband in the west of Ireland: small, bitter trails in the woods, giving out into a nothingness that made as true a comment on the Famine as any other visible sign of it.

It was late spring, really the first hours of summer. Or perhaps, more accurately the season between seasons. As a Dubliner I knew this time. I had come to wait for it: those twenty or so days when the roads, side roads, front gardens, avenues and alleys of the city were full of blossom. Apple. Pear. Plum. The early purples of lilac and the defiant, poisonous yellow of the laburnum. They coloured the distances and made driving a small drama of surprise and pleasure. Then in the final few days, kerbs and gutters seemed to be the perpetual site of a summer wedding. A debris of confetti-like petals lay everywhere. Finally, with a few final showers of rain, it was over.

Until then I had taken that time for granted, beautiful as it was. Early summer. The end of spring. The start of more light, more leaves, more warmth. But also as it happened the time when the first news of the potato crop went like wildfire through the stricken Ireland of the Famine years. In May and June of 1846 the sun shone continuously. The *Freeman's Journal* reported that the "icy, continuous, drenching rain" of the early spring was over and stated that there was "every appearance of an abundant harvest". By August the fields were blackened, shrouded in mist, afflicted by mysterious thunderstorms. The Lieutenant of Sligo summed it up. "From Mullingar to Maynooth," he wrote, "every field is black."

How do we make history? Maybe the question should be, how do we unmake it? Searching for some correlative to the question, I start to imagine those Hollywood directors deciding early on in the business that they wanted to put snow in the movies. Beginning, in the first place, to speak about a natural event. The snow of their childhood perhaps. The sled rides under sparkling stars and wintry skies. The drifts that reached halfway up the front door. Not just an element therefore, but the myth of an element, with all the fear and hearsay that attended it. Or maybe they talked about the absence of childhood snow. The clear Christmas skies of southern California. A missing element, but still mythic. And then the talk must have shifted from the element to its representation. How to take the grainy, icy substance—not to mention its legend of lost Christmases and impassable driveways—and put it on a small screen. That, I imagine is how the talk must have gone. And then somewhere, after the resolution of it all, the snow was decided on. And then of course the problem came up that there was no snow where they lived. No snow likely ever under the amiable, seasonless skies. And that was the way they worked. From remembrance to craft, from the momentous to the problematic, from the actual to the reductive.

It would be frivolous to say that a poet comes at history the way those film makers came at snow. But that is the risk. The risk of contrived power and mechanical magic. The risk also—although I will here stop extending the comparison—that in the process of contrivance a great and elemental thing will be reduced, turned into something much less for an ornamental purpose. As soon as I knew I was a poet and wanted to write my Irishness into my poetry, I knew history had to be part of it. Too much had happened in Ireland, and to Ireland, for me to exclude that from my sense of Irishness. It was only gradually that I came to suspect my own sense of history. What after all was it made up of? I knew of the obvious events—the rebellions, battles, speeches. But the more I looked at them the more I realised that Irish history was largely a story of heroes. Perhaps it was inevitable. The painfully-made construct of a new state demanded it and in many instances the facts seemed to support it. When I left school and went to Trinity, the images of Irish identity were those images: stereotypes of individual victories, of guerrilla triumphs. My thoughts were not clear about all this. They may not be clear to this day. To the displaced teenager, there was a welcome power in that story of heroes. And yet some part of me resisted it. I felt that if I were to take that narrative I would become like the film-makers—moving with suspicious ease from process to product.

It must be plain by now that I am trying to make an argument. So at this point I should set it out clearly. The argument is this: the past is not the same as history. And in my case at least, the discovery of their difference came as a series of defining moments.

The making of history. The unmaking of it. Both are processes familiar to scholars and historians. In a strict sense, neither process comes within my competence as a poet. The time insisted on by a poem is quite different from the human fiction of time, and in some cases depends on its disruption. Nevertheless, because my childhood and adolescence involved a strange reversal of the common experience, in that it involved coming back to Ireland rather than leaving it, I got a definite and in some ways unwanted insight into those very processes. And since the story of the Famine is linked with the unmaking of history, at some point I began to realise that I needed to understand one to accept the other.

When I returned to Ireland at the age of fourteen I came back to a strange country. A place whose name I had heard, a land whose presence had never left our house. A place I had regretted and yearned for as a child, simply because to belong to it would have given me a thousand small excellences of ownership of place and purpose. In those teenage years I occasionally wandered around Dublin. I listened to the accents around me—vowel sounds that were the flourish and signature of place itself. I felt, in some obscure and unrational way, cheated of that effortless ability

to blend in with my surroundings. I began to feel that I had been
subtly disfigured by a chance exile. That the chance of being out
of Ireland as a child was going to turn into an unwanted destiny
of difference: different speech, different memories.

I began to believe that the disfigurement went even deeper
than that. Childhood is an elusive place. The powerlessness a child
feels is an elusive state of mind. And certainly—I would realise this
more as time went on—whatever power a child feels is intimately
connected to place. I had lost my place, in the real and metaphoric
sense. To that extent, I felt a peculiar powerlessness. Out of that
strange mixture of chance and loss, and childhood feelings of
bewilderment, came other feelings that I felt at that time, without
being able to articulate them clearly. I was a teenager in my own
place at last, wandering, in my weekends off school, around neighbourhoods of Dublin which I scarcely knew. Sometimes I stopped
in front of statues and looked curiously at the inscriptions under
them. Charles Stewart Parnell in O'Connell Street. Daniel
O'Connell himself. Henry Grattan. Sometimes I found there the
words I had hungered for. Ireland. Hero. And here, I felt, were
the instruments of history. The scaffold. The speech from the
dock. The place where destiny conquered chance, rather than the
other way around.

What was I looking for? It seemed harmless enough at the
time, that mixture of wandering and searching. Now I see it more
clearly in the context of that making and unmaking of history.
Because that was what I was doing. Walking from street to street,
ignorant of contexts or locations, stopping in a light summer driz-
zle in O'Connell Street, staring at a bronze plaque five feet above
my head. Random and uninformed as my wanderings often were,
I was doing something as old as human invention: I was making
history. Making it moreover from the depths of my childhood.
Making it from a thousand wishes and dreams and angers. Making
it in the image of my exclusion and with the determination to hide
my confusion in a larger dignity. I could not bear that the powerlessness I had felt as a child should be reflected in the powerlessness of my country. Now that I could belong, I wanted to belong
to something worth the wait. I wanted to be part of a story of
heroes. If anyone had come up to me at that stage and told me
that the defining event in that history was not a gallows or a song

or a speech but a frightening laying waste of a people, I would have turned away. I did not want silence or waste to be defining energies in the story of Ireland. In my story.

And then my mother told me a different story. And this is where I came in. Out of the blue that summer night someone's voice—a loved and authoritative voice—intervened in my search for an heroic narrative. Infinitesimally, someone began to shift my sense of what I belonged to. Her story did not stay with me. But the fact of her story-telling did. The edge of pain and survival, the details of human endurance, the hopelessness and dignity—someone had honoured the existence of those things by taking one fragment of it and making it into a narrative.

After my mother's story, after my visit to Achill, somewhere in the lost land between girlhood and womanhood, I began to make more sense of Irish history. Or perhaps, in some finite and practical way, I began to see that my own relationship to it was both central and unresolved. And yet in the very years when I was beginning to understand such things, I was actually starting out on a life which seemed to have no place for them. I married. I moved out to a suburb with freshly laid roads and a house with raw wooden floors. To a world which invited new beginnings, where the outlines were trans-national, distinctly un-tribal. Where remembrance seemed an unlikely and even unwelcome act.

And now I have to make an argument which must make sense and be persuasive, and yet—because it comes out of my least coherent instincts about my country, my history, my poetry—resists precisely that shape. I have to argue that in a house at the edge of a city, at a time when Ireland was turning more and more towards a modern Europe and away from a dark past, I began to turn back to that past. And the truth is I did. But why? I can't say that I understood hunger better, or emigration, or fever. It would be wrong to assert I did. But I understood something else. As a woman poet, I was beginning to find out just how much of what I valued was excluded from Irish history and from whole sections of Irish literature. This gave me no more insight than before into the human suffering of the Famine. If anything it made me look inward rather than outward. But it made me more sceptical than before of the received version of what was worth preserving through our history. I began to deduce how much, in both the present and past, was left in shadow by the pitiless glare of selective heroics. Inasmuch as I began to doubt the fictions of history I became more open to the possibilities of an alternative version. Inasmuch as I began to question the heroics of nation-making I began to see just how exclusive are the stories a people can tell themselves.

And so I began a tentative journey. My sense of exclusion led to my questions about expression. My doubts about expression led me finally to realise that one of the only dissenting traditions which a writer in Ireland could intellectually adhere to was silence. And not just the silence named by Joyce as an equal partner to exile and cunning. But an even deeper silence: a human one. In which the images of shame—of women devouring their own babies, of land profiteering—had somehow to co-exist with the poignant sense of endurance and survival during a great ordeal. A silence in which stories were not told, in which memories were not handed on, in which the ordinary sorrow and devastation of a people was neither named nor recorded.

I have no idea what my own ancestors did during the Famine. Like everyone else, those people were consigned to a place outside history. As a poet, simply through being a woman, simply because I now put less value on that heroic narrative which had so attracted me when I was young, I already deemed my poetic life to be outside Irish history. The blue hills, the nearby trees, the school runs and broken bicycles of my neighbourhood belonged to a world heroes never visited. A word, for that reason, ironically safe from the suppressions which one history intends for another. And there at last I could listen again to those voices. To my mother on a summer night. To the woman looking out the window in Achill. To my own voice asking myself how to imagine a past without first remembering it.

Gradually and diffidently, I began to include the Famine in my poems. Never extensively, but with increasing purpose. Within the technical and ethical world of my poems, which is private to every poet, I construed it as narrative and not imagery. Somehow I wanted to make a distance and respect for the event which would prevent language appropriating it. Even so, when I first began to write poems where the Famine was included, I knew I was not truly writing about the human suffering which the event signalled.

I could not. Nor would I presume that I could. I was fully aware how separate the vastness of all that misery was, how impossible to take into a lyric poem.

And yet my hesitations were two-edged. Through a process of dialogue with a difficult and sometimes exclusive literary tradition, I now had a much stronger sense of the limits and possibilities of the Irish poem. If that poem could not be an agent of empathy, it could be an instrument of memory. If it could not change forgetfulness, and poetry does not have that power, it could question the machinery of suppression. The story of heroes—that iron determination to have extraordinary actions as our exemplars rather than human survival—was responsible for many of the silences I found most oppressive as a younger poet. But if I found them oppressive I was still free to question them. The people of the Famine, with their dreams, their hopes for the future, their beautiful children, were not. And so it seemed to me right that a poet of their own history, in a poem of their country, should break the silence which shrouded us both.

What will I tell my daughters? Strangely enough, little enough. There will be no summer rooms and snow machines for them. There is no need. The Famine is now less and less part of our fugitive consciousness. More and more it has become a clear narrative of our survival. Through stories, images, arguments and educational programmes, the Famine is now almost as honoured in Irish official life as once it was obscured. There are still questions, however, and they should still be answered. Among them, why the stories we told ourselves for more than a hundred years—stories of endurance, exuberant defiance and even violence—so resolutely excluded a generation and its unspoken witness. Why we shaped our expression with so little regard to their silence. Why we preferred a self-made heroism to the complex humanity they offered us as example. Despite this, it seems that I will not have to tell my daughters, as my mother implied to me in that story, that the Famine was one of the twofold trials of the Irish people—once in the happening and once in the remembering. Times have changed. Hopefully, they will not have to remember because they will never have forgotten.

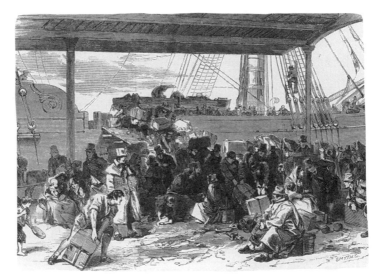

Irish emigrants embarking for America, Waterloo Docks, Liverpool
(Illustrated London News, 6 July 1850; *courtesy of the National*
Library of Ireland.)

CHAPTER TEN
A Spreading Evil

"What Shall I Wear, Darling, *to* The Great Hunger?"
BY PAUL DURCAN

"What shall I wear, darling, to The Great Hunger?"
she shrieked at me helplessly from the east bedroom
Where the west wind does be blowing betimes.
I did not hesitate to hazard a spontaneous response:
"your green evening gown—
Your see-through, sleeveless, backless, green evening
    gown."
We arrived at the Peacock
In good time for everybody to have a good gawk at her
Before the curtain went up on The Great Hunger.
At the interval everybody was clucking about, cooing
That it was simply stunning—her dress—
"Darling, you look like Mother Divinity in your see-
    through,
Sleeveless, backless, green evening gown—it's so visual!"
At the party after the show—simply everybody was there—
Winston Lenihan, Consolato O'Carroll-Rivera, Yves St.
    Kirkegaard—
She was so busy being admired that she forgot to get drunk.
But the next morning it was business as usual—

Grey serge pants, blue donkey jacket—driving around
 Dolphin's Barn
In her Opel Kadett hatchback
Checking up on the rents. "All these unmarried young
 mothers
And their frogspawn, living on the welfare—
You would think that it never occurs to them
That it's their rents that pay for the outfits I have to wear
Whenever The Great Hunger is playing at the Peacock.
No, it never occurs to them that in Ireland today
It is not easy to be a landlord and a patron of the arts.
It is not for nothing that we Fáil Gael have a social con-
 science;
Either you pay the shagging rent or you get out on the
 street.
Next week I have to attend three-and-a-half Great
 Hungers,
Not to mention a half-dozen Juno and the Paycocks."

Famine Roots

BY TERRY GOLWAY

Lately my family has been laying claim to Famine roots. The Golways, we say, left Ireland during the hunger and settled on Staten Island, a green and pleasant place in New York harbour where the sick and the dying were taken off the coffin ships and brought to a dreary quarantine station to recover or to die. I was born on Staten Island, as were my father, grandfather and great-grandfather.

We are Famine immigrants, the sons and daughters of outcasts. We say it with a mixture of reverence and awe, in the same prideful tone a Yankee dowager will use to describe how her ancestors landed at Plymouth Rock. "You know, our family came here during the Famine," we'll say in a breathless voice expecting listeners to nod solemnly, knowingly. They always do.

There is a slight problem with all of this, one we acknowledge to ourselves from time to time. We actually don't know if the Golways were Famine immigrants. We've traced the line to the 1880s or so, but there the paperwork fails us, and truth be told, we simply haven't had time to press the issue. Somebody in the family, a distant cousin perhaps, once told us that we are the descendants of Famine immigrants, and that's all the proof we need. But the reality is, we're just making it up. In fact, we don't even know if we're spelling the family name correctly—check the Irish telephone directory, and you'll find plenty of Galways, but no Golways. An Ellis Island mistake, the family says.

But Ellis Island was built after the Famine. Long after. We choose to ignore the contradiction.

So, fine, the Golways are Famine immigrants. The question is why we would wear such a designation as a badge of honour. That would surely puzzle our ancestors, if they were who we think they were. If they indeed were among the walking skeletons who stumbled onto the South Street docks in lower Manhattan, or if they were among the lepers dispatched to Staten Island's terrible limbo, they certainly would prefer that we not dwell on their suffering. Our odd pride would horrify them—don't they know, you can hear them asking each other, what we went through? Why dwell on it? Forget it, and move on. That's why the family came to America, where the immigrant agent changes your name and your identity and your life.

They would be right, of course, for they surely knew there was nothing romantic or charming in their flight from starvation. The Famine immigrants were ashamed of their plight and would have seen our family's half-truths, murmured over dining tables groaning with defrosted and microwaved delicacies, as an indecent obsession.

Decent or not, it is something of an obsession all right. The Famine suddenly has become a mainstay of conversation with friends and family, if only to discuss a news clipping or the latest commemorative dinner-dance. This would have been unthinkable twenty-five years ago, when, after years of Catholic education, I took my rightful place in the family and in society as a freshly minted, utterly assimilated American cold warrior, stripped of folk memory and all but the shallowest ethnic identity. In the 1950s and 1960s, American schools—and Catholic schools in particular—saw it as their duty to soothe the beast of ethnicity, generally with the soft music of patriotism and civics.

So successful were the Catholic schools in this critical bit of socialisation that a degree from a Church-affiliated university conferred mainstream, all-American status on its holder. So it came to pass, as Daniel Patrick Moynihan wrote in *Beyond the Melting Pot*, that during the 1950s, the era of security clearances, "to be an Irish Catholic became *prima facie* evidence of loyalty. Harvard men were to be checked; Fordham men would do the checking." If "Fordham men" (this was before the feminist revolution) meant Irish-Catholic men, well, this notion of unquestioned patriotism was a far cry from the accusations of disloyalty which Woodrow Wilson had hurled scattershot at Irish-American nationalists during and after World War I.

I've concluded only recently that the schools and America itself were afraid of ethnicity during the height of our twilight struggle with the Soviet Union. To suggest hyphenation was to imply differences that ought to be brushed aside in the name of common cause. So, even such a singular episode as the Famine was judged to be too dangerous (and not, incidentally, as too shameful

or even too painful) to discuss. If during my grammar school days
of the 1960s or my high school days of the '70s, the Famine
received anything more than a casual mention, it escaped me. As I
recall suffering no penalties for having failed to memorise the bare
details, I believe it is safe to say that this most profound human
tragedy, this terrible purge of Ireland's Catholics, went unmen-
tioned in the Catholic schools of New York. Well, at least we had a
day off on St. Patrick's Day.

Perhaps I'm not being entirely fair to a generation of well-
meaning educators, since I'm taking the educational philosophies
of the 1990s and applying them to the 1960s. Back then, the
notion of multiculturalism would have been dismissed as laughable
(as it, regrettably, often still is). American school children in the
middle of the so-called American Century were not embarking on
a journey of cultural self-awareness. They were learning the skills
needed to send men to the moon, bring freedom to the oppressed
and opportunity to the disadvantaged. The America of my elementary school years had a lot on its mind. The ancient wounds of
a single ethnic group, and a white European ethnic group at that,
paled in comparison to the larger task of creating a great society.

Besides, hadn't John Kennedy's election changed everything? For some, it probably had. Kennedy's election was the
supreme moment of Irish-Catholic arrival in the American mainstream. The Irish presence in American politics on 22 November
1963 was astonishing. As Moynihan pointed out, on John
Kennedy's last day of life, "the President of the United States, the
Speaker of the House of Representatives, the Majority Leader of
the United States Senate, the Chairman of the (Democratic)
National Committee were all Irish, all Catholic. . ." The Irish-
American yearning for acceptance, a cultural counterpoint to chip-
on-the-shoulder, Jimmy Cagney-style Irishness, finally was
satisfied. The memory banks, filled to overflowing, could at least
be purged. All was forgiven. All was forgotten.

So it was. And there's the pity. By forgetting who we were,
by suppressing the folk memory of the struggle on both sides of
the Atlantic, and by forsaking history in pursuit of acceptance, we
have betrayed the memories of those hundreds of thousands of
exiles, perhaps a Golway or Galway among them, who came here
in hopes of satisfying their great and terrible hunger.

We have forgotten that the Famine Irish exiles were
America's original huddled masses, tired, hungry and indeed yearning to be free. Their true brothers and sisters are not the well-fed,
middle-class success stories who can afford an odd pride in having
Famine roots, but the black and brown and yellow immigrants who
drive cabs, pick fruit, clip bushes and otherwise attempt to make
something for themselves in a hostile land. This should be self-evident. But those who draw comparisons between the Irish of the
1840s and the Haitians, Mexicans and Vietnamese of today very
likely forfeit whatever chance they might have had of leading their
local St. Patrick's Day parade. In fact, an author-friend of mine who
spoke in California in the midst of Proposition 187 fever[1] made
such a comparison to an Irish-American audience—the reaction
was such that he might as well have argued in favour of high taxes,
military base closures and the Mediterranean fruit fly.

Unlike the Irish in Ireland, who often seem imprisoned by
history, we are masters of our past, for we have rewritten it and
reshaped it, adding a happy ending played out in a comfortable
suburban Cape Cod. We have banished the hunger, the suffering
and the bitter realities in favour of a triumphant saga of assimilation through hard work, character and talent. No wonder we were
ripe for the picking when the Republican Party figured out that
there were votes to be had in blaming the poor, the outcasts, the
aliens and the forsaken for America's plight. In our rewritten version of the past, cleansed as it is of struggle and failure, we no
longer recognise the faces of our ancestors.

A century and a half ago, the scowling Victorian free-trader
Charles Trevelyan dispatched our families to hell or America with
the following words: "The great evil with which we have to con-
tend is not the physical evil of the famine, but the moral evil of the
selfish, perverse and turbulent character of the people." The echo
you hear is the rhetoric of America's new free traders, who, like the
colonial administrators in Ireland, believe that poverty is a sign of
poor character and that an economy free of government interfer-
ence is the best assurance of a good society. Trevelyan, like George
Bush, believed in charity for the poor—a thousand points of light
for the starving millions. As for government-financed relief, well,
Trevelyan wisely wrapped up such wasteful public expenditures in
Black '47. He was worried that the Irish might grow dependent

on government handouts. "If the Irish once find out there are any circumstances in which they can get free government grants. . .we shall have a system of mendicancy such as the world never saw," he wrote.

The political debates of late-century America would sound chillingly familiar to my ancestors, to all our ancestors. The contempt and fear of the poor, the well-fed adoration of the free market, the reflexive suspicion of government-assisted solutions—these hallmarks of nineteenth-century English colonial policy have been revived and revamped in the name of a new American revolution. What *The Times* of London saw in Famine Ireland, many of our leading statesmen see in our inner cities: not privation, but "thoughtlessness (and) indolence."

If political analysts have it right, among those cheering on this new revolution are large numbers of Irish Americans who have made the journey from the ghetto to the split level, and who have persuaded themselves that their success is a tribute to their own initiative and talent, and has precious little to do with the sacrifices of dead generations and the remarkable struggles of the trade unionists, civil servants and neighbourhood politicians who pushed aside America's barriers of bigotry and hatred. The Irish-American embrace of free marketeers, social Darwinists and hayseed evangelists is historically ridiculous, but there you have it. History clearly is not our strong suit anyway. Trevelyan's successors are setting the American agenda with the support of the middle-class, suburban Irish-Americans, those quintessential Reagan Democrats.

I was almost one of them, I must admit. In the early 1980s, I, like many others, was taken in by Ronald Reagan's sunny disposition, fervent optimism and soft reassurances. I had no ties to the old urban machine, and although I was a registered Democrat, I thought the party was tired and corrupt. The great dreams of my elementary school days had been shattered by assassins' bullets, the heartless vicissitudes of borderless capitalism and the stubborn realities of crime, violence and social injustice. We hadn't built a great society after all, so maybe it was time to try something new.

Just as these thoughts were beginning to take shape, a prisoner in a bit of hell called Long Kesh stopped taking his daily bread and captured the attention of the world. I became transfixed by the plight of Bobby Sands and his comrades, who chose to deny themselves food for the sake of a political principle. Who were these men, and what drove them to such an end? I knew very little. The turmoil of Northern Ireland during the 1970s had passed without comment in my house, for we had turmoil enough in America. Bobby Sands and his problems were in another, unknown world.

With the help of my parish priest, a remarkable man named Maurice Burke, a native of County Waterford who had been transferred to Staten Island from Nigeria because of poor health, I immersed myself in everything the family and the schools had chosen to forget. It was a memorable and infuriating baptism, and I still recall being struck dumb as I read for the first time accounts of the unspoken, forgotten Famine, and saw for the first time what the likes of Thomas Nast thought of the Irish who washed ashore in the mid-nineteenth century. Revelation came sweeping over my ignorant and naive soul. What they were saying about us back then, I thought with the wide-eyed incredulity of youth, we are now saying about these others!

Such was the end of my flirtation with America's new Trevelyans, with the neo-nothings who would close down our borders because these others are too poor, have too many children and expect too many handouts. America's Trevelyans actually believe they are revolutionaries, that they are the first to embrace charity for all, and malice for some. Because Irish-America has varnished over the Famine experience, it is cheering on the soulmates of yesterday's tormentors. History is a terrible thing to lose.

My late discovery of Famine history has left its mark in ways I could hardly have imagined back in my assimilated-American days. My business puts me in constant contact with politicians and policy makers; in the eyes of too many of them I see the hard look of Charles Trevelyan and his ilk, who see character flaws in every empty pocket. I do not enjoy their company, nor, I suspect, do they long for mine. It is just as well.

Luckily, I have found more agreeable company in recent years. My interest in the Famine and its impact on America has taken me on a journey down the cul-de-sacs, back alleys and side streets of Irish-American nationalism, and I'm putting the finishing touches on a biography of the great Fenian conspirator, John Devoy. He was himself a Famine survivor, although the same cannot be said of his precocious older brother, James, dead of cholera in 1849 at the age of fourteen. Devoy's life was one of bitter controversy, and his writings were drenched with the most terrible anger and bitterness. Oddly, he is silent on the Famine. But in his case, it is the silence of the wounded, not of the ignorant. Irish-America's forgetfulness probably has served it well, as, to an extent, America's forward-looking spirit has helped it to avoid the clutches of remorseless history so evident in places such as Bosnia. The march to assimilation probably was made easier by leaving historical baggage along the roadside.

But at such a moment as the mid-1990s, when commemorations of the Famine coincide with the accession to power of America's Trevelyans, Irish-America's amnesia has become troublesome and, in fact, infuriating. If the Irish in America had the courage to confront their history, with all its unpleasant and perhaps unsettling truths, they—we—would be rushing to the defence of those the great global marketplace has left behind. We would hear the echoes of the righteous Victorians in the jargon-spewers of the 1990s. The arguments are the same. If we were confident about our own narrative, we would point to ourselves as the all-American proof that the huddled masses of today are tomorrow's strivers, and tomorrow's strivers are the future's leaders.

But we don't know our own history. It's a pity.

NOTES

1 Proposition 187 was a 1994 initiative approved by California voters denying basic services like health care and education to illegal immigrants.

Closets Full of Bones

BY PETER QUINN

Our own ancestors
Are angry ghosts
Closets so full of bones
They won't close.
—Tracy Chapman

A spectre is haunting the West: immigration. From the passage of Proposition 187 in California, restricting basic human rights for illegal immigrants, to the growing anti-immigrant movements in Europe, there is a widespread attempt by economically advanced societies to seal themselves off from the less fortunate. The imagery used to describe these immigrants is almost always the same: immigrants are to hordes what sheep are to flocks, or lions to prides. They swarm rather than arrive, their faceless uniformity evoking the insect world and its ceaseless, relentless capacity to reproduce.

There is no better description of the passions and fears that immigration engenders than the hysterical vision of approaching apocalypse contained in Jean Raspail's novel, *The Camp of the Saints.* First published in 1973, *The Camp of the Saints* tells what happens when a million diseased, crippled, impoverished inhabitants of the Indian subcontinent board a ragtag armada of decrepit ships and descend on the south of France. In Raspail's story, a weak and effete France, awash in liberal guilt and gushing Christian sentimentalism, finds it doesn't have the power to resist.

Neglected for decades, Raspail's book has recently received much attention in Europe and was the subject of a cover article ("Must It Be the Rest Against the West") in the December 1994 issue of *The Atlantic Monthly.* Co-authors Matthew Connelly, a graduate student of history at Yale, and Paul Kennedy, the author of *The Rise and Fall of the Great Powers* (1988), offer a qualified endorsement of the Malthusian and Spenglerian fatalism that is at the heart of Raspail's novel: "Readers may well find

Raspail's vision uncomfortable and his language vicious and repulsive, but the central message is clear: we are heading into the twenty-first century in a world consisting for the most part of a relatively small number of rich, satiated, demographically stagnant societies and a large number of poverty-stricken, resource-depleted nations whose populations are doubling every twenty-five years or less."

On the face of it, Raspail's notion of a conscience-stricken West being overwhelmed by an army of dishevelled immigrants is less discomforting than laughable. The West has shown itself perfectly capable of using sufficient force whenever its vital interests are at stake—or perceived as being so—as it did most recently in the Gulf War. Indeed. For all the handwringing over immigration and the future of the West, there seems little appreciation that for the last five hundred years at least, it has been the West that has been threatening and battering the rest of the world, colonising entire continents and waging war to secure the resources it needs. The current virulent reaction against immigrants in France, Austria and Germany or, for that matter, the US's recent treatment of Haitian refugees, is hardly a sign of societies suffering from terminal humanitarianism.

The pessimism evinced by Connelly and Kennedy is mitigated somewhat by their call for international co-operation to deal with the underlying causes of the present population crisis. But as with so many descriptions of the threat posed by the Third World, the authors' underlying sense of the West's vulnerability before the procreatic puissance of the world's nameless poor is far more vivid and forceful than any formulaic list of possible solutions. The threat is from below, from Raspail's "kinky-haired, swarthy-skinned, long-despised phantoms", from the teeming races that Rudyard Kipling once described as "lesser breeds without the law".

In the United States, the question of intelligence as a distinguishing characteristic between greater and lesser breeds has come to centre stage with *The Bell Curve* (1994), the best-selling treatise by Charles Murray and the late Richard J. Herrnstein. Unlike *The Camp of the Saints*, this sedate and statistics-laden book is not directly concerned with immigration, and its central thesis—that I.Q. is a function of race—is more subtle and complex than the horrific vision evoked by Raspail.

Despite their differences, however, there are similarities. At the heart of *The Bell Curve* and *The Camp of the Saints,* as well as of Connelly's and Kennedy's article, is a world in which the central divisions are racial and in which, when all is said and done, the white race is endangered. In fairness to Murray and Herrnstein, they credit Asians with higher I.Q.'s than white Americans. Yet here again is found the implicit threat of a Caucasian community being challenged by another race, one that has been traditionally credited with being shrewder and craftier—in its own "inscrutable" way, smarter—than Westerners.

The fear that white civilisation is growing steadily weaker and is at risk of being overwhelmed by barbarians from within and without marks a new life for an old and ugly tradition. The most infamous manifestation of the tradition is the Ku Klux Klan and the host of so-called Aryan resistance groups that continue to spring up on the periphery of American political life. But its most powerful and enduring effect was not limited to cross burnings or rabble-rousing assaults against blacks and immigrants. There was a far more respectable, educated version of this tradition that clothed itself in the language of science and not only won a place in the academy, but helped to shape our laws on immigration, inter-racial marriage and compulsory sterilisation (of the mentally ill and retarded).

The movement derived its authority from the work of an Englishman, Francis Galton—Darwin's cousin—who in 1883 published his masterwork, *Inquiries into Human Faculty and Its Development.* In it, Galton advocated the modification and improvement of human species through selective breeding and coined a name for it as well: eugenics. In Galton's view, which was shared by many of his Victorian contemporaries and buttressed by a wealth of pseudo-scientific skull measuring and brain weighing, the races were totally distinct. Eugenics, he believed, would give "the more suitable races or strains of blood a better chance of prevailing speedily over the less suitable."

At the start of the twentieth century, the United States was ripe for the gospel of eugenics. The country's original immigrants—Anglo-Saxon and Scots-Irish Protestants—were feeling battered and besieged by the waves of newcomers from southern and eastern Europe (i.e., Italians, Slovaks and Ashkenazi Jews) who were judged so immiscible in appearance and conduct that

they would undermine the country's character and identity.
According to the eugenicists, the racial "germ plasm" of these
groups was riddled with hereditary proclivities to feeblemindedness, criminality and pauperism. These suspicions were given scientific justification by studies that purported to trace family
behaviour across several generations and discern a clear pattern of
inherited behaviour.

By the end of World War I, eugenics was taught in many colleges. Its research arm was generously funded by some of America's
wealthiest families, including the Harrimans, Rockefellers and
Carnegies. Alfred Ploetz, the German apostle of "racial hygiene",
hailed the United States as a "bold leader in the realm of eugenics",
a leadership that consisted of the widespread ban on inter-racial
marriage and the growing emphasis on compulsory sterilisation.

In the wake of the First World War, the eugenicists helped
direct the campaign to halt the "degeneration" of the country's
racial stock by changing its immigration laws. As framed by
Henry Fairfield Osborn, the president of the Museum of Natural
History (at that time a centre of eugenics fervour), America
would either stop the influx from southern and eastern Europe or
it would perish:

> Apart from the spiritual, moral and political invasion
> of alienism, the practical question of day-by-day competition between the original American and the alien
> element turns upon the struggle for existence between
> the Americans and aliens whose actions are controlled
> by entirely different standards of living and morals.

The eugenicists played an important role in achieving the
Immigration Restriction Act of 1924, a victory noted and
approved by Adolf Hitler in his book of the same year, *Mein
Kampf*. In fact, nine years later, when the Nazis took power in
Germany, they would hail US laws on immigration, inter-marriage
and sterilisation as models for their own legislation.

As successful as the eugenicist crusade was, it was not the
first time that the United States had experienced a broad and
widely supported campaign against the influx of intractable foreigners whose essential alienism—their alleged lack of moral or
mental stamina—would, it was believed, eat away the foundations

of American democracy and sink the country into a permanent state of pauperism.

The country's first great immigrant trauma (that is, aside from the forced importation of African slaves) began in 1845, with the failure of the potato crop in Ireland and the onset of a catastrophe that would result in the death of a million Irish from hunger and disease, and force millions to flee. "The volume of Famine emigration," writes historian Kerby Miller, "was astonishing: between 1845 and 1855 almost 1.5 million sailed to the United States. . .In all, over 2.1 million Irish—about one-fourth of Ireland's pre-Famine population—went overseas; more people left Ireland in just eleven years than during the preceding two-and-a-half centuries."

The flight of the Famine Irish produced an immigrant experience unlike any other in American history. There was no web of emigration societies or government agencies to encourage or cushion the process of resettlement abroad. In effect, traditional Irish society—the life of the townlands and the rudimentary agriculture that supported the mass of the Irish tenantry—came apart, dissolving into a chaotic rout. Faced with the simple choice of flee or starve, or in many cases left by eviction with no choice at all, the Irish abandoned the land.

From Liverpool to Boston, contemporary observers remarked on the utter destitution of the Irish who poured into their streets, many of them ill and emaciated and, in the words of one eyewitness, "steeped to all appearances in as hopeless barbarism as the aboriginal inhabitants of Australia".

The dislocation that resulted was enormous. Although the memory of what happened has been softened by the romantic haze that obscures much of our true immigrant history, the passage of the Famine Irish was stark and bitter. Their arrival was the major impetus to the growth of the largest third-party movement in American history, the American or Know-Nothing Party, which was predicated on a loathing for Catholics in general and Irish ones in particular. In the popular mind, the Irish became identified with poverty, disease and violence, a connection strengthened by events like the New York City Draft Riots of 1863. The scale of social turmoil that followed the Irish into America's cities would not be seen again for another century, until the massive exodus of African-Americans from the rural south to the rural north.

Today the sense of the Catholic Irish as wholly alien to white, Christian society seems, perhaps, difficult to credit. But, in mid-nineteenth-century America, the unalterable otherness of the Irish was for many an accepted belief. Indeed, the experience of the Famine Irish seems to be the historical event closest to the visionary nightmare contained in Jean Raspail's novel. Here, in flesh rather than fiction, was the descent of a swarming horde of the gaunt and desperate poor on the shores of a smug and prosperous West.

Although eugenics was still a generation away, the theory of Irish racial inferiority was already being discussed in the mid-nineteenth century. In 1860, Charles Kingsley, English clergyman and professor of modern history at Cambridge University, described the peasants he saw during his travels in Ireland in Darwinian terms:

> I am haunted by the human chimpanzees I saw along
> that hundred miles of horrible country. . .to see white
> chimpanzees is dreadful; if they were black, one would
> not feel it so much, but their skins, except where
> tanned by exposure, are as white as ours.

Three years later, in 1863, Charles Loring Brace, the founder of the Children's Aid Society and a prominent figure in the American social reform movement, published a book entitled *Races of the Old World*. Drawing on the claims of Anglo-Saxon racial superiority found in popular historical works such as Sharon Turner's *History of the Anglo-Saxon* and John Kemble's *The Saxon in England*, Brace located the cause of Irish mental deficiency in brain size, a measurement that served for Victorian ethnologists as an iron indication of intelligence:

> The Negro skull, though less than the European, is
> within one inch as large as the Persian and the
> Armenian. . . The difference between the average
> English and Irish skulls nine cubic inches, and only
> four between the average African and Irish.

As with so many of his contemporaries, Brace was wrong in his theory of an Irish "race" stigmatised by shared physical and mental deficiencies. This is not to deny the prevalent poverty of the Irish of Brace's era or the real and formidable problems their poverty presented. The migration of the rural poor was, is and will always be problematic. But the challenges it presents can only be aggravated by doomsday fearmongering that casts the issue in terms of a vast and imminent Volkerwandering in which the wretched of the earth will infest and overrun Western civilisation.

Writing in 1866, Charles Wentworth Dilke recorded his journey across America, Africa and much of Asia. A recent university graduate with high political ambitions, Dilke saw the world caught up in the struggle of light and dark. He framed the future in terms of the competition for survival between the "dear races" (Europeans of Teutonic origin) and the "cheap races" (the hordes of Irish, Indians, Chinese, etc.). For Dilke, "the gradual extinction of the inferior races" was not only desirable but would be "a blessing for mankind."

Dilke was a lofty-minded imperialist. Though contemptuous of other cultures and a racial alarmist, he was no proponent of genocide. Yet we know the kind of final solutions these vicious and simplistic scenarios of racial struggle and survival can lend themselves to. Maybe the Victorians did not. We do.

We need to remind ourselves that immigrants are not a single genus. They come in all shapes and sizes. They have immense strengths and talents as well as liabilities. Their potential for enriching and enlivening the societies that receive them is every bit as real as the difficulties their presence can create.

Certainly, those of us who descend from the Famine Irish would seem to have a special responsibility to look past the current evocation of innumerable, anonymous hordes threatening our borders, or the latter-day recycling of theories of ethnic and racial inferiority, to see in the faces of today's immigrants the image of our ancestors: those hungry ghosts who, though dispossessed and despised, passed on to us their faith and their hope.

Emigration vessel—scene between decks (Illustrated London News,
10 May 1851; courtesy of the National Library of Ireland.)

CHAPTER ELEVEN
Our Dark Fathers

My Dark Fathers
BY BRENDAN KENNELLY

My dark fathers lived the intolerable day
Committed always to the night of wrong,
Stiffened at the hearthstone, the woman lay,
Perished feet nailed to her man's breastbone.
Grim houses beckoned in the swelling gloom
Of Munster fields where the Atlantic night
Fettered the child within the pit of doom,
And everywhere a going down of light.

And yet upon the sandy Kerry shore
The woman once had danced at ebbing tide
Because she loved flute music—and still more
Because a lady wondered at the pride
Of one so humble. That was long before
The green plant withered by an evil chance;
When winds of hunger howled at every door
She heard the music dwindle and forgot the dance.

Such mercy as the wolf receives was hers
Whose dance became a rhythm in a grave,
Achieved beneath the thorny savage furze

That yellowed fiercely in a mountain cave.
Immune to pity, she, whose crime was love,
Crouched, shivered, searched the threatening sky,
Discovered ready signs, compelled to move
Her to her innocent appalling cry.

Skeletoned in darkness, my dark fathers lay
Unknown, and could not understand
The giant grief that trampled night and day,
The awful absence moping through the land.
Upon the headland, the encroaching sea
Left sand that hardened after tides of Spring,
No dancing feet disturbed its symmetry
And those who loved good music ceased to sing.

Since every moment of the clock
Accumulates to form a final name,
Since I am come of Kerry clay and rock,
I celebrate the darkness and the shame
That could compel a man to turn his face
Against the wall, withdrawn from light so strong
And undeceiving, spancelled in a place
Of unapplauding hands and broken song.

On "My Dark Fathers"

BY BRENDAN KENNELLY

What matters is vision and the ever-asked, ever-unanswered question involved with it: what is poetry? There have been many attempts to define it. Ultimately, each poet must define it for himself. I find it impossible to define, fascinating to describe. I see it basically as a celebration of human inadequacy and failure. I know that in the deepest sense poetry educates the poet; it leads him through confusion into clarity and simplicity. It teaches the poet about himself, telling him about things in himself such as dedication and hypocrisy. It leads him into severe definitions. It outlaws vagueness. Because it wants to be pure, purely itself, not concerned with deceiving or flattering or making an impact, it towers above him like a judge who, hearing the poet's case over and over, and appraising it constantly and with total fair-mindedness, is incapable of giving a wrong judgement. Poets may deceive; poetry cannot.

In "My Dark Fathers", I tried to define my own relationship with Irish history. One day I attended a talk given by Frank O'Connor about the Famine that happened in Ireland in the nineteenth century and has such harrowing effects on the Irish character. I was trying, at the time, to write a poem about that history which I had lived with since childhood. During his talk, O'Connor spoke of a traveller's (Mrs. Asenath Nicholson's) description of a woman dancing on the Kerry shore:

> This woman who danced before me, was more than fifty, and I do not believe that the daughter of Herodias herself was more graceful in her movements, more beautiful in her complexion or symmetry, than was this dark-haired matron of the mountains of Kerry.

This image struck me immediately. The woman was the entire people, capable of spontaneous artistic expression; capable of it, that is, before the Famine. But then came the terrible desolation.

O'Connor made me aware of Peadar O Laoghaire's *Mo Scéal Féin*
where there is the following description of the dead and dying:

> You saw them every morning after the night out,
> stretched in rows, some moving and some very still,
> with no stir from them. Later people came and lifted
> those who no longer moved and heaved them into
> carts and carried them up to a place near Carrigastyra,
> where a big deep pit was open for them, and thrust
> them into the pit.

This is the "pit of doom" in my poem. There is a description of a man named Paddy bringing his wife Kate from the workhouse back to his hut:

> Next day a neighbour came to the hut. He saw the
> two of them dead and his wife's feet clasped in Paddy's
> bosom as though he were trying to warm them. It
> would seem that he felt the death agony come on Kate
> and her legs grow cold, so he put them inside his own
> shirt to take the chill from them.

In the poem I identify this woman dead from Famine disease, her "perished feet nailed to her man's breastbone", with the
woman comparable to the daughter of Herodias, dancing on the
shore in Kerry. Perhaps the most frightening consequence of
Famine is described in George Petrie's collection of *The Ancient
Music of Ireland*—the terrible, unbearable silence. To my mind,
this meant not only the silence that followed racial suffering akin
to what Hitler inflicted on the Jews, but it means that Ireland
became the grave of song. I was witnessing the death of the dance:

> This awful, unwanted silence which, during the
> Famine and subsequent years almost everywhere pre-
> vailed, struck more fearfully upon their imagination,
> as many kind Irish gentlemen informed me, and gave
> them deeper feeling of the desolation with which the
> country had been visited, than any other circumstance
> which had forced itself upon their attention.

These images of the pit, the woman, the rows of dead, the
terrible silence, were in my mind after hearing O'Connor talk.

Shortly afterwards, I was at a wedding and a boy was asked to sing. He did so, but during the song he turned his back on the wedding party. In his averted figure, I saw the woman who forgot the dance, the land that rejected its own singers. I think I understood then the sad farce of Irish censorship, the modern middle-class commitment to complacency and swinish apathy, Joyce's nightmare, the ferocious bitterness of many Irish poets and artists I have met, the contemporary fear of the silence of the self (a grotesque parody of song is preferable to no song at all), and behind it all, the responsibility of the poet to explore and celebrate the entire thing. If "My Dark Fathers" achieves the clarity I hoped it would, that is what it means. Or at least, that is part of its significance, because no human being can say exactly what a poem means. Only the poem can say that.

*"The Famished", Grosse Isle. The inscription at the emigrant cemetery
tells that 5,294 people, flying from pestilence and famine in Ireland in
1847, "found in America but a grave". (John Falter, 1974; courtesy of
3M, Saint Paul, Minnesota)*

CHAPTER TWELVE
Recognising the Victims

The Emigrant Irish
BY EAVAN BOLAND

Like oil lamps, we put them out the back,

of our houses, of our minds. We had lights
better than, never than and then

a time came, this time and now
we need them. Their dread, makeshift example:

they would have thrived on our necessities.
What they survived we could not even live.
By their lights now it is time to
imagine how they stood there, what they stood with,
that their possessions may become our power:

Cardboard. Iron. Their hardships parcelled in them.
Patience. Fortitude. Long suffering
in the bruise-coloured dusk of the New World.

And all the old songs. And nothing to lose.

Doing Justice to The Past: The Great Famine and Cultural Memory

BY LUKE GIBBONS

Only that which does not cease to hurt remains in memory. — *Nietzsche*

On 20 September 1845, *The Nation* newspaper appeared in a special edition edged in black. The sombre design registered the grief felt at the sudden death of Thomas Davis, the co-founder and guiding spirit of the newspaper who died of scarletina four days earlier at the age of thirty. But the black border on each page was appropriate for another reason, as reports from English newspapers in the agriculture section confirmed the seriousness of the blight which had just struck the potato crop—"a fearful calamity for the country as it appears to pervade nearly all parts of England".[1] The full force of that calamity, as we now know, was averted in England, but unfolded in all its horror in Ireland over the next five years. It was, wrote Aubrey de Vere from Ireland in 1847:

> intimated to us that from the beginning the calamity
> had been regarded as an imperial one, and that there
> had been a latent intention to meet it in that manner
> which would have been deemed just had it fallen on
> Yorkshire or Cornwall.[2]

That famine did not stalk the English countryside is sufficient by itself to rebut suggestions that it was primarily a natural calamity, which governments were powerless to control or alleviate. Mass starvation would have been unthinkable in the imperial heartland, not just for humanitarian reasons, but for reasons of national pride. The elimination of famine and pestilence on a mass scale was one of the key indicators of social progress, and was central to England's claim to be the most advanced economy in the world, the model to which other civilisations should aspire. That it did break out in Ireland only confirmed English suspicions that the Irish, with their indolent reliance on the potato and a subsistence economy, did indeed possess an inferior civilisation, and as such were authors of their own calamity.

"PASSIVE INJUSTICE" AND PUBLIC RESPONSIBILITY

It is from this point of view that political economists and their apostles in the British Treasury, operating within the dominant paradigms of the day, could convince themselves in the face of unspeakable horror that the Famine was an act of Providence, a "fortunate fall" which would deliver the Irish from evils of their own making. The Famine had concentrated in a short, sharp shock a painful modernisation process that might have taken generations, and as such was to be welcomed as a desperate remedy for a recalcitrant Irish economy. "It is hard upon the poor people," commiserated Sir Charles Trevelyan, "that they should be deprived of knowing that they are suffering from an affliction of God's providence." This providentialist belief that, in Trevelyan's own words, "supreme wisdom has educed permanent good out of transient evil",[3] was bound up with a particular evangelical strand of Protestantism which informed the application of *laissez faire* principles during the Famine, and, as such, is crucial to an understanding of the motivation of key figures at the British Treasury such as Trevelyan and Sir Charles Wood.[4] The fact that a benign outcome was anticipated, however perversely, and that, accordingly, there need by no imputation of direct genocidal intent towards the Irish, has misled some commentators into seeking to absolve officials at the Treasury, and the British administration, of any responsibility for the catastrophe in Ireland.

According to Kevin B. Nowlan, in his foreword to the centenary volume of essays *The Great Famine*, which was published belatedly in 1956:

> In folklore and political writings the failure of the British government to act in a generous manner is quite understandably seen in a sinister light, but the private papers and the labours of genuinely good men tell an additional story. There was no conspiracy to destroy the Irish nation.[5]

In a similar vein, the pioneering economic historian of the period, Austin Bourke, has written of Trevelyan in his "Apologia for a Dead Civil Servant" that:

> The pillorying of Sir Charles, ungrateful though it may be to "by far the ablest man connected with Irish

relief," has value as a cautionary example of how one can transfer guilt from a responsible minister of government to a public servant who faithfully implements and defends his master's policy without regard to his own opinions or preferences.[6]

The implication here seems to be that out of good (if the motives of senior officials and ideologues were indeed such) can come no evil, as if following orders and doing one's duty in implementing the orthodoxies of the day is sufficient to remove any culpability for wrong-doing. But, as Jasper Becker has recently argued in relation to the "secret famine" which devastated China between 1958 and 1962, Mao's conviction that his disastrous experiments in agricultural innovation would constitute a Great Leap Forward is not sufficient in the eyes of Western commentators to absolve him from blame for the deaths of countless millions. By the same token, the Soviet Famine of 1931–4 was seen by its perpetrators as an unfortunate by-product of a rapid modernisation policy, but again that has not stopped critics of Stalinism from condemning this forced modernisation out of hand.[7] This is usually accompanied by more sensational designs of disordered personalities and deliberate intent, but the point is that such ascriptions of malevolence are not necessary for injustice, even of a profound kind, to take place.

Crucial to an understanding of this is the concept of "passive injustice", as elaborated by Judith N. Shklar in her powerful study *The Faces of Injustice.* This indicates a form of injustice whose corrosive effects may be all the greater precisely because it passes for normality, for propriety on the parts of well-intentioned people (however mistaken or ill-advised). Active injustice involves the breaking of rules but passive injustice may ensue from simply doing nothing, or from an over-zealous adherence to rules and accepted routines. In its most familiar forms, passive injustice is displayed by the apathy which enables citizens to turn a blind eye in the face of acute suffering or even matters of life and death, as in the notorious case of Kitty Genovese, who was murdered while her neighbours watched from nearby windows.[8]

Shklar is pointing to a fundamental flaw in conceptions of justice as they have evolved in the West with the rise of individualism and market economics. Prior to this, under medieval

Christendom and Renaissance civic humanism, what was termed the "right of necessity" or subsistence took precedence over the absolute right to property, which meant that in cases of famine or distress, those with surplus goods were obliged to share them with the destitute, or to assist those whose lives were otherwise endangered. Concern for others in extreme situations was not discretionary, a matter of private charity or philanthropy, but was part of the underlying connective tissue of society. So far from being obsolete in Ireland, moreover, these sentiments formed the basis of the moral economy of the countryside as exemplified by the communalism of the "Rundale" system in Irish agriculture, and the close webs of affiliation through which rural townlands wove their identities. When the spectre of famine hovered over the west of Ireland once more in 1897, fifty years after the Great Famine, James Connolly and Maud Gonne issued a pamphlet, *The Rights of Life and the Rights of Property*, which sought to reinstate for a radical politics these teachings of the early Church fathers and Christian morality. "In case of extreme need of food," the pamphlet quoted Cardinal Manning, "all goods become common property."[9]

The point of citing this is to show that alternative moral and economic philosophies were indeed available throughout the nineteenth century to those who wished to avail of them. The revisionist view that the proponents of *laissez faire* were trapped within the value systems of their own time, and could not have thought otherwise, ignores the historical fact that these doctrines were the subject of debate in their heyday.

As succinctly expressed by Adam Smith, the new *laissez faire* code entailed that while "a man shuts his breast against compassion, and refuses to relieve the misery of his fellow sufferers", he may still "often fulfil the rule of justice by sitting still and doing nothing"[10]—a dictum tragically echoed in Lord Clarendon's rueful comment during the Great Famine that he was unable "to shake Charles Wood and Trevelyan that the right course was *to do nothing* for Ireland".[11] Such codes of conduct do not evince simply a lack of compassion for Shklar, but a lack of justice, and her concept of "passive injustice" is designed to close off the fatal dissociation between justice and concern for others which has disfigured the rise of western liberal democracies.

If the problems presented by dominant concepts of justice raise serious questions over notions of responsible citizenship in the private sphere, the full gravity of these inherent shortcomings is not apparent until they are extended to public life, where many lives are affected. As Shklar expresses it:

> By passive injustice I do not mean our habitual indifference to the misery of others, but a far more limited and specifically civic failure to stop private and public acts of injustice . . . Public servants are even more likely to be passively unjust [than private citizens in this respect], being by training unwilling to step outside the rules and routines of their offices and peers, afraid to antagonise their superiors or to make themselves unduly conspicuous.(6)

It was not just bureaucratic indifference, however, which presided over the famine, but a specific variant of it pledging unquestioning allegiance to *laissez faire* principles in their most rigid, doctrinaire form. Not least of the consequences of this was that the laws of commerce were presented as the laws of nature, and calamities that could have been averted accordingly construed as misfortunes, accidents of nature, or "acts of Providence". It is precisely this attachment of a sense of normality and inevitability to what is essentially a preventable disaster which deprives its victims of even the therapeutic consolation of attaching blame, and hence of exonerating themselves from complicity in their own destruction.

PASSIVE INJUSTICE AND CULTURAL MEMORY

One response to this by the victims, found in much of the folklore sources, is to acquiesce in one's own helplessness or incomprehension by attributing the famine to "God's will", or "Fate" of a more malignant cast. But a very different response sought to fill the moral void by discerning a pattern in the disaster traceable to previous acts of destruction visited upon the Irish by British rule. From this point of view, the true horror of the Famine derived not from its uniqueness but from its *repetition*, its tendency to strike again and again with lethal effect. Writing in the aftermath of the Great Famine, a commentator in *The Irish Quarterly Review* ruefully observed:

To say that Ireland of all the European nations, presents the most difficult problems for the statesman,
the strangest anomaly to the political economist, and
the saddest spectacle to the philanthropist, is only to
utter what has grown trite by the melancholy repetition of ages... [T]he history of no other people presents us with so great a uniformity of suffering and
misfortune. The famines and tumults of one age are
only equalled by those which succeed them in
another; the devastating wars of Elizabeth are only
surpassed in atrocity by the desolating massacres of the
Commonwealth—the harrowing details of Archbishop Boulter, Bishop Nicholson and other writers,
who describe the terrible years of scarcity endured by
the Irish people in the middle of the eighteenth century [during the devastating famine of 1741], are only
thrown into the shade by the horrors of the famine in
the middle of the nineteenth![12]

The mention of the traumatic legacy of the Elizabethan wars
is salutary here, for while there may be no direct evidence of genocidal intent during the Great Famine, it was during this early
period that Edmund Spenser sent a notorious memorandum to
Queen Elizabeth I, expressing the conviction that "unless the Irish
be famished, they will never be subdued". Speaking at a Repeal
meeting in January 1846, Daniel O'Connell summoned up this
revenant of conquest, warning that it was not inconceivable for the
English to "starve the Irish nation", for Spenser, "with all the
vividness of poetic imagination", has already proposed such a
course of action.[13]

Vestiges of this policy of extermination also lingered on in folk
memory, as is clear from William Hackett's report from the Cork
countryside in 1849 that the peasantry "have a tradition that the
reign of a Queen is portentous of evil to Ireland", citing popular
recollections of dispossession in the time of Mary Tudor, and what
was referred to as the "fire sword famine" of her sister, Elizabeth I.[14]
This linking of the Famine with the colonial experience of persecu-
tion and confiscation is a recurrent motif in later histories of the
period, and it is this, I suggest, which was primarily responsible for
the perception that the Famine was itself a conspiracy, consciously

brought about by the British government.[15] As Judith Shklar
argues, the difficulty in apportioning responsibility in cases of passive injustice nurtures rather than allays a sense of grievance, and the
need to identify specific individuals as authors of the catastrophe is
accordingly accentuated and intensified:

> It is one of the failings of the normal model [i.e.
> "active injustice"] that it looks only to agents, not to
> the inactive contributors to injustice . . . we ought to
> direct our sense of injustice less towards the search for
> possible initiators and the immediate causes of disas-
> ters than towards those who do nothing to prevent
> them or to help the victims . . . Even though the dis-
> astrous burdens left us by our deceased predecessors
> or the work of the invisible hand and a harsh but pre-
> dictable nature cannot be identified as actively unjust,
> they are amenable to improvement.(40, 56)

On Shklar's terms, the incorporation of the catastrophe into
wider historical narratives of colonialism may be more beneficial
in the long run than direct imputations of conspiracy and pre-
meditated atrocity. Many public officials, as she points out in her
discussion of the Great Famine, did all within their power to
relieve the situation, and "no one could charge them personally
with callousness or indifference". But it does not follow from this
that no human agencies were responsible, and that it was purely a
misfortune, or natural disaster:

> Was it . . . purely a misfortune that so many Irish peas-
> ants lived off a single crop, and that the landlords
> imposed rigid obstacles to agricultural improvement?
> This might raise the impossible question of historical
> injustice, but in this case there is every reason to
> recognise passive injustice. It is not only in retrospect
> that one sees many policies that the government might
> have pursued . . . The immense contempt that most
> Englishmen felt for the Irish was also not to be
> ignored.(68)

This recognition of "historical injustice", moreover, is
advanced not only by placing events in a wider Irish context, but

in an extended comparative frame which expresses solidarity with the suffering of other peoples, while being sensitive to both the similarities and differences to the Irish situation. As Laurence Mordecai Thomas comments in his thoughtful comparative study of the evils of the Holocaust and American Slavery:

> A person who focuses upon the moral suffering of some, and not others, does no one an injustice if that person is sufficiently mindful that the suffering of those about whom he writes does not even begin to exhaust the topic of suffering, and if, in any case, the writer's aim is not one of invidious comparisons.[16]

REMEMBRANCE AND REPRESENTATION

In this respect, a small advertisement under the masthead on the issue of the *Nation* which announced the death of Thomas Davis and the first ominous portents of the Famine is of interest:

AMERICAN SLAVERY

> FREDERICK DOUGLASS, recently a slave in the United States, intends to deliver another lecture in the MUSIC-HALL, Lower-abbey street, on TUESDAY evening next, 23rd instant, at Eight o'clock. Doors to be open at Half-past seven o'clock. Admission, by tickets, to be had at the door. Promenade—fourpence. Gallery—twopence.

Frederick Douglass, escaped slave and outstanding champion of the abolitionist cause, travelled to Ireland in late August 1845 to deliver a series of lectures in Dublin, Wexford, Waterford, Cork, Limerick, and Belfast—"from the Hill of Howth to the Giant's Causeway", as he put it, "and from the Giant's Causeway to Cape Clear". In a letter to William Lloyd Garrison in the United States, he writes that "instead of the bright, blue sky of America, I am covered with the soft, grey fog of the Emerald isle":

> I can truly say, I have spent some of the happiest moments of my life since landing in this country. I seem to have undergone a transformation. I live a new life. The warm and generous co-operation extended

to me by the friends of my despised race; the prompt
and liberal manner with which the press has rendered
me its aid; the glorious enthusiasm with which thousands have flocked to hear the cruel wrongs of my
down trodden and long-enslaved fellow countrymen
portrayed; the deep sympathy for the slave, and the
strong abhorrence of the slaveholder everywhere
evinced. . .I gaze around in vain for one who will
question my humanity, claim me as his slave, or offer
me an insult.[17]

But, he goes on to say, it is not all pleasure, and he has experienced "very much that has filled me with pain. I will not in this
letter attempt to give any description of those scenes which have
given me pain". Douglass had in fact arrived in Ireland in the first
throes of the Famine, and in another letter, he conveys the dreadful impressions it made on him:

I have heard much of the misery and wretchedness of
the Irish people. . .but I must confess, my experience
has convinced me that the half has not been
told. . .Here you have an Irish hut or cabin, such as
millions of the people of Ireland live in. . .in much the
same degradation as the American slaves. I see much
here to remind me of my former condition, and I confess I should be ashamed to lift my voice against
American slavery, but that I know the cause of humanity is one the world over. He who really and truly feels
for the American slave, cannot steel his heart to the
woes of others.[18]

Douglass's sympathy for the plight of the Irish poor may be
seen as a reciprocal gesture, complementing the key role played by
Daniel O'Connell and other leading abolitionists in the anti-slavery cause in Ireland and Britain. But it was not all magnanimity
and mutual support. Instead of expressing common causes with
Douglass, some Irish newspapers, with the kind of insularity which
has often characterised expressions of Irish identity both at home
and abroad, ventured the opinion that "white slaves" are in no
position to make common cause with their American counterparts:
"when we are ourselves free, let us then engage in any struggle to

erase the sin of slavery from every land. But, until then, our own liberation is that for which we should take council, and work steadily".[19] As David Roediger has written, it would be heartening to think that groups on the bottom rung of the social ladder would offer mutual support, sympathising with each other's condition because of a shared history of oppression.[20] But unfortunately, the structures of competition in society see to it that the reverse is frequently the case, as advances by one disadvantaged or marginalised group are achieved at the expense of others. In the case of Irish-America, as has been documented by Roediger, Noel Ignatiev and others, social mobility and the determination to prove one's whiteness, often—but not always, it is important to emphasis—meant stepping on those with whom they previously shared a common burden.[21] As another Irish newspaper wrote in relation to Frederick Douglass's lecture tour, a "people in serfdom cannot afford to make new enemies" by criticising those who victimise others.[22]

It is one thing to come across these sentiments in a nineteenth-century provincial newspaper, but another thing to find them in the multiculturalist milieu of the *Village Voice*. In a recent polemic against post-colonial (or multi-cultural) pretensions on the part of the Irish, Lawrence Osborne takes Declan Kiberd's book, *Inventing Ireland*, to task for suggesting that Ireland's colonial history has any bearing on present day Ireland, let alone anything to offer to other peoples with a colonial past. In Kiberd's book, he tells us:

> There are plenty of "liberationist" heroes, [and] fragile Third World solidarities . . . Ireland, he contends, has more in common with Kenya and Algeria than with France or Germany. To be Irish is to be iconclastic relative to "imperial Europe". The Irish can claim to be the "niggers of Europe", in Roddy Doyle's phrase, and reap a certain politically correct credibility thereby.[23]

Mary Robinson, he goes on to say, had even the temerity to relate famine in Somalia to the Great Irish Famine on a visit to Africa. The Irish, he says, are white, fullstop, and should stick to their own caste. Whatever propagandists might say, the Irish and the British, for "all intents and purposes", are "the same race, indistinguishable from each other". If this is so, one wonders why, to revert to Aubrey de Vere's question at the beginning of this essay, the British authorities were so slow to spot the obvious similarities, and did not respond to the Irish Famine the way they would have if a similar catastrophe threatened Yorkshire and Cornwall.

Rather than being forced or tendentious, the analogies between the impact of the Famine on Irish culture, both at home and abroad, and the African-American response to slavery and the horrors of the Atlantic passage, testify to the painful negotiation of popular memory in cultures encumbered with the ordeal of colonisation. While it is true that slavery gave rise to some remarkable exercises in retrieval—for example, the narratives of Frederick Douglass—there is a sense in which it has taken one hundred and fifty years for the lived experience of black culture to come out from under the shadow of the past. This did not mean that the time lag in between was one of silence and forgetting, but that, due to continuing discrimination and the absence of civil rights, it was not possible to create the cultural space—and the confidence—to engage fully with the unwritten epitaphs of another era.

By the same token, it may well be that the long term repercussions of the Famine were such that it is only in this generation that Irish society is able to come to terms with the full scale of the disaster. The spectre of famine haunted successive generations, precipitating, within a few decades, the Land War in the late 1870s, and, as we noted above, a similar prospect of famine on the western seaboard in 1897–8. This fear of hunger persisted into the twentieth century until the centenary itself, when, in the midst of war-rationing and food shortages, a threatened crop failure in 1946 prompted the Irish government to mobilise 250,000 men and women—the so-called "Harvest army"—to bring in the crops from the waterlogged fields. For this reason, the failure of the government to commemorate the Famine need not be put down to bad faith, but may have been due to the fact that the memory was still too close to the bone.

As Judith Shklar has suggested, one of the consequences of the low visibility of passive injustice, the facility with which it eludes the nets of criticism or accountability, is that sense of outrage remains unrequited, and the voices of victims are simply not heard. In these circumstances, in Paul Ricouer's words, to be forgotten and written out of history is to die again. Memory, then, is not just a matter of retention or recollection but of finding the narrative forms that will do justice to this troubled inheritance without sanitising it, but also without succumbing to it. There are those who insist that all these events are firmly behind us, but the cultural experience of catastrophe demonstrates, on the contrary, that the past is not over until its story has been told.

Notes

1 "The Potato Crop", *The Nation*, 20 September 1845, p.814.

2 Aubrey de Vere, *English Misrule and Irish Misdeeds*, (London: Murray, 1848), p.14.

3 Charles Trevelyan, *The Irish Crisis*, (London: 1848), p.1.

4 See Peter Gray, "The Triumph of Dogma: Ideology and Famine Relief", *History Ireland*, Vol. 3, no. 2, Summer 1995; "Potatoes and Providence: British Government's Responses to The Great Famine", *Bullan*, Vol. 1, no. 1, Spring 1994.

5 "Foreword"[under the initials of the editors R. D. E. and T. D. W.] to R. Dudley Edwards and T. Desmond Williams, (eds.), *The Great Famine*, (Dublin: Browne and Nolan, 1956), p.xi.

6 Austin Bourke, "Apologia for a Dead Civil Servant", *The Irish Times*, 5-6 May 1977, reprinted in Jacqueline Hill and Cormac O Grada (eds.) *The Visitation of God? The Potato and the Great Irish Famine*, (Dublin: The Lilliput Press, 1993), p.170.

7 Jasper Becker, *Hungry Ghosts: China's Secret Famine*, (London: John Murray, 1996).

8 Judith N. Shklar, *The Faces of Injustice*, (New Haven: Yale University Press, 1990), p.42. (All subsequent references in parentheses in text.)

9 See the remarkable chapter, entitled "Famine", in Maud Gonne MacBride's *A Servant of the Queen*, (London, 1938).

10 Adam Smith, *The Theory of Moral Sentiments*, (1759), (ed.) D. D. Raphael and A. L. Macfie (Oxford: Oxford University Press, 1976), pp.81, 82.

11 Cited in Cecil Woodham-Smith, *The Great Hunger: Ireland 1845-1849*, (New York, 1962), p.375.

12 'A Glance at the Past and Present Condition of Ireland', *The Irish Quarterly Review*, no. iv. December, 1851, p.579.

13 *The Nation*, 24 January 1846, p.228.

14 Cited in Neil Buttimer, "A Stone on the Cairn: The Great Famine in Later Gaelic Manscripts", in Chris Morash and Richard Hayes, (eds.), *Fearful Realities: New Perspectives on the Famine*, (Dublin: Irish Academic Press, 1995), p.96.

15 See comparison made by P. A. Sillard, the biographer of John Mitchel, who relates Lord Clarendon's role during the Famine to the scorched earth policy of Lord Mountjoy in the Elizabethan period—a comparison that draws the wrath of the editors of the 1956 collection of essays, *The Great Famine*, (p.vii).

16 Laurence Mordecai Thomas, *Vessels of Evil: American Slavery and the Holocaust*, (Phildelphia: Temple University Press, 1993), p.3-4.

17 Frederick Douglass, *My Bondage and My Freedom*, [1855], with an introduction by Philip Foner (New York: Dover Publications, 1969), pp.370-1.

18 Philip Foner, (ed.), *The Life and Writings of Frederick Douglass*, vol. 1 (New York: International Publishers, 1950), pp.140-1.

19 Cited from the *Waterford Freeman*, 10 September 1845, in John W. Blessingame, (ed.), *The Frederick Douglass Papers*, vol. 1: 1841-46 (New Haven: Yale University Press, 1979), p.77.

20 See David Roediger, "Irish-American Workers and White Racial Formation in the Antebellum United States", *The Wages of Whiteness*, (London: Verso, 1991), p.134. I have discussed this point in greater detail in "Unapproved Roads: Ireland and Post-Colonial Identity" in *Transformations in Irish Culture*, (Cork: Cork University Press, 1996).

21 Roediger, ibid., Noel Ignatiev, *How the Irish Became White*, (New York: Routledge, 1995), and Dale T. Knobel, *Paddy and the Republic: Ethnicity and Nationality in Antebellum America*, (Middletown, CT: Wesleyan University Press, 1986).

22 *Frederick Douglass Papers*, Op cit., p.77.

23 Lawrence Osborne, "The Uses of Éire: How the Irish Made up a Civilisation", *The Village Voice*, June 1996.

The Famine of Feeling

BY TOM HAYDEN

To be the present of the past. To infer the difference with a terrible stare.
But not to feel it. And not to know it.
— Eavan Boland[1]

All my great-grandparents were Famine immigrants. Inevitably, there were other relatives whose names I will never know who died of fever or starvation. Others wept to the heavens when their children were exiled to America on the coffin ships. Their mournful keening, Frederick Douglass wrote after a visit to Ireland, reminded him of the "wild notes" of African mothers during the slave trade.[2]

I am an orphan to this history. My parents never told me of it. Though they were shaped and influenced by the Famine, I don't know if they themselves were aware of it.

Unlike the horrific experiences of other people, there has been an ocean of silence over the trauma these millions of Irish suffered. To be sure, there is a folk awareness that lingers. But there are thousands of unmarked Famine graves under the green fields of Ireland. Ireland's first Famine museum opened only a few years ago. Until recently, academic histories and popular literature on the Famine has been sparse. The Famine is neglected in school curriculums too.

When the Famine is recalled at all, it usually is as "the *potato* famine", which seems to imply an unfortunate agricultural accident beyond human control or responsibility. It is not seen as the intentional thinning and removal of a whole rural population considered "surplus" by a foreign power.

A Famine repressed, however, breeds an incipient hunger of its own, a hunger to know, to grieve, to hold accountable, to resolve, and to honour. This hunger for memory is stirring. Our stories are being recovered. In William Kennedy's *Very Old Bones*, the character Peter Phelan came to this recognition: "that individuals, families or societies that willfully suppress their history will face a season of reckoning, one certain to arrive obliquely, in a dark place, at a hostile hour, with consequences for the innocent as well as for the conspirators."[3] For the Famine descendants, this is "a season of reckoning".

*   *   *   *   *

My great grandparents found their way to the farmlands of Wisconsin and Ohio (one was born in Boston just after her parents arrived). According to scant records, my Irish great-grandfather Thomas Emmet Hayden (born 1845) married an Alice Foley (born 1848). Their son Thomas was born in 1868 and died in 1941, his life spanning the successful growth of America as a world power. That Thomas Hayden was a lawyer immersed in Milwaukee ward politics. He married Mary Agnes Ducey, and their child, my father John, was born in Milwaukee in 1906.

My mother's family can be traced to Emmett Owen Garity, who came to Ontario, married Mary Ethel Olwell, and settled in Jefferson County, Wisconsin, with only the barest necessities of life. He was a principled man; during the US Civil War, his farm was a station on the Underground Railroad of escaping slaves.

My grandfather, also Emmett Garity, was killed in a cannery accident in small-town Wisconsin in 1920, leaving my grandmother ("Nannie Ethel") to raise twelve children, including my mother, through the Great Depression. If those times were cruel, no one spoke of it, for crueller times lay in the past, and there was the next generation to look forward to.

The Irish arrived in America impoverished, disoriented, and surrounded by Nativist bigotry. From the members of the Know-Nothing Party to an intellectual eminence like Ralph Waldo Emerson, they were scorned as inferior, "a mongrel mass of ignorance and crime and superstition".[5] They competed, often violently, with blacks over the worst, most oppressive jobs. The average emigrant lived only six years.[6] Infants died by the tens of thousands. Insane asylums filled with the Irish. And yet they came, and slowly, painfully, they stayed. And in time, large numbers began to succeed. By the early 1900s, the time of my parents' birth, two-thirds of five million Irish-Americans were born in the US.

The fictional drunkard Studs Lonigan spoke for my parents' generation: "The effects and scars of immigration are upon my life. The past was dragging through my boyhood and adolescence

. . . But for an Irish boy born in Chicago in 1904, the past was a tragedy of his people, locked behind '*the silence of history*.'"[4]

Why did my parents make a secret of the past? Did they think it best to forget? Or did they themselves not know? I will never know, because when history is not inherited, questions cannot be asked. There was only a present and a future in the existence they provided me.

In my parents' youth, US President Woodrow Wilson had campaigned against "hyphenated Americans" like the Irish. My parents had no desire to be hyphenated. In my entire life, they never mentioned Ireland. Total assimilation was the goal. I was their little pride and joy, the only child, the one who would attend university and succeed. They expected me to become a professional, perhaps a lawyer or doctor. My father was an accountant, my mother a school film librarian. The poets, story-tellers, musicians and mystics of the Irish past were being toppled for the ideal of the white collar middle-manager. But as my mother noted later, "Tommy always had a nose in his book." It was true, and when I took a college interest in literature and writing, my parents were concerned. When I turned down a job at the Detroit *News* to join the civil rights movement, they thought I was throwing my life away. Why work against hunger and discrimination?

* * * * *

The threat of historical amnesia due to shame, denial, and the pressures of assimilation has faced the Indians, the African-Americans, the Jews, the Armenians, every community that has experienced uprooting, enslavement, or genocide. By comparison, the Irish Famine seems more suppressed in consciousness, not only of the Irish but Americans as a whole. The writer Peter Quinn thinks that people who look back at their Irish origins are particularly subject to criticism and dismissal. He speculates that "maybe people are afraid that if the Irish—the grandparents of all ethnic groups—dissent from the assimilationist myth, the country will fall apart."[7]

What little Irish culture I encountered growing up was distant, trivial, sentimentalised. I have dim childhood memories of St. Patrick's Days where every quaint stereotype of the Irish was repeated and acted out. As late as my fortieth birthday, a close friend held a surprise party complete with Hollywood dwarfs he hired to play leprechauns.

To be cut off from one's past, however, doesn't mean that the past has lost its hold. It only means the ghosts are masked.

". . .their demonic yells are still ringing in my ears, and their horrible images are still fixed upon my brain."
—a writer in Cork, 1846 [8]

". . .the cataclysm stunned many of its victims into traumatised muteness..."
—Terry Eagleton, historian [9]

"Starving families boarded themselves into their cabins, so that their deaths might go decently unviewed."
—Terry Eagleton[10]

"How to gain pride from the ditches?"
—Seamus Cashman, Dublin publisher and writer

"Ireland is "pretty *small potatoes* by contrast with the present conflict between the East and West."
—U.S. State Department official, 1949[11]

"The struggle of life is between memory and forgetting."
—Milan Kundera[12]

In the Irish past I dwell
Like sound implicit in a bell.
—Seamus Deane, poet[13]

Does trauma and its denial stay with us, only repressed through time? What is the continuing effect? Or can these matters be wiped from memory, without damage or loss? Is that the meaning of "starting over"?

As the Irish writer John Waters points out, "by blandly insisting that we 'leave the past behind us', we prevent ourselves from doing so."[14] There is unfinished business with the ghosts.

> *O Headon, Hayden, Oh Eideain in Irish*. . .is of frequent occurrence in the Ormond Deeds from the year 1374. . .the name must be regarded primarily as belonging to Co. Carlow. . .one of the principal Irish surnames in that county at the time of the 1659 census. . .Peter *Hayden* of Boleycarrigan, Co. Wicklow. . .elected *captain of the insurgents* in preference

to Michael Dwyer, was with *35 other prisoners
killed... in 1798.*
—Irish genealogy book

Was this Peter Hayden, martyred in the 1798 rising of the
United Irishmen, a relation of mine? It seems impossibly fanciful.

But what I need to know, and never will, is whether I am
named for Thomas Emmet, brother and co-conspirator of Robert
Emmet, who was considered "the most dangerous man in
Ireland" by a British agent, and who was hanged for leading the
1798 rebellion.

Thomas Emmet also was sentenced to death for high trea-
son in 1798, but was banished to America instead, where he
became a respected political refugee, a friend of Thomas Jefferson,
attorney general of New York, and, according to one text, "a
revered link between the frustrated hopes of the Irish Revolution
and the opportunities offered by the political freedom of the
American Republic." After Emmet's death in 1827 his cause was
taken up by many of the Famine generation.

I was named Thomas Emmet Hayden *the fourth*. When I
asked my parents about the others I was named after, my mother
could only say, merrily, "the first, second, and third". In retrospect, it clearly seems that someone in my family meant to honour
and preserve the legacy of Thomas Emmet. Who was that?

One root of my family was from County Monaghan, on the
southern border of today's Northern Ireland. When I visit
Monaghan, which closely resembles rural Wisconsin, I wander,
imagine, and stare at local faces in the city centre, trying to understand how history cast us apart. I try tracing my ancestors in the
county museum, but am overwhelmed by the task. The archival
records from 1849 sound like an account of cattle herds. Careful
handwriting records the "Paupers who were admitted into, or discharged from, the Workhouse; and the Number of the Sick, and
the number Born, or who died therein, during the week ended
Saturday ___, day of ___." Below this explanation are columns
marked "Admitted", "Discharged", "Died", and the count of
"Sick and Lunatic Paupers". In June 1849 the Workhouse over-
flowed with 2,000 people.

In 1995, I became gripped with a need to search out the
grave sites of this "disappeared" people of Monaghan. With the

help of a local historian, Theo McMahon, I drove to the north side
of Monaghan city, where the white stucco flats give way to hillside
farms. Although Theo knows more than anyone in Monaghan
about genealogical records, he never had brought himself to look
for Famine graves. We walked up a hill into a field of stones and
rubble and, detecting no visible graves, sought the help of an
elderly passer-by. We learned from him that we were standing on
the abandoned site of the Monaghan fever hospital. Soon more
neighbours were sharing their folk knowledge and asking questions. The graves were right over there, they said, pointing across
several small hills into a little knoll. "And what's being done about
it?" they wanted to know. Hundreds of bodies were over there in
unmarked graves. The Famine victims were never included in the
annual blessing of the graves (and thus, from a strict Catholic view-
point, could not ascend to Heaven). Cows made paths across the
field of the dead, dropping dung on Irish ancestors.

   My ancestors! Was this all I could know of them? I crossed
the long hillside with Theo, following the cattle trails, scanning
fields ahead. I was feeling lost when Theo suddenly said, "here
they are", and all about us were the overgrown remains of burial
mounds. Some had small trees growing from their centre. The rest
seemed utterly. . . abandoned, from sight, from history, from the
simplest reverence. Here wagons had carried them from the fever
hospital above, to be dumped in shallow graves, sometimes singly
and sometimes together, covered in lime. I had finally traced my
"family" history to its resting place in a muddy, degraded and
neglected field. I sat down. I knelt. I took a picture. Except for
dizziness, I could not feel the emotions I wanted to feel. The history that was buried in the field was too buried inside me to be
released.

   Monaghan lost nearly forty percent of its population, about
60,000 people, in the Famine decade, suffering the most of any
county in traditional Ulster. According to *The Monaghan Story*, an
out-of-print history, the local people called the blight "the
Blackness".[15] Reading the anecdotes gives a sense of the world of
my great-grandparents that the statistics cannot supply. But how
can "blackness" be recalled?

   Monaghan had four workhouses, the inmates separated
from their families and doing hard labour for two meals a day.

According to an 1845 Monaghan county record, these institutions were "repulsive to the habits and feelings of a people". The "intolerable overcrowding" was relieved in only two ways: through emigration, or "when death helped to empty the workhouses through fever and disease".

The story of Mary Ann McDermott of Monaghan, who supported her two children by doing chores rather than submitting to the workhouse, reminded me of the fierce, frugal pride of my mother and grandmother.

> On Friday March 12, 1847, (she) walked from Killeveen to Clones on an errand and she received a cupful of meal which she divided among her children . . . She returned from Clones and got weak and sat down . . . (someone) gave her food but she was unable to eat it. She died on the spot of starvation.[16]

There was callousness bred by hunger, too.

> The fever changed the whole attitude of people to their neighbours. Peter Coogan of Cornamucklagh carried out the beggar, Laurence Daly, first from his own house and then from the house of his cottier, Terry Hughes, and dumped him on the roadside to die. This was a change in Ireland.[17]

The Famine experience is about hidden impacts. I have tried, for example, to identify the print of the Famine experience on my parents. But I wonder now if there was a Famine echo as well. They both hated welfare or dependency of any kind. My mother showed up for work every single day for twenty-seven years. When she died, I found that she had carefully placed a modest $6,000 in life savings in no less than three banks in her small town of Oconomowoc, Wisconsin. Inside the security of the banks, inside their vaults and safety deposit boxes, she still wrapped her money in tinfoil, to protect against a level of catastrophe I could not imagine. A catastrophe like Famine.

My parents believed the world was harsh. "Mourning and weeping in this valley of tears"—the prayers of the Catholic Irish carried this sense of harshness. Not even neighbours or relatives could be trusted, for they would take advantage if they could.

Preserving appearances was crucial. My mother often whispered
"sshhh" while holding a finger to her lips, even when no one was
around. She didn't trust her own sisters. To the end of their lives,
she and my father suspected everyone was out to take advantage
of me. Deep within both my parents was the post-Famine distrust
described by Kerby Miller as a "covert competitiveness which
found poisonous expression in. . .incessant gossip and obsessive
attention to the most minute indices of comparative status or
respectability."[18] "'What will the neighbours think?' became lace-
curtain Irish America's secular catechism."[19]

Achieving comparative status or respectability was the end of
the rainbow for my parents, what they struggled to obtain. And,
"what will the neighbours think?" was a nagging fear. What was the
source of this fear of *un*-respectability? I think it was connected to
a horrific immigrant nightmare they still were fleeing. It was flight
from respectability's opposite, which is *shame*. But they didn't
know what trauma pushed them forward, buried as it was in the
dynamics of "making it".

> What we need is not to dominate the Irish but to
> absorb them. . .We want them to become rich, and
> send their sons to our colleges, to share our prosper-
> ity and sentiments.
> —Boston Wasp, 1887[20]

> . . .the Irish will, before many years are past, be lost in
> the American. . .there will no longer be an 'Irish ques-
> tion' or an 'Irish vote'. . .
> —editorial, *The Atlantic Monthly*, 1896[21]

> In terms of education, income, and occupational
> achievement, Irish Catholics are the most successful
> gentile group in American society. . .
>   Their college attendance rate. . .is now roughly
> comparable to that of Episcopalians. . .only the Jews
> are more likely at the present time to produce pub-
> lishing academic scholars.[22]

My parents grew up when Irish-Americans were poised to
overcome the more blatant and violent prejudice that they had suffered in America. A middle class life was possible. My mother

became a working woman, a secretary, in the Flapper generation of the 1920s. My father was a hotel doorman who attended accounting school at night. They were neither shanty Irish nor the lace-curtain kind. They were ready for the venetian blinds of the suburbs. The American Dream could begin. The experiences of famine, eviction, banishment, and Fenian nationalism were receding. A twenty-six county modern Irish state existed across the sea, and an Irish establishment was planted here in America. Normalcy beckoned after decades of trauma. The old Thomas Emmet could be forgotten. The Hibernians were putting American flags in every parochial school classroom. By 1900, the nationalist hymn "A Nation Once Again" was being eclipsed by the new ballad, "When Irish Eyes Are Smiling" (a sad song of total denial, which begins "There's a tear in your eye/And I'm wondering why/For it never should be there at all. . .")

My parents moved from Milwaukee to Detroit and my father became an accountant at Chrysler Corporation. I was born in 1939. Our household bliss was disrupted by World War II, when my father was drafted into the Marines. But he remained stateside, and we lived with him in San Diego until the war ended. After World War II, we moved to a new suburb of Detroit, Royal Oak, which symbolised this transition.

Then, at the beginning of the Golden Age of the 1950s, my parents divorced.

> ". . . romanticism seems to have been pretty well crushed out by the famines and the Penal Laws . . . Since the Great Famine, it would seem, both Irish and Irish-American women and men have had a much harder time in being affectionate than they used to."[23]

Neither of them ever tried to explain what happened. It was something after the War. My father took over a year to return from the coast. My mother said he was hitch-hiking across the country. When he came home, I recall him spending night after night at the American Legion hall, a kind of pub for veterans. From my bedroom, I would hear him stumbling up the staircase.

One night I heard my father yelling and my mother crying. While I lay silently under my sheets, he was fifteen feet away smashing a hammer against their bedroom door, which was locked.

Though our whole house was shaking with their pain and violence, the incident was never mentioned. Then came a night when my father opened the door, sat down on my bed, and told me he was leaving in the morning. He kissed me on the cheek for the last time.

They were good parents, I thought then, and I think so today. After the divorce, we ate dinner together every weekend, and my parents remained amicable in front of me. I took summer vacations with my father and lived with my mother year round. But the silence never lifted from what had happened between them. Feelings were not expressed, and I don't know if we were in touch with any. I assumed that such silent family failures were normal, internal setbacks on the path to external success.

I thought being drunk was normal too; it was strongly approved of in the circles I grew up in, despite the destructive effects of alcohol on my father that I could see as a child. My father's Legion drinking buddies were like the "bachelor boys" of post-Famine Ireland, young men dispossessed from traditional roles and reassembled around the ideal of being a "hard drinker". Obviously the Famine can't be blamed for every disorder in life. But what else but the disintegration of their cultures makes Native Americans and Irish Americans have the highest percentages of alcoholism? Why else do the Irish have the highest rates of mental illness in the world, and why the massive rates of alcoholism and schizophrenia among Irish-Americans? It is thought that the Irish drink for escape, for denial, that numbness might conquer an ancient depression.[18]

There was other family denial too, some that took me fifty years to uncover. I have a child's image, for example, of an "Uncle Bill", my father's younger brother. In an off-moment of candour while I was growing up, my mother smiled and, with her finger over her lips, hinted that Uncle Bill was not well. I took this to mean he was in an insane asylum, never to be seen or mentioned again. Recently, however, I learned that Bill was a gay fireman who lost his job and lived alone in Milwaukee all his life. Without telling anyone, my father sent Bill a cheque every month. In his mind, support for a "queer" brother had to be kept secret.

* * * * *

". . .the intense level of religious devotion characteristic of the Irish on both sides of the Atlantic is a rather recent phenomenon, dating to the time of the Great Famine."[25]

"The cataclysm of the Great Famine convinced most peasants not only that their old beliefs were ineffectual in staving off disaster, but that God had punished them for their wicked resistance to the Church's teaching."[26]

While their Irishness was bleached away by this time, my parents still were motivated by their inherited Catholicism. Though there was little or no talk of spiritual matters around the house, it was extremely important to my parents that I have a Catholic education.

In the 1920s, when Royal Oak was a virulent anti-Catholic centre of the Ku Klux Klan, the Church sent a crusading young priest to establish our parish. His name was Father Charles Coughlin, an Irishman from Canada who spoke in a fearless brogue. He became the most powerful priest in America in the 1930s, a populist with an audience of several million radio listeners.

What I remember as a small boy was Father Coughlin's ability to paint a picture of Heaven and especially Hell that was more vivid and dramatic than my own picture of life on earth. His was an Augustinian/Puritan theology that viewed sin as our sickness and obedience as the cure. Life was brief, the fires of Hell eternal. Obedience was the key, and when any of us forgot this lesson, the priests were waiting with rulers and rods to lash our hands while we knelt, arms outstretched, on painfully hard floors. The good news was that devout Catholics could reach Heaven; but as for Protestants and Jews, that was another matter.

My parents told me nothing of the earthly political controversies surrounding Father Coughlin. He was more powerful than any other priest or teacher in my life, and completely a mystery.

Coughlin embodied key contradictions of the Irish assimilation. On the one hand, he preached of social justice for the dispossessed, the small businessmen, farmers and workers of Depression America. They were, in the Catholic view, whole human beings with souls, not cogs in the industrial machine. Receiving as many as 400,000 letters per week after his Sunday radio sermons, he was a powerful advocate for the kinds of relief that eventually constituted the New Deal.

On the other hand, he violently opposed secular movements
for socialism and industrial unionism, and he demonised the Jews
at the time of Nazi ascent in Germany. The Communists and the
Jews were enemies of the Christian God, unlike Nazism which
professed a Christian root. Ironically, while castigating the "international Jewish bankers", Father Coughlin speculated in the silver
market himself. His own secretary held 500,000 ounces of silver,
making her the largest owner in Michigan. Finally in 1939, after
Coughlin's personal emissary met with Count Von Ribbentrop in
Berlin, our pastor was instructed to end his political activities by
the Vatican, under US government pressure.

I knew none of this until researching a book twenty years
later. But the Irish-Americans knew. The "radio priest" had tens of
millions of listeners every Sunday afternoon. The "Studs Lonigan"
Irish not only knew, they approved of this "Father Moylan", as
James T. Farrell fictionalised Father Coughlin.

> "Well, I know what we ought to do. Put all the for-
> eigners we got taking jobs away from Americans, *pack
> them in boats*, and say to them, 'Now see here,
> America belongs to Americans.'"
>
> "It's only right, America is America, and it
> should be for Americans," Studs said.
>
> "You're damn right it should be. And you know
> who's going to wake Americans up? It's men like
> Father Moylan who speaks on the radio every Sunday.
> He tells 'em and he talks straight."
>
> "And he's a Catholic, too," Studs said proudly.[27]

In supporting Father Coughlin, many Irish were following
the immigrant path from a culture of inferiority to its opposite
extreme: super-patriotism.

> "[Catholic] societies seemed merely Irish Catholic
> replicas of native Protestant institutions, proclaiming
> American patriotism. . .the Ancient Order of Hiber-
> nians (AOH) by providing American flags for every
> parochial schoolroom in the country. . .the Knights of
> Columbanus by being conspicuously patriotic in
> wartime."[28]

In 1960 the Irish immigrant success story culminated in the

election of a Roman Catholic, John Fitzgerald Kennedy, to the Presidency. It was the first time in my life that I actually heard the subject of Irish Catholics being discussed in public, as if one's heritage was an issue. I did have a dim memory of hearing my mother express disappointment about the defeat of Al Smith in 1928. Kennedy was a redemption for that earlier wrong. But since by 1960 I was so assimilated, I simply dismissed the attacks on Kennedy's religion as obsolete, irrelevant echoes from a past that no longer mattered. I was so Americanised that I did not feel any ethnic heartbeat. My primary connection with John F. Kennedy was generational, not an Irish one.

When I went away to university, to be swept up in the civil rights and anti-war movements of my time, my parents' world was turned upside down. Instead of assimilating, I was seceding. Instead of conforming, I was defying. I was causing shame and destroying the respectability they did everything to build.

My father blamed the world for what had gone wrong. "I don't know who influenced him when he went away, but it's not the way he was raised," he told a reporter. A tight-lipped man to begin with, he simply stopped talking to me for fifteen years, even after he re-married and raised a new daughter. As for my mother, she never broke our connection but neither did she ever stop reminding me how I had embarrassed and nearly ruined her life. Secretly, I thought she liked my friends and even became drawn to the controversies I was always in. She just didn't want the neighbours to know, and prayed I would grow out of it.

At the time, I was unaware of any Irish dimension to my radical discontent. As I would discover later, the Irish tradition is filled with poets and political leaders supportive of progressive, often radical, causes. They were heavily involved in American labour radicalism, producing such personalities as Mother Jones and Helen Gurley Flynn. They were stalwart supporters of the New Deal, which wouldn't have happened without the support of the Irish political machines. But during the new movements of the Sixties, I mainly thought of Irish-Americans as propping up the status quo, their politics mired in traditional ethnic machines, out of step with the modern currents of change I was experiencing. I didn't know it, but such assimilationist politics had been the great fear of Irish nationalists like Jeremiah Donovan Rossa, who condemned those "whose shamrocks blossomed like diamonds", and James Connolly, who called Irish-American politicians "descendants of the serpents St. Patrick banished from Ireland".[29]

The most famous of the Irish machines was that of Major Richard Daley of Chicago, described by Father Greeley as "an Irish chieftain governing through a complex system of clan loyalty".[30] He was born and lived all his life in the Chicago neighbourhood of Bridgeport, originally the site of a canal built by Irish labour. This was the ethnic neighbourhood culture of Studs Lonigan, and the source of Finley Peter Dunne's stories of "Mr. Dooley", the bachelor philosopher from County Roscommon. Daley's Chicago was home to America's most durable political machine, until a fateful clash of destinies in 1968.

From New York to San Francisco, the political machine was a gift of the Famine Irish to American culture. In Famine Ireland, the Irish had no vote, no government of their own to represent and defend their interests. On a political level, they were beggars. Seán O'Faoláin's biography of their leader, Daniel O'Connell, was entitled *King of the Beggars*. In the new land, they would beg no more.

"Living in a new country, in the aftermath of the Famine, the Irish employed political power as a buckler of community solidarity. . .a means with which to shield themselves. . .and a sword with which to fight back."[31] Perhaps there was a moment after the Famine when Irish-American politics could have mixed militant Irish nationalism with social radicalism in the new homeland. I can imagine myself working for the banished Fenian Rossa, for example, in his 1870 campaign for the New York state senate. Rossa apparently defeated Boss Tweed himself, only to have his election stolen by fraud. After that, the Democratic Party gradually became the vehicle of assimilation, not a broader vision of change.

According to Kerby Miller, "Irish-Americans henceforth voted with their stomachs. . .repeatedly rejecting nationalist pleas to desert and punish the Democratic Party for its indifferent or hostility to Irish freedom."[32] Who could blame them? Faced with destitution and prejudice, the Irish needed whatever protection the Democratic Party ultimately offered. Ethnic politics was a protective reaction against a world in which true justice was impossible, but additional *in*justice was preventable. If there was no hope for the redistribution of wealth, the saying went, at least the Irish could redistribute the graft.

There were heavy costs for this Irish assimilation via the patronage system. For one, while the Irish didn't bring racism to America, they learned it here. From the first, Irish labour was pitted against blacks in brutal competition. Irish maids took the jobs of black women in the North. While Irish nationalists like O'Connell preached passionately against slavery, others defended the Confederacy which kept blacks from competing for jobs as freemen. While 100,000 Irishmen fought on the Northern side, the Irish also sparked mass riots against the draft, including attacks on black New Yorkers. The same Democratic Party which opened its doors to Irish immigrants was pro-slavery at the time. While many Irish today prefer to believe that the Irish-black conflict was only economic in nature, the Famine suggests a sadder dynamic as well: the Irish-Americans transferred to black people the very racial stereotypes long used against the Irish. Having been stigmatised as chimpanzees, wild animals and bog-creatures, the Irish chose whiteness when the chance came along. They wounded the heart of Frederick Douglass.[33]

A second cost of striving to assimilate after the Famine, I believe, was the exaggerated patriotism and super-loyalty summarised in the philosophy of so many former immigrants: "America, right or wrong". It was not enough for the Irish to change their accents or names. For most, it seemed necessary to conform culturally, for one's Americanism to exist beyond question. The quest for respectability ended with the defence of conservative law-and-order. The Cold War against communism was also a religious war against atheism, a chance to assert a new Irish-Americanism in the form of McCarthyism.

The tragic outcome of such politics was Vietnam, where American military involvement from 1954 to 1964 was shaped by a newly-powerful Catholic lobby. Several hundred thousand Catholics streamed out of the Communist North in 1954 at the urging of Catholic missionaries (and the American CIA), only to become the doomed and loyal base of the Catholic dictatorship of Ngo Dinh Diem in Saigon. The rest is history. The irony was that the war left millions of dead, wounded and uprooted refugees on a level as devastating as the Irish Famine a century before. To the extent that

Irish-Americans supported US policies, it was a replay of what the Irish had been through themselves. But the mirror was broken.

Looking back I see the Irish Catholic conservatism that surrounded my growing up as an unconscious but ongoing response to the Famine. The immigrants brought with them a religious Jansenism, a stern doctrine of shame that very nearly blamed the Irish for their own starvation. In the wake of Famine horror, the Church promoted an "otherworldly fatalism", in Oscar Handlin's phrase. The Irish-Americans formed intensely-tribal political associations based in their parishes. They translated their shame into silence, and fiercely forgot the Famine as the possibilities of a better life materialised before them.

But by its very nature, this repressive drive for a secure assimilation ultimately brought about its own demise in the 1960s. For one thing, the Irish achieved a level of success in America that permitted a relaxation of the old ways. For another, the rigid conformity demanded by the post-Famine church and political machines conflicted with an underlying Irish soul. At a mystical moment in the early 1960s, the authoritarian ice began to thaw. Pope John XXIII's "*Pacem in Terris*" found its way into the Port Huron Statement, the founding manifesto of Students for a Democratic Society. The hard-line doctrines of Cardinal Spellman were challenged by priests like the Berrigans and politicians like the Kennedys. The burning of Vietnamese villages was met with the burning of American draft cards, the first by David Miller, a Catholic Worker. Finally, the Irish law-and-order machine of Mayor Daley was to confront new rebels like myself on the streets of Chicago.

It was almost an Irish civil war within the larger divisions of the decade. By the end of the 1960s, Father Coughlin even came out of retirement to attack priests like the Berrigans as "swingers" and "loud-mouthed clerical advocates of arson, riot and draft card burning". He added "that he tremendously admires the youth of today, even the Chicago Seven, one of whom, Tom Hayden, had attended the Shrine of the Little Flower. On the other hand . . . Father Coughlin said that the man he admires the most on the contemporary scene is Judge Julius Hoffman, the presiding judge in the Chicago Seven trial."[34]

* * * * *

The sixties made me Irish. Partly it was an identification with Robert
Kennedy. His older brother, President Kennedy, seemed to be an
icon of assimilation, while Robert Kennedy became a raw Celtic
spirit. It is interesting, however, that President Kennedy decided to
make his 1963 visit to Ireland against the advice of his Boston Irish
advisers who saw "no political or diplomatic advantages to be gained
by such a *sentimental excursion*".[35] The President was moved by visiting the cottage of his great-grandfather, Patrick Kennedy, an 1848
Famine emigrant from Dunganstown. Upon his leaving, the
President quoted a poem of an exile's pain:

> 'Tis the Shannon's brightly glancing stream,
> Brightly gleaming, silent in the morning beam
> Oh! the sight entrancing.
> Thus return from travels long, years of exile,
> Years of pain
> To see old Shannon's face again,
> O'er the waters glancing.

After his brother's assassination, Robert Kennedy became
identified with an Irish persona I had not known before. It was
not a crusty, conservative and old-fashioned Catholicism. This
Bobby Kennedy had long since evolved from his days as legal
counsel to Joseph McCarthy. He could hold the traditional Irish
vote, but there was also a wild Irishman in Bobby Kennedy, who
identified with nonconformists, resisters, farmworkers, ghetto
dwellers, the Sioux on their desperate reservations. For the first
time I felt there was such a thing as an Irish soul.

Robert Kennedy spoke of the Famine experience in the first
speech he gave after his brother's murder to the Friendly Sons of
St. Patrick, in Scranton, Pennsylvania. "There was," he recalled,

> that black day in February 1847 when it was
> announced in the House of Commons that fifteen
> thousand people a day were dying of starvation in
> Ireland. . .So the Irish left Ireland. Many of them
> came here to the United States. Many left behind
> hearts and fields and a nation yearning to be free. It is
> no wonder that James Joyce described the Atlantic as
> a bowl of bitter tears.

Reminding his audience of times when no Irish could vote, he said that

> there are Americans, who—as the Irish did—still face discrimination in employment. . .There are walls of silent conspiracy that block the progress of others because of race or creed without regard to ability. *It is toward concern for these issues—and vigorous participation on the side of freedom that our Irish heritage must impel us. If we are true to this heritage, we cannot stand aside.*[36]

Bobby Kennedy was the last national political leader who bridged the gap between white ethnics like Irish-Americans and the disaffected minorities of the ghettos and fields.

On the night that his body was flown back to New York, I wandered into St. Patrick's Cathedral for the first time. The largest cathedral in the US, St. Patrick's was built by the Famine generation, completed in 1879. Its famous Archbishop John Hughes was the most powerful leader of the Irish in New York City, providing famine relief, battling the Know-Nothings, and holding "firm in his belief that the Irish-Americans should be concerned first and foremost with the affairs of their adopted country."[37] Having started as the spiritual fortress of the immigrant Irish, St. Patrick's now was the symbol of their success and power.

But now another Kennedy lay in wait for eulogy. It was late, the end of a dark night. I sat in a back pew, staring at the small wooden coffin in the centre of this vast historical space, and began to cry. America was not what my parents promised it would be. Even the symbols of Irish success were dead.

* * * * *

The identity which I received from my parents continued to unravel during 1968, finally ending on the streets of Chicago. Assimilation led to emptiness. All around me others were realising new identities for themselves, as liberated women, black or Chicano nationalists, even gay people. They were leaving the melting pot to regain their roots. But who was I?

History tells of a "hidden Ireland", of a native character behind the Anglicised facade. I was beginning to understand that there was a hidden Irish-America too. There was not only Cardinal

Spellman but Bobby Kennedy; not only Charles Coughlin, but the Berrigan brothers; not only George Meany, but Elizabeth Gurley Flynn. The figures in American life who most repelled and most attracted me, who warred for my soul, seemed all to be Irish.

Then a "hidden Ireland" across the sea came alive. Precisely at the peak of the protests in Chicago, on 24 August 1968, several thousand civil rights marchers took to the streets in Northern Ireland, singing "We Shall Overcome" for the first time. On 5 October, in a scene that resembled Chicago, 400 marchers were blocked from protesting in Derry, beaten into the ground with batons, hosed with water cannons, and began street battles in the Bogside. While the whole world may have been watching in Chicago, now I was watching, for the first time in my life, *these Irish who seemed and looked so much like me.*

Now I knew I was Irish too. But what did it mean, how to describe it? Being "Irish-American" sounded a bit too settled and middle class. I wasn't just "Irish". Maybe I was an exiled Irishman, an *Éireannach Éigin*. A recovering Irishman? After almost thirty years, I still am not sure. But the recognition that arose in 1968 continued to grow and surprise me.

In 1969, a friend of mine from the Bobby Kennedy campaign arrived in Los Angeles from Belfast, where he spent the year after the murder of his hero. He regaled me with stories of republican activists, tapes of Bernadette Devlin speeches, books of nationalist history, recordings of rebel songs, which I consumed with Irish whisky. The romantic phase of my Irish identification was underway.

* * * * *

FEDERAL BUREAU OF INVESTIGATION

Dec. 15, 1971

Urgent

To: Director From: Los Angeles

THOMAS EMMET HAYDEN
SOURCE ADVISED DECEMBER FIFTEEN INSTANT. THOMAS EMMET HAYDEN DEPARTED LOS ANGELES EVENING OF DECEMBER FOURTEEN LAST, FOR NEW YORK CITY, ULTIMATE DESTINATION, IRELAND.

SOURCE STATED HAYDEN PLANS ON GOING TO NORTHERN IRELAND THROUGH SOUTHERN IRELAND

AND ANTICIPATES TAKING PART IN PRESENT
REVOLUTION.
ROUTE OF TRAVEL FROM LOS ANGELES TO NEW
YORK UNKNOWN BY SOURCE. SOURCE STATED HAYDEN
MAY BE UTILIZING THE NAME EMMET GARITY, MAIDEN
NAME OF MOTHER.

In 1971, I decided to experience Ireland for the first time. Instead of the emigrant's return, however, I was banished.

The Irish authorities acted on US and British intelligence cables warning that I was a dangerous radical on a subversive mission to Belfast. All I wanted to do was experience the island of my ancestors. After twenty-four hours of fruitless argument in Shannon airport, I was placed on a plane, my romantic desire for roots abruptly terminated.

The emigration official who stamped my expulsion papers form Shannon was named Garity, my mother's name. For all I knew, he was a relative of mine, part of the family tree I was trying to explore. When my son was born eighteen months later, Jane Fonda and I decided to name him Troy O'Donovan Garity, for his grandmother and for Ireland. For expulsion and return.

Five years later, the Irish authorities finally admitted me, and I took my two-year-old son to Ireland. Where my parents had erased Ireland from my past, I wanted it to be my son's earliest possible memory. That it was. In Belfast, he experienced camouflaged British soldiers sticking automatic weapons into his father's face at checkpoints. In Dublin, while happening to walk by the General Post Office, Troy started pointing at people and asking, "are those my ancestors?"

Each of us carries a legacy of the past that stretches back far before our parents' time. While most therapists or biographers focus only on our parents' effects on us, we also carry the legacies, spirits, traumas, and qualities of our invisible and even unknown ancestors. While this "hidden Ireland" within is largely lost, we can create an image of the life of our ancestors before they were uprooted. At the very least, we can honour the memory of those Famine relatives who died in ditches or were cast from coffin ships. We can complete the journey they began. And in gaining access to the texture, the *feeling*, of this past, it may be

possible to discover the sources of scars in ourselves that we need
to open and heal.

If there could be an archaeology of the past self, you might
find below the comfortable hillside home of an Irish-American
today a single-family suburban one, and below that an inner-city
apartment, and below that a cellar in New York, and before that a
cargo hold, and finally, the burned decaying ruins of a stone cottage in an Irish field of shallow graves. Those ruins, those graves,
are deep in ourselves. We cannot go home again, but we will never
be at home in our present lives until our memories can return to
the places from which we have been severed. Through this process
I have begun to end the famine of my feelings.

The Irish Canadian novelist, Jane Urquhart, ends her novel
Away with the universal consciousness that is the gift of knowing
one's particular self:

> Then she saw the world's great leavetakings, invasions
> and migrations, landscapes torn from beneath the feet
> of tribes, the Danae pushed out by the Celts, the
> Celts eventually smothered by the English, warriors
> in the night depopulating villages, boatloads of
> groaning African slaves. Lost forests. The children of
> the mountain on the plain, the children of the plain
> adrift on the sea. And all the mourning for aban-
> doned geographies.[38]

In 1996, Irish President Mary Robinson, who has led the
Irish national effort to commemorate the Famine, was kind
enough to welcome me home to the Ireland my family had forgotten. She took special care to show me the permanent light in
her window for all the Irish who are away.

I am coming to realise that the Famine experience has not
ended, and will not end until forgotten ghosts of our past are
finally at rest in our reverence, until the world's children are safe
from famine today, until we live in a world where all of us are truly
home, and none of us feel away.

NOTES

1 Eavan Boland, "The Dolls' Museum", from *In a Time of Violence*, (Manchester: Carcanet Press Limited, 1994)

2 Ronald Takaki, *A Different Mirror—A History of Multi-Cultural America*, (New York: Little Brown, 1993), p.139.

3 William Kennedy, *Very Old Bones*, (London: Penguin Books, 1993)

4 James T. Farrell, *Studs Lonigan*, [1966] (University of Illinois, 1993), p.iv.

5 Kerby Miller and Paul Wagner, *Out of Ireland, The Story of Irish Emigrants to America*, (Washington DC: Elliott and Clark, 1994), p.54.

6 Ibid., p.41.

7 Personal correspondence.

8 Cited in Helen Litton, *The Irish Famine, An Illustrated History*, (Dublin: Wolfhound Press, 1994), p.52.

9 Terry Eagleton, *Heathcliff and the Great Hunger, Studies in Irish Culture*, (London: Verso, 1994) p.13.

10 Ibid., p.8.

11 Cited in Sean Cronin, *Washington's Irish Policy, Independence, Partition, Neutrality*, (Dublin: Anvil Press, 1987), p.243.

12 Milan Kundera, *The Unbearable Lightness of Being*, (New York: Harper & Row, 1984)

13 Seamus Deane "Return", from *Selected Poems*, (Gallery Books, 1988)

14 John Waters article "We Cannot Escape Our History No Matter How Hard We Try", in the *Irish Times*, 12 October, 1995.

15 Peadar Livingstone, *The Monaghan Story, A Documented History of the County Monaghan from the Earliest Times to 1976*, (Enniskillen: Clogher Historical Society, 1980), pp.211-222.

16 Ibid., p.218.

17 Ibid., p 217.

18 Kerby Miller, *Emigrants and Exiles, Ireland and the Irish Exodus to North America*, (New York and Oxford, 1985), p.414.

19 Ibid., p.498.

20 Miller, *Emigrants and Exiles*, op cit., p.497.

21 Miller, ibid., p.497.

22 Andrew Greeley, *The Irish Americans, The Rise to Money and Power*, (New York: Harper & Row, 1981), p 2.

23 Greeley, *The Irish Americans*, op cit., p.122.

24 On Irish and alcoholism, see Niall O'Dowd, "The Myth and the Reality", *Irish America* magazine, October 1988. O'Dowd reports a National Institute of Mental Health study showing 36 percent of Irish men drink "nearly every day", twice the figure for WASPs and Jews. Also, according to the World Health Organisation, the Irish in Ireland have the highest rate of mental illness in the world, and Irish

Americans have the highest hospital admission rate from alcoholism and schizophrenia of all ethnic groups in the US. Monica McGoldrick has written in *Irish Families* that "more than other ethnic groups, the Irish struggle with their sense of sin and guilt. Irish schizophrenics, for example, are commonly obsessed with guilt for sins that they might not even have committed."

25 Greeley, *The Irish Americans*, op cit., p.144.

26 Miller and Wagner, *Out of Ireland*, op cit., p.101.

27 James T. Farrell, *Judgement Day*, op cit., p.735.

28 Miller, *Emigrants and Exiles*, op cit., p.534.

29 Miller, *Emigrants and Exiles*, op cit., pp.536, 544.

30 Greeley, *The Irish Americans*, op cit., p.155.

31 Peter Quinn, Introduction to William L. Riordan, *Plunkitt of Tammany Hall*, (New York: Penguin, 1995), p.xvi.

32 Miller, *Emigrants and Exiles*, op cit., p.537.

33 On Frederick Douglass' speaking tour in Cork, Belfast and elsewhere in Ireland, see William S. McFeely, *Frederick Douglass*, (New York: Touchstone, 1991), p.126, 318. Douglass, travelling during the Famine, "saw what his anti-slavery hosts seemed blind to. . .The anti-slavery people stepped around these Irish poor as they made their way into Douglass' lectures about mistreated Africans in America." But Douglass recorded in his diary that "I see much here to remind me of my former condition. . ." Later, in America, he spoke against British tyranny in Ireland, comparing it to slavery, in a powerful image: "We want no black Ireland in America!" Nevertheless, most Irish immigrants entered the pro-slavery Democratic Party, fearing that freed former slaves would take back the menial jobs which they had taken from blacks in the North. Douglass noted in 1853 that "every hour sees us elbowed out of some employment to make room for some newly-arrived emigrant from the Emerald Isle, whose hunger and colour entitle him to special favour. These white men are becoming house-servants, cooks, stewards, waiters and flunkies. . .If they cannot rise to the dignity of white men, they show that they can fall to the degradation of black men. . ." See Noel Ignatiev, *How the Irish Became White*, (London: Routledge, 1995), p.111. Meanwhile, although Daniel O'Connell continued to denounce American slavery in the 1840s, many Irish nationalists, including the revered John Mitchel, supported the slave-holding Confederacy, to Douglass' great sadness.

34 Sheldon Marcus, *Father Coughlin, The Tumultuous Life of the Priest of the Little Flower*, (New York: Little Brown, 1973), p.223.

35 Kenneth O'Donnell, *"Johnny, We Hardly Knew Ye"*, Memories of John Fitzgerald Kennedy, (with David Powers and Joe McCarthy), (New York: Little Brown, 1970), p.358.

36 Edwin Guthman and Richard Allen, *Robert F. Kennedy, Collected Speeches*, (New York: Viking, 1993), pp.107-08.

37 John A. Barnes, *Irish American Landmarks, A Traveller's Guide*, (Detroit: Visible Ink Press, 1995), p.107.

38 Jane Urquhart, *Away*, (New York: Viking, 1994) p.128.

BIOGRAPHICAL NOTES

Eavan Boland, a Dublin poet and author, whose collections have received several Poetry Book Choice Awards. Her works include *In a Time of Violence*, *The Journey*, *Outside History*, and *Object Lessons*.

Jimmy Breslin, Irish-American novelist and journalist, whose works include *Table Money* and *World Without End, Amen*.

Gabriel Byrne, actor-writer whose sixteen films include *The Usual Suspects*, *Into the West*, *Miller's Crossing* and *In the Name of the Father*, which he executive-produced and which received seven Oscar nominations.

James Carroll, author of several books including *An American Requiem: God, My Father*, and the *War that Came Between Us*, for which he won the 1996 National Book Award for non-fiction.

Tim Pat Coogan, journalist and writer, was editor of the Irish Press for twenty years. Among his many books are *The IRA: A History*, *The Troubles*, and *Michael Collins: The Man Who Made Ireland*.

Seamus Deane, professsor of English at University of Notre Dame, Indiana, writer whose debut novel, *Reading in the Dark*, was short-listed for the Booker Prize.

Luke Dodd, founder and director of the Famine Museum in Strokestown, County Roscommon.

James Donnelly, professor of history at University of Wisconsin; past president, American Conference on Irish Studies; author of Famine chapters in A *New History of Ireland*.

Paul Durcan, Irish poet, whose works include *Going Home to Russia, A Snail in my Prime, Daddy, Daddy*, and *Christmas Day*.

Luke Gibbons, professor in Communications at Dublin City University, and member of Field Day, among the editors of the *Field Day Anthology of Irish Writing*.

Terry Golway, Irish-American journalist and historian at the *New York Observer*.

Tom Hayden, California state senator, known and respected for his radical political activities during the sixties, author of *The Lost Gospel of the Earth*.

Seamus Heaney, Nobel-prize winning poet from Derry, Northern Ireland, whose many works include *North*, *Death of a Naturalist*, *Seeing Things*, and *The Spirit Level*.

Brendan Kennelly, professor in English at Trinity College, Dublin, has received international acclaim for many books of poetry including *Cromwell* and *The Books of Judas*.

Seán Kenny, educated in Dublin and emigrated to Los Angeles. Now based in New York, he is author of the contemporary Famine novel, *The Hungry Earth*.

Brian Lacey, director of the Heritage Museum in Derry.

Helen Litton, Dublin, Irish researcher and editor, author of *The Irish Famine, An Illustrated History*.

David Lloyd, author of *Nationalism and Minor Literature: James Clarence Mangan and the Emergency of Irish Cultural Nationalism*.

Nell McCafferty, Northern Irish journalist and well-known spokesperson on various controversial or topical issues, author of *Woman to Blame* and *The Best of Nell: Selected Writings*.

Nuala Ní Dhomhnaill, poet whose collections of poetry include *An Dealg Droighean* (1981), and *Pharaoh's Daughter* (1990), with translations by Seamus Heaney and others.

Peter Quinn, New York author of the historical novel of the New York Irish, *Banished Children of Eve*, former speech writer for New York Governor Mario Cuomo, and now chief speech writer at Time Warner.

Carolyn Ramsay, is a Los Angeles based journalist, who writes for *People* magazine.

John Waters, a Dublin columnist for the *Irish Times*, former editor of *In Dublin* and *Magill* magazines, and author of the highly-praised *Jiving at the Crossroads* and *Race of Angels: Ireland and the Genesis of U2*.

Ray Yeates, Irish theatre director and acting teacher who currently teaches and directs at the American Academy of Dramatic Arts in New York.

SOURCES AND BIBLIOGRAPHY

D. H. Akenson, *The Irish Education Experience: The National System of Education in the 19th century*, (London, 1970)

D. H. Akenson, *A Mirror to Kathleen's Face: Education in Independent Ireland*, (Montreal and London, 1975)

David Arnold, *Famine: Social Crisis and Historical Change*, (Oxford and New York, 1988)

Matthew Arnold, *On the Study of Celtic Literature*, (London: Smith, Elder & Co., 1867)

A. T. Atkinson, *A Review of the Main Principles of History Teaching Applied in British and Irish Schools*, (M.Ed. Thesis, TCD, 1973)

Peter Balakian, *Black Dog of Fate* (New York: Broadway Books, 1998)

John A. Barnes, *Irish American Landmarks, A Traveller's Guide*, (Detroit: Visible Ink Press, 1995)

Jasper Becker, *Hungry Ghosts: China's Secret Famine*, (London: John Murray, 1996)

R. D. Collison Black, *Economic Thought and the Irish Question, 1817–1870*, (Cambridge, 1960)

Robert Bledsoe et al, (eds.), *Rethinking Germanistik: Canon and Culture*, (New York: Peter Lang, 1991)

John W. Blessingame, (ed.), *The Frederick Douglass Papers*, Vol. 1, 1841–46 (New Haven: Yale University Press, 1979)

Eavan Boland, *In a Time of Violence*, (Manchester: Carcanet Press Ltd., 1994)

Eavan Boland, *Outside History*, (Manchester: Carcanet Press Ltd., 1990)

Angela Bourke, "Performing not Writing", *Graph*, 11, Winter 1991–2

P. M. Austin Bourke, "The Irish grain trade, 1839–48", *Irish Historical Studies*, xx, No. 78, Sept. 1976

P. M. Austin Bourke, *"The Visitation of God"? The Potato and the Great Irish Famine*, (Dublin, 1993)

Thomas A. Boylan and Timothy P. Foley, *Political Economy and Colonial Ireland: The Propagation and Ideological Function of Economic Discourse in the Nineteenth Century*, (London: Routledge, 1992)

Charles Loring Brace, *Races of the Old World*, (1863)

Brendan Bradshaw, "Nationalism and Historical Scholarship in Modern Ireland", *Irish Historical Studies*, xxvi, No. 104, Nov. 1989

Ciaran Brady (ed.), *Interpreting Irish History: The Debate on Historical*

Revisionism, 1938–1994 (Dublin, 1994)

Bullan, Vol. 1, No. 1, Spring 1994

Patrick Callan, "Aspects of the transmission of history in Ireland during the latter half of the 19th century" in *Irish Educational Studies*, Vol. 6, No. 2, 1986–7

Patrick Callan, "Irish History in Irish National Schools 1900–08" in *Proceedings of the Educational Conference 1980*

William Carleton, *The Black Prophet: A Tale of Irish Famine*, (London: Simms and McIntyre, 1847)

James Carney, *The Irish Bardic Poet*, (Dublin: The Dolmen Press, 1967)

James Carty, *A Class-Book of Irish History*

Christian Brothers, *History of the Institute*, (4 vols.) (Private circulation only)

James Clifford and George E. Marcus, *Writing Culture: The Poetics and Politics of Ethnography*, (Berkeley and Los Angeles: University of California Press, 1986)

B. M. Coldrey, *Faith and Fatherland: the Irish Christian Brothers and the Development of Irish Nationalism 1838–1921*, (Dublin: Gill & Macmillan, 1988)

Matthew Connelly and Paul Kennedy, "Must It Be the Rest Against the West", *The Atlantic Monthly*, December, 1994

Tim Pat Coogan, *The IRA*, (London: Harper Collins, USA: Roberts Rinehart, 1996)

Tim Pat Coogan, *The Troubles*, (London: Hutchinson, USA: Roberts Rinehart, 1995)

John Coolahan, *Irish Education, History and Structure*, (Dublin: Institute of Public Administration, 1981)

T. Crofton Croker, *Researches in the South of Ireland, Illustrative of The Scenery, Architectural Remains, and the Manners and Superstitions of the Peasantry*, (London: John Murray, 1824)

The Croker Papers. The Correspondence and Diaries of John Croker, (Vol III, 1884)

Sean Cronin, *Washington's Irish Policy, Independence, Partition, Neutrality*, (Dublin: Anvil Press, 1987)

Tony Crooks, (ed.), *The Changing Curriculum: Perspectives on the Junior Certificate*, (Dublin: The O'Brien Press, 1989)

Edmund Curtis, *A History of Ireland*, (London, 1936) "Irish History and its Popular Versions" in *The Irish Rosary*, Vol. 29, No. 5, 1925

L. P. Curtis, Jr., *Anglo-Saxons and Celts: A Study of Anglo-Irish Prejudice in Victorian England*, (Connecticut: University of Bridgeport, Conference on British Studies, 1968)

L. P. Curtis, Jr., *Apes and Angels: The Irishman in Victorian Caricature*, (Washington, D.C., 1971)

L. P. Curtis, Jr., "The Greening of Irish History", *Eire-Ireland*, xxix, No.

2, Summer 1994

M. F. Cusack, *A History of the Irish Nation*, (London, 1876)

M. Daly, and D. Dickson, (eds), *The Origins of Popular Literacy in Ireland: Language, Change and Educational Development 1700–1920*, (TCD/UCD 1990)

Michael Davitt, *The Fall of Feudalism in Ireland, or the Story of the Land League Revolution*, (London and New York, 1904)

Seamus Deane, *A Short History of Irish Literature*, (Notre Dame: UNDP, 1994)

Seamus Deane, *Selected Poems*, (Gallery Books, 1988)

Sean de Peitid, "Teaching Irish History" in *The Secondary Teacher*, (Autumn 1972)

Aubrey de Vere, *English Misrule and Irish Misdeeds*, (London: Murray, 1848)

Benjamin Disraeli, *Life of Lord George Bentinck*, (1852)

James S. Donnelly, Jr (ed.), "The Journals of Sir John Benn-Walsh Relating to the Management of His Irish Estates, 1823–64", *Journal of the Cork Historical and Archaeological Society*, lxxx, No. 230, July-Dec. 1974

Frederick Douglass, *My Bondage and My Freedom*, [1855], with an introduction by Philip Foner (New York: Dover Publications, 1969)

Paul Durcan, *Poems: Going Home to Russia*, (Belfast: The Blackstaff Press, 1987)

Thomas J. Durcan, *History of Irish Education from 1800*, (Dragon Books, 1972)

Terry Eagleton, *Heathcliff and the Great Hunger, Studies in Irish Culture*, (London: Verso, 1994)

Ruth Dudley Edwards and T. Desmond Williams (eds.), *The Great Famine: Studies in Irish History, 1845–52*, (Dublin: Browne and Nolan, 1956, New York, 1957)

Norbert Elias, *Power and Civility: The Civilizing Process, Vol. 2*, (New York: Pantheon, 1982)

James T. Farrell, *Studs Lonigan*, [1966] (University of Illinois, 1993)

Sean Farren, "Curriculum Developments in Ireland North and South in the period 1945–1960" in *Irish Educational Studies*, Vol. 1, 1981

Samuel Ferguson, *Nationalism and Minor Literature*, (Berkeley and Los Angeles: University of California Press, 1987)

Philip Foner, (ed.), *The Life and Writings of Frederick Douglass*, Vol. 1 (New York: International Publishers, 1950)

Roy F. Foster, *Modern Ireland 1600–1972*, [1988] (London: Penguin Books, 1989)

Thomas Gallagher, *Paddy's Lament: Ireland 1846–1847. Prelude to Hatred*, (New York: Harcourt Brace Jovanovich, 1982)

Francis Galton, *Inquiries into Human Faculty and Its Development*,

(1883)

Luke Gibbons, *Transformations in Irish Culture*, (Cork: Cork University Press, 1996)

Maud Gonne MacBride, *A Servant of the Queen*, (London, 1938)

Peter Gray, "Punch and the Great Famine", *History Ireland*, Vol. I, No. 2, Summer 1993

Peter Gray, Paper delivered at the NYU International Conference on Hunger, May 1995.

Peter Gray, "British Politics and the Irish Land Question, 1843–1850" (Ph.D. Dissertation, Cambridge University, 1992)

Andrew Greeley, *The Irish Americans, The Rise to Money and Power*, (New York: Harper and Row, 1981)

Edwin Guthman and Richard Allen, *Robert F. Kennedy, Collected Speeches*, (New York: Viking, 1993)

Mr. and Mrs. S. C. Hall, *Ireland: Its Scenery, Character, and History*, Vols. I and II [1841] (Boston: Nicholls and Co., 1911)

Seamus Heaney, *Death of a Naturalist*, (Faber & Faber, 1966, 1991)

Jacqueline Hill and Cormac O Gráda (eds.) *The Visitation of God? The Potato and the Great Irish Famine*, (Dublin: The Lilliput Press, 1993)

History Ireland, Vol. 3, No. 2, Summer 1995

History Ireland, Vol. 3 No. 4, Winter 1995

T. F. Holohan, *Analysis of Factors influencing Current Status of History in the Senior Cycle*, (M.Ed Thesis, TCD 1981)

T. F. Holohan, "History in the Post-Primary Curriculum" in *Studies in Education*, Vol. 1, No. 2, 1983

Noel Ignatiev, *How the Irish Became White*, (London, New York: Routledge, 1995)

Illustrated London News, 22 December 1849

In Dublin, 13 December 1984

The Irish Quarterly Review, No. iv., December, 1851

P. W. Joyce, *An Illustrated History of Ireland*, (Dublin: The Educational Company, 1923)

William Kennedy, *Very Old Bones*, (London: Penguin, 1993)

Brendan Kennelly, *My Dark Fathers*, (Dublin: New Square Publications, 1964)

Christine Kinealy, *This Great Calamity: The Irish Famine 1845–52*, (Dublin: Gill & Macmillan, 1994, USA: Roberts Rinehart, 1995)

Dale T. Knobel, *Paddy and the Republic: Ethnicity and Nationality in Antebellum America*, (Middletown, CT: Wesleyan University Press, 1986)

Milan Kundera, *The Unbearable Lightness of Being*, (New York: Harper & Row, 1984)

J. J. Lee, *Ireland 1912–1985, Politics and Society*, (Cambridge University

Press, 1989)

J. J. Lee, *The Modernisation of Irish Society 1848–1918*, (Dublin: Gill & Macmillan, 1973)

Charles James Lever, "St. Patrick's Eve", (London: Chapman & Hall, 1845)

Helen Litton, *The Irish Famine, An Illustrated History*, (Dublin: Wolfhound Press, 1994)

Peadar Livingstone, *The Monaghan Story, A Documented History of the County Monaghan from the Earliest Times to 1976*, (Enniskillen: Clogher Historical Society, 1980)

F. S. L. Lyons in *Irish Historical Studies*, Vol. xiv, No. 53, Mar. 1964

Gerard Mac Atasney, *This Dreadful Visitation: The Famine in Lurgan/Portadown* (Belfast, 1997)

A. S. Mac Shamhrain, "Ideological conflict and historical interpretation: the problem of history in Irish primary education c.1900–30" in *Irish Educational Studies*, Vol. 10, 1991

Henry Mangan, "Clio in Ireland" in *O'Connell School Centenary Record*, (Christian Brothers, 1928)

James Clarence Mangan, "Siberia", *The Nation*, 18 April 1846

Sheldon Marcus, *Father Coughlin, The Tumultuous Life of the Priest of the Little Flower*, (New York: Little Brown, 1973)

William S. McFeely, *Frederick Douglass*, (New York: Touchstone, 1991)

John Stuart Mill, *On Representative Government*, [1863] (London: J. M. Dent, 1910)

Kerby Miller, *Emigrants and Exiles, Ireland and the Irish Exodus to North America*, (New York and Oxford, 1985)

Kerby Miller and Paul Wagner, *Out of Ireland, The Story of Irish Emigrants to America*, (Washington DC: Elliott and Clark, 1994)

Kate Millett, *The Loony Bin Trip*, (London: Virago Press, 1991)

John Mitchel, *The Last Conquest of Ireland (Perhaps)*, [1861] (Glasgow: Cameron, Ferguson, & Co., n.d.)

Chris Morash and Richard Hayes, (eds.), *Fearful Realities: New Perspectives on the Famine*, (Dublin: Irish Academic Press, 1995)

Laurence Mordecai Thomas, *Vessels of Evil: American Slavery and the Holocaust*, (Phildelphia: Temple University Press, 1993)

William O'Connor Morris, *Ireland 1494–1905, Cambridge Historical Series*, (Cambridge University Press, 1909)

Anthony Motherway, "Developing the History Curriculum in the Primary School 1922–86" in *Irish Educational Studies*, Vol. 7, No. 2, 1988

Anthony Motherway, "The Textbook Curriculum: the status of the textbook in the teaching of History and English at senior primary level" in *Irish Educational Studies*, Vol. 6, No. 1, 1986–7

Charles Murray and Richard J. Herrnstein, *The Bell Curve*, (1994)

Dominic Murray, "Identity: a covert pedagogy in Northern Irish schools" in *Irish Educational Studies*, Vol. 5, No. 2, 1985

The Nation, 20 September 1845

The Nation, 24 January 1846

The Nation, 7 March 1846

Asenath Nicholson, *Lights and Shades of Ireland*, (London: Gilpin, 1850)

W. Nolan, L. Ronayne and M. Dunleavy (eds.), *Donegal History and Society*, (Dublin, 1995)

T. P. O'Connor, *The Home Rule Movement, with a Sketch of Irish Parties from 1843*, (New York, 1891)

Kenneth O'Donnell, *"Johnny, We Hardly Knew Ye"*, *Memories of John Fitzgerald Kennedy*, (with David Powers and Joe McCarthy), (New York: Little Brown, 1970)

Niall O'Dowd, "The Myth and the Reality", *Irish America* Magazine, October 1988

Liam O'Flaherty, *Famine*, [1937] (Dublin: Wolfhound, 1984)

Tim O'Flaherty, *The Teaching of History in the Primary School*, (M.Ed. thesis, UCD)

Cormac O Gráda, *An Drochshaol - Béaloideas agus Amhráin*, (Baile Atha Cliath, 1994)

Cormac O Gráda, '"Making History" in Ireland in the 1940s and 1950s: The Saga of *The Great Famine*', *Irish Review*, No. 12, Spring/Summer 1992

Cormac O Gráda, *The Great Irish Famine* (Basingstoke, Hampshire, 1989)

Séamus O Grianna, *Caisleáin Óir*, (Corcaigh, 1976)

Rev. John O'Hanlon, *Catechism of Irish History to the death of O'Connell*, (Dublin, 1868)

Fr. Peadar O'Laoghaire, *Mo Scéal Féin*, (*My Story*), [1915], translation by Cyril T. O Céirín (Cork: The Mercier Press, 1970)

"Race under Representation", *Oxford Literary Review*, 13, Spring 1991

Patrick Pearse, *The Murder Machine*, (1912)

George Petrie, *The Ancient Music of Ireland*, (Dublin University Press, 1855)

Cathal Portéir, *Famine Echoes*, (Dublin: Gill & Macmillan, 1995)

Cathal Portéir, (ed.), *The Great Irish Famine*, (Cork: Mercier, 1995)

E. Randles, *Post-Primary Education in Ireland 1957–70*, (Dublin: Veritas, 1975)

Jean Raspail, *The Camp of the Saints*, (1973)

William L. Riordan, *Plunkitt of Tammany Hall*, (New York: Penguin, 1995)

David Roediger, *The Wages of Whiteness*, (London: Verso, 1991)

Rourke, *History of the Great Irish Famine*, (1845)

John G. Rowe, *The Romance of Irish History*, (Longman, Green and Co.,

1913)

Robert James Scally, *The End of Hidden Ireland, Rebellion, Famine, and Emigration*, (New York: Oxford University Press Inc., 1995)

Nassau W. Senior, *Journals, Conversations, and Essays Relating to Ireland*, (2 vols., 2nd ed., London, 1868)

Judith N. Shklar, *The Faces of Injustice*, (New Haven: Yale University Press, 1990)

Rev. A. M. Skelly, OP, *The Sorrows and Glories of Ireland*, Joseph F. Wagner Inc., New York 1935

Adam Smith, *The Theory of Moral Sentiments*, (1759), (ed.) D. D. Raphael and A. L. Macfie (Oxford: Oxford University Press, 1976)

A. M. Sullivan, *New Ireland*, (2 vols.) (London, 1877)

A. M. Sullivan, *The Story of Ireland*, (Dublin: Gill, 1867)

Ronald Takaki, *A Different Mirror – A History of Multi-Cultural America*, (New York: Little Brown, 1993)

A. J. P. Taylor, *Essays in English History*, (Harmondsworth, Middlesex, 1976)

Charles E. Trevelyan, *The Irish Crisis*, (London, 1848)

Charles E. Trevelyan, "The Irish Crisis", *Edinburgh Review*, January 1848

Jane Urquhart, *Away*, (US: Viking, 1994)

W. E. Vaughan (ed.), *A New History of Ireland*, v: *Ireland under the Union*, pt. I, 1801–70 (Oxford, 1989)

The Village Voice, June 1996

J. P. (Lorcan) Walsh, *Comparative Analysis of Reading Books of Commissioners of National Education & of Christian Brothers 1831–1900*, (M.A. Thesis, UCD, 1983)

J. P. (Lorcan) Walsh, "Nationalism in the textbooks of the Christian Brothers" in *Irish Educational Studies*, Vol. 6, No. 2, 1986–7

P. J. Walsh, *The Teaching of History in Irish Schools*, (M.A. Thesis UCD, 1941)

Waterford Freeman, 10 September 1845

Kevin Whelan, "Come All Your Staunch Revisionists – Towards a Post-Revisionist Agenda for Irish History", *Irish Reporter*, ii (Second Quarter, 1991)

Cecil Woodham-Smith, *The Great Hunger: Ireland 1845–1849*, (London, New York: Hamish Hamilton, 1962, Penguin, 1991)